33

chp 2-HG
Regine-read

A Dragon's Progress

A Dragon's Progress

Development Administration in Korea

editors
Gerald E. Caiden
Bun Woong Kim

Kumarian Press

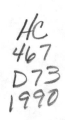

Copyright © 1991 by Kumarian Press, Inc.
630 Oakwood Avenue, Suite 119, West Hartford, Connecticut 06110-1529 USA

Printed in the United States of America

94 93 92 91   5 4 3 2 1

Edited by Barbara A. Conover
Cover design by Laura Augustine
Proofread by Cornelia Bland Wright

Library of Congress Cataloging-in-Publication Data

A Dragon's progress : development administration in Korea / editors, Gerald E. Caiden, Bun Woong Kim.
    p.   cm. — (Kumarian Press library of management for development
  Includes biographical references and index.
  ISBN 0-931816-90-4. — ISBN 0-931816-89-0 (pbk.)
  1. Korea (South)—Economic policy. 2. Korea (South)—Economic conditions. 3. Korea (South)—Politics and government. I. Caiden, Gerald E. II. Kim, Bun Woong. III. Series.
HC467.D73 1990
338.95195—dc20   90–21333

Contents

Introduction: Drawing Lessons from Korea's Experience ix
    Gerald E. Caiden

Part I   **Two Korean Perspectives on Development Administration**

1.   Systemization of Knowledge on Public Administration: 3
The Perspective of Development Administration
Hahn Been Lee

2.   Alternative Social Development Strategies   9
for Korea in the 1990s
Dong Hyun Kim

Part II   **Korea Is Different**

3.   The Theory and Applicability of Democratic Elitism   19
to Korean Public Administration
Bun Woong Kim and David S. Bell, Jr.

4.   The Administrative Culture of Korea: 26
A Comparison with China and Japan
Mahn Kee Kim

Part III   **The Nature of Korean Leadership**

5.   The Formation of the Governing Elites   43
in Korean Society
Wan Ki Paik

6.   Crisis, Regime Change, and Development: 58
A Quantitative Analysis of South Korean
Political Transformation 1945–1987
Suk Joon Kim

7.   Korean Democracy and the Limits of   67
Political Engineering
Jung Suk Youn

Part IV   The Government and Economic Development

8.   Government Direction of the Korean Economy   85
     In Joung Whang

9.   The Structure of the Economic Policy-making   95
     Institutions in Korea and the Strategic Role of the
     Economic Planning Board
     Byung Sun Choi

10. The Korean Economy Toward the Year 2000   107
     In Joung Whang

Part V   The Role of the Public Bureaucracy

11. Merits and Demerits of Public Administration   123
     in Korea's Modernization
     Wan Ki Paik

12. An Assessment of Government Intervention in   135
     Korean Economic Development
     Bun Woong Kim

Part VI   Uneven Development

13. The Territorial Dimension of the Developing   147
     Capitalist State: Measuring and Planning
     Centralization in Korea
     Yong Duck Jung

14. Financial Structure and Management: 161
     The Case of the Seoul Metropolitan Region
     Dong Hyun Kim

15. Decentralization and Implementation of   181
     Social Development at the Local Level in Korea
     Dong Hyun Kim

Part VII   Public Administration Education in Korea

16. Education Policy Changes in Korea: 199
     Ideology and Praxis
     Shin Bok Kim

17. Korean Public Administration: 210
     Education and Research
     Jong S. Jun

18.   The Study of Public Administration in Korea   220
       Jong Hae Yoo

19.   A Critical Evaluation of Education for   224
       Public Administration in Korea
       Chong Bum Lee

Part VIII Administrative Reform Strategy

20.   Two Critical Combinations for Successful   239 —
       Administration Reform
       Hahn Been Lee

21.   Democratization and Administrative Reform   246 —
       in Korea: A New Direction
       Bun Woong Kim

Selected Bibliography   253

Contributors   259

Index   265

Drawing Lessons from Korea's Experience

Gerald E. Caiden

THIS IS A collection of readings in English by some of Korea's leading authorities on development administration in the Republic of Korea. It is based on the conviction that although every country has to follow its own path to modernization and development, all countries can learn from each other's experiences. They can learn either what to avoid as being totally out of character and beyond realization or what might be worth copying and adapting to local conditions. Here is a new state, born in possibly the worst of circumstances that has arisen out of ashes like a modern-day phoenix. Yet it is the first so-called less developed country (LDC) and newly industrializing country (NIC) to host the Olympic Games. It did so in such a way as to be universally acclaimed as the best managed Olympics to date.

Even before this success, Korea had been attracting increasing global attention as one of the four dragons that had come from nowhere after World War II to join the world's largest trading nations in the 1980s. It was by far the largest of the four dragons in land size and population, and while it did share some cultural traits with the predominantly Chinese dragons, it had its own distinctive national character worthy of study in its own right.[1]

Some forty or so years ago, no one could have predicted such future success. Then, war raged in the peninsula and much of the physical infrastructure was being destroyed. The two newly created Korean states were hopelessly and irreconcilably split and just to ward off even greater disaster and suffering had to rely on external military support and massive international assistance. Whatever the real outcome of the Korean War (1950–1953), there appeared little future for either side, particularly the southern state, which seemed condemned to be a poverty-stricken backwater of Asia, dependent on Western, predominantly American, aid. Even

---

[1] A good introduction to Korea is Donald S. MacDonald, *The Koreans: Contemporary Politics and Society* (Boulder, Colo., Westview Press, 1988).

before the hostilities it had been desperately poor, with an annual per capita income not much above that of the Indian subcontinent and a long way behind that of Africa's rising star, Ghana. Yet forty years later, it has left Ghana and its richer northern neighbor behind. Depending on the source, the per capita income of the Republic of Korea certainly rose forty-fold, perhaps even fifty-fold, while in the same period life expectancy increased from fifty to seventy-one years. When it first joined the International Monetary Fund in 1955, its per capita gross national product (in current dollars) was only $65; by 1988 it was well over $6,000. No other state experienced such a rapid transformation on such a scale for such an extended stretch. In less than two generations the Republic of Korea (hereafter Korea) has well and truly modernized and in the process has overcome crippling obstacles to become the envy of many a country still enmeshed in abject poverty.

How this was achieved is described in detail elsewhere (see Bibliography). This volume singles out one aspect only, that of development administration. Korea was not blessed with abundant natural resources or a modern education system or a Westernized business elite or any other advantage that would easily explain how it managed to develop so quickly. Although it may have received U.S. aid and assistance on a larger scale than other poor countries, it never was a vassal state and Koreans eventually came to take business away from the United States. No, Korea pulled itself up by its own efforts, making best use of what it had, a poor but aspiring people eager to escape dire poverty and rebuild their country in their own way. Statistics attest to a strong work ethic, a thrifty population, a disciplined labor force, wise investments (and some foolish ones, too, but few), careful professional planning, effective management, and rising living standards and consumerism. But these do not tell the full story. They record the achievements well enough but they do not tell how economic growth occurred or at what price.

Undoubtedly the figures are impressive, even awe-inspiring to better-placed countries that have long been overtaken and left behind in Korea's wake. But many Koreans regret the disappearance of a life style whose memories are being kept alive in museums and by special commemorative events. Like virtually everything else, values have changed. Foreigners presented with only a skewed balance sheet of Korean modernization would not be aware of what has been lost and how the new gets only a mixed reception. While rightly proud of what has been accomplished in so short a time, Koreans are also circumspect and critical. Their astounding successes have not prevented them from providing a more balanced picture of what has been happening. In this spirit, the contributors to this volume give both sides of the story of various aspects of development administration in what has been an exceptional experience, running counter to what has taken place among poor countries.

An Unusual Success Story . . .

When Korea emerged in the early 1950s, it could go only upward. Temporary relief provided by postwar reconstruction and international assistance would ensure its survival. But what else? How could the talents and energies of its war-scarred population best be mobilized to build a better future? After some initial stumbling, Korea's elite came to a difficult realization. Korea would have to look outward, to shake off its insularity, in order to seize whatever opportunities came its way and compete in the global economy.

North Korea had chosen a different path and, typical of the day, had opted for import substitution, greater self-sufficiency, bureaucratic centralism, and protection from international competition in ways that discouraged enterprise and initiative. At first, the Republic of Korea had also pursued similar goals, beginning with the management of demand. But in the early 1960s it switched to an efficiency of supply and export orientation based on devaluation, industrialization, cheap labor, entrepreneurial incentives, reduced domestic protection, and government regulation. It switched just at the right time—when world trade in manufactured exports was about to boom. The Korean government, or rather its economic technocrats, proved to be successful at picking the winners and channeling credit to them. In the process, it favored a relatively small number of large producers (*chaebol*), thereby combining politics with business in "Korea, Inc." At the same time, the gains were not frittered away by incompetence and mismanagement but were reinvested and nurtured.

At first glance, Korea's policy seemed much like that of its closest friendly neighbor (and former colonizer), Japan. After all, it had been Japan that had first set Korea on its path of modernization by promoting industrialization, urbanization, literacy, and Western influence, and later had kindled a fierce desire among Koreans to equal and overtake those who had exploited them. Both states believed in economic liberalism. Both maintained strong partnerships between government and business in a collaborative effort joining public action and private initiative. Both stressed domestic protection and export industries. Both relied on market competition and price incentives. Both encouraged education and technology. Both emphasized political and social stability. Both developed distinctive homegrown styles of national economic management that to a greater or lesser extent relied on public initiatives (in Korea from the Economic Planning Board and in Japan from the Ministry of International Trade and Industry) and private sector implementation.

But here the similarities stop. Japan was already well developed and a much more powerful entity. After World War II it was to all intents and purposes well Westernized, democratized, and to a lesser extent demilitarized. It was one of the economic front-runners that had taken advantage

of the Korean War to bounce back and mount a challenge even to the
United States. In contrast, Korea was so backward that it could not be
considered any kind of threat—until it took advantage of the Vietnam War
to begin to compete with Japan. Even so, the gap between the two countries was so wide that it was Japan that virtually monopolized attention
for those seeking the magic formula to economic success and the myster-
ies of effective management. In fact, Korea's rise was, if not virtually overlooked, certainly overshadowed by "Japan, Inc."

Nevertheless, Korea's path to modernization has been different from that
of Japan's. Its formula for economic success and effective management has
been self-made. It may resemble Japan in several respects but it is no pale
imitation. It stands on its own merits. The lead was taken by a distinctive
technocratic military-political elite that was Western-influenced, American-
ized yet jealously nationalistic, and determined to make the world notice
their latter-day phoenix. Members of this elite would do it their own way.
They would take the risks and the blame for the mistakes they might make.
The personal costs would be high if they failed, but the rewards would
be higher if they succeeded. In no way would they follow North Korea
or Japan, nor could they have if they had wanted. They would have to
find uniquely Korean solutions to their country's predicaments. They opted
for rapid economic growth directed from above through authoritarian
government; central economic planning and management; the proletari-
anization of labor; agrarian reforms and rural emigration to mushroom-
ing industrializing cities; and unequal development, regional disparities,
class differentiation, and uncompensated social costs. With their firm grip
over the country, they could impose their will, discount opposition, and
take advantage of rising expectations to get the rest of the population to
go along with them. Whether they succeeded depended on whether they
could increase the economic pie so that more people could share larger
pieces. In this way they could promise increasing relief from abject poverty and growing opportunities for the ambitious and talented, providing they avoided too much dislocation, too much uncertainty, and too
much discontent in the process. Despite setbacks and mistakes, they have
largely succeeded, perhaps beyond their wildest dreams.

... Which Should Be Seen in All Its Complexity ...

This volume concentrates on key elements of Korea's development administration in such a way as to explain to those who did not directly participate in or experience what took place between 1950 and 1990 the
thinking, strategies, and instruments that were employed, and to point
to certain lessons that they might learn from Korea's experience.

The book is divided into eight parts. Part I presents two specifically Korean views of development administration. One recounts what actually

happened in Korea—the push to modernization through economic growth directed from above by an authoritative technocratic elite. The other regrets that so much emphasis was placed on economic development to the detriment of political and social development, and would like to see in the future more emphasis on a people-centered model of development that would preserve the uniqueness of a culture rather than transform it into a pale imitation of the West. The emphasis in development administration should have been on the quality of life, and not on the gross national product. On the other hand, had the emphasis at the outset not been placed on rapid economic growth, there would have been so little to share that the quality of life for the average person would barely have improved.

Part II deals with the uniqueness of Korea, emphasizing that a country may borrow foreign ideas but has to indigenize them and adapt them to local circumstances. Korea should not be measured against the standards of Western pluralism, because it is not Western or pluralistic. It is still authoritarian and elitist. It is also East Asian, sandwiched between China and Japan, with which it shares many cultural characteristics. Yet it has evolved its own peculiar version of patrimonial bureaucracy and its own administrative style of formalism, familism, law-abidingness, and pragmatism. Part III directs attention to the patrimonial bureaucracy or guided democracy of Korea's neomercantile security state led by a submissive unrepresentative governing elite clearly biased toward military and economic development. This bias allows it to maintain its monopoly of power through electoral manipulation, political patronage, and bureaucratic spoils, although its very successes promote pluralism and democratization.

Parts IV and V examine the leadership role of government and the public bureaucracy in Korea's modernization. The state has been the instigator and primary agent of development projects. Until a deliberate shift in economic policy in 1979, it had attracted some of the country's most capable managerial talent. By that time, it had succeeded in changing social values in favor of technology, productivity, and efficiency. It had promoted state protégés in cozy patron-client relations that had taken Korea well beyond economic liftoff, which was largely attributable to economic policy planners on the Economic Planning Board. They also engineered the 1979 Comprehensive Measures for Economic Stabilization, which liberalized the economy and stressed private enterprise. But, as the public bureaucracy's role in economic enterprise diminished, it increased in social welfare, education, research and development, and international affairs.

Part VI looks into the consequences of uneven development, that is, the concentration on economic growth over social and political concerns, the centralization of decision making to the neglect of local autonomy, the exaggeration of the public bureaucracy and its protegés at the expense of other social institutions, regional disparities, the gap between haves and have-nots, and the contrast between urban and rural development. The Seoul metropolitan region, which has come to contain about one quarter of Korea's population, has not been able to cope adequately but remains shackled with an outmoded urban administration system. Indeed, the whole structure of public administration needs overhauling to overcome the deficiencies of central planning and to provide greater access to government.

Part VII outlines the nature of public education in general as the background to the evolution of public administration education in particular. The demand for education has placed tremendous strains on all facilities, and competition has been fierce. Unfortunately, quality has been sacrificed and government intervention has resulted in further constraints. Korean studies have yet to emerge from out of the shadow of American public administration and management and from the narrow focus of preparing candidates for public service examinations. A new generation of scholars is now reshaping the discipline to local requirements.

That a specifically Korean public administration could be of global value is illustrated in Part VIII, where Korea's initial experience in gearing up for economic takeoff through islands of innovation within a traditional public bureaucracy is recounted and lessons drawn for countries attempting similar administrative transformation. Also emphasized is that administrative reform would enhance the capacity not only of the public sector but of the whole state and society. It should be directed at more balanced development and toward a more democratic, socially just, and prosperous Korea.

. . . Owing Much to Competent Development Administrators . . .

The collection is headed and concluded by selections from the bountiful writings of Hahn Been Lee, who played an active part as the Deputy Prime Minister and Minister of the Economic Planning Board during a particularly critical stage and as Korea's most internationally renowned scholar of development administration. Possibly no one else has so successfully combined theory and practice, bridged East and West, and insisted that countries can learn from one another's experiences. Clearly his views on public administration in general and development administration in particular have been influenced by his experiences in Korea's modernization. In Chapter 1, "Systematization of Knowledge on Public Administration: The Perspective of Development Administration," he states that the prime business of government at an early stage of development should include the initiation of public education and the promotion of agriculture; in midstream it should turn to higher education and industry, and after that to social services, community development, and urban redevelopment.

Accordingly, the first task of development administrators is to propose and advocate policy ideas and prepare decisions for future action directed at achieving desired goals by optimal means within the agenda of a particular society. Their second task is to marshal available resources and energize participants and organizations to translate policies and plans into concrete programs and projects. Their third task is to introduce administrative changes and innovations by applying the requisite reform instruments and strategies to the substantive programs and projects. Their fourth task is to sustain new programs and reforms through institution-building that routinizes innovations. In contrast to more traditional approaches to public administration, the emphasis throughout development administration should be placed on values and goals, initiatives and motivations, resource mobilization and cultivation of support. Development administrators, therefore, are proactive. They have to push for their ideas, educate their political masters, and cooperate with other power centers as they arise. To do this effectively, they must possess more than traditional bureaucratic skills. They must be skilled in both policy formulation and public management, which require interdisciplinary knowledge, a breadth of view, and probably experience outside the public sector. The great challenge is to change the attitudes of all public administrators from seeing themselves as masters of the public to viewing themselves as public servants and embracing the idea of public service.

Hahn Been Lee recognizes in Chapter 1 that every country has to decide for itself *what* it wants to develop, *where* to place its priorities, and *which* institutions and instrumentalities it prefers, according to its own peculiar situation, resources, and constraints. But once it has made up its mind, it needs to implement its decisions through an enterprising, entrepreneurial, results-oriented cadre of developmental administrators culled from all walks of life. These leaders must have the energy and drive to get things done; they must also formulate policies, plans, and programs and institutionalize their innovations and changes. They have to be missionary in the way they approach their tasks, mobilizing resources and support, convincing doubters, and overcoming resistance and inertia. While commanding government power themselves and marshaling and coordinating other power centers, they must not lose sight of the fact that they are serving the public, not the other way round. Though politically active, they must remain politically subordinate; while enterprising and creative, they should stay bound by the norms of public accountability and rectitude. Throughout, they drive the engines of development.

Dong Hyun Kim does not wholeheartedly approve the path on which development administrators in Korea have been driving the engines of development or the particular engine they have been driving (Chapter 2). Although they have achieved remarkable economic success, it has been at the cost of lagging social development, because they have relied uncritically on deterministic economic concepts of development. The pie has been increased but it has not been shared evenly. The gap between rich and poor has increased, and problems of poverty have not been solved. Authoritarianism remains intact while democratization struggles. The economic model of development has failed and should be replaced with a social model that captures the fullness of social reality, that sees people not just as resources in development but as the beneficiaries of development, as active participants in the development process, as dynamic cultural products. The three components of social development—economic, political, and sociocultural—are interrelated and together form a culturally unique whole. The goal of social development should be to maintain a balance between the uniqueness of the local culture and development plans based on specific local realities, not slavishly following universalistic (i.e., Western) models. Korea has relied too heavily on Western development models and shown too little creativity in designing its own to suit local circumstances. Despite appearances, in reality Korea suffers acute problems because it has concentrated too much on the development of things—not institutional infrastructures and not people as self-reliant human beings. Emphasis should switch from gross national product (GNP) to the quality of life of the common person. The engine for development should shift from money to people.

... in a Uniquely East Asian Setting ...

Each country is unique. Before any other country can derive lessons from Korea's experiences in development administration, it has to realize how it differs from Korea and what Korean features cannot be replicated elsewhere. As Bun Woong Kim and David S. Bell, Jr., state in Chapter 3, "The Theory and Applicability of Democratic Elitism to Korean Public Administration," each country "must be viewed in its historical, socioeconomic nexus" in and of itself. There is no historical law that compels every country to evolve and develop exactly the same as any other. A country may borrow foreign ideas and practices but it has to refashion them to local circumstances, to "indigenize" them through interaction with existing concepts and practices and overall cultural patterns which will eventually lead to change and assimilation. Those who have applied, at least formally, a Western pluralist model to Korea have been confronted with Korea's propensity toward authoritarianism, bureaucratic elitism, and "paralytic centripetalism" and have overlooked the weaknesses of pluralism as a model for developing countries.

In the case of Korean society, the elite-masses class division has not lent itself to a polity maintained by pluralist interest group balancing but to one maintained by domination and regulation. Consequently Korea's bureaucratic elite has not conformed to democratic norms. Nonetheless, this has not made it ineffectual in facilitating economic and social development, although it may have impeded political development. The elite has maintained that the masses have not yet been ready for democracy. Thus public policy has been confined to a few select leaders operating within a quasi-democratic institutional framework, and expecting and exacting obedience, conformity, and passivity from their followers. In Korea's version of guided democracy, elite preferences have dominated, with political passivity of the people "as a necessary condition for allowing for the creative functioning of the elite." In short, Korea has never been a Western democracy or functioned like one. Public administration in Korea has not operated as if it were in a Western democracy but has evolved its own administrative style and culture in keeping with locally prevailing "democratic elitism." Applying Western norms of public administration does not make sense. Korea is not Western.

On the contrary, Korea belongs to an exclusive group of countries sharing a strong tradition of Confucianism that has shaped their administrative cultures. This facet is examined by Mahn Kee Kim in Chapter 4, "The Administrative Culture of Korea: A Comparison with China and Japan." It is more meaningful to compare Korean public administration with that of its East Asian companions with whom it has been linked for centuries rather than dwell upon its fleeting contacts with the West. In all three countries, although less so in Japan than in the others, Confucianism has promoted a tradition of patrimonial bureaucracy, a well-educated, privileged, respected guardian class that is prudent, conservative, ritualistic, and morally self-effacing. All three have preserved a strong measure of bureaucratic elitism, a high respect for officialdom, a rather formalistic mode of operations, and a special sense of public duty and personal example. Familism is still strong, possibly strongest in Korea, where family lineage and blood relationships count and make for rampant nepotism. Authoritarianism is also strong, although it has been much weakened in Japan, where officials actually feel threatened by other power centers. The rule of law has always been weaker in China and Korea in favor of a sense of appropriateness of rules, although Koreans are more law-abiding. On the other hand, the Japanese have the strongest acceptance of social hierarchy and are the most deferential. The Chinese worry most about "face" (*mentzu*) and suffer most from bureaucratic inertia. Though at one time Koreans shared more traits with the Chinese, they probably now share more with the Japanese, given their emphasis on efficiency and pragmatism.

In any event, Chinese communism and Japanese liberalism have taken these countries much further away from traditional Confucianism than authoritarian elitism has the Koreans. Nonetheless, their distinctive East Asian administrative cultures set them off from other countries and their different political regimes set them off from one another. Korea merits special attention because Japan has gone beyond development administration, China has barely entered it, and Korea has progressed through most of its stages within living memory and its experiences are still fresh. Although none of their specifically East Asian features can be replicated, Korea's approach to administrative development is worthy of study by developing countries.

... Modernized by a Singular Technocratic Elite ...

In the process of national development, particularly of a newly independent state, leadership is the crucial variable. In Korea, leadership has always been concentrated in a definite, identifiable governing elite or minority ruling class and has remained so under the charismatic dictatorships of Rhee and Park that lasted over thirty years, according to Wan Ki Paik in Chapter 5, "The Formation of the Governing Elites in Korean Society." As development proceeded, growing pluralism demanded a more representative elite, but in the meantime absolute power was wielded through a strictly instrumental, submissive governing elite selected on the basis of personal loyalty. Because such an elite could not be replaced peacefully when it became spoiled and corrupted, opposition was driven underground. Such an elite may have accomplished what the dictator wanted done, but it was inherently unstable, divorced from the populace, passive, and certainly unrepresentative. Each leader tended to rely on people he trusted, people from his home region, those educated at the leading universities, and loyal military officers and business associates. The high presence of the military reflected the perceived outside threats to the state, the early modernization of the military, and the "can-do" managerial attitude of senior officers. To them were added experts with scientific and technical knowledge and skills. Sudden changes in leadership brought about disruption in the elite and the replacement of its members.

It would have been much better for Korea had the governing elites been more representative, had the functional business, professional, intellectual, and educational elites been less subservient to the governing elites, had there been political processes that would have permitted the peaceful transfer of leadership, and had the monopolization of political power not generated internal conflicts and conspiracies that disrupted national unity. On the other hand, the dictator could push through anything he wanted and could rely on submissive instruments dominated by his chosen loyal followers to carry out his decisions efficiently and effectively, even if they were not the best decisions that could have been made. What was decided was done, which is more than can be said of countries where leaders complain that little gets done.

The elite's clear bias was military and economic development, not political and social development or, as Suk Joon Kim prefers in Chapter 6, "Crisis, Regime Change, and Development: A Quantitative Analysis of

South Korean Political Transformation, 1945–1987," an economic miracle with political underdevelopment. Rejecting both the bureaucratic authoritarianism and dependent development theories as being inapplicable to Korea, he proposes that such contradictory development has been due to a neomercantile security state arising out of a series of crises and regime changes. Korea has actively sought economic rather than political goals externally while pursuing security rather than welfare internally, although in recent years it may have been moving toward a neomercantile welfare state. The military has played a key role in determining the nature of development. For any change in the nature of the state to occur, there would have to be a significant shift in ideology and policy or state institutions. But with the growth of pluralism, the prospect of regime change increases.

The same conclusion is arrived at by Jung Suk Youn in Chapter 7, "Korean Democracy and the Limits of Political Engineering." He also believes that an advanced economy automatically generates pluralism and demands for wider participation in decision making. The more the governing elite succeeds in transforming the economy, the more it is threatened with political failure. Eventually, growing pluralism should lead to genuine democratic choice. In the meantime, the mass ratification of elite determinations (which exclude some groups altogether, such as the radical and the poor, and exaggerate others, such as the conservatives, the military, and the rich) and the charade of democracy will continue through electoral manipulation, political patronage, and bureaucratic spoils. The majority is so tied to the status quo (or fears losing personally by change) that the elite has only to concede the minimum necessary to remain in power. As this situation is likely to continue in the absence of externally induced crises, the elite will retain its remarkable staying power.

... Dependent on Effective State Instrumentalities ...

The technocratic elite, or more accurately the technocratically oriented elites, have relied on a strong state apparatus to get things done. The military had to be strong to ward off possible invasion from the north. The police and intelligence networks had to be strong to preserve internal security. The economy had to be strengthened if abject poverty was to be overcome. The infrastructure had to be reconstructed and the education system improved. Modernization required the restructuring and superceding of traditional institutions. Until private resources, private energies, and private initiatives could be mobilized, harnessed, and developed, the state would have to take the initial burden of nation building and national development. Since 1960, the Korean government has been determined to lift the nation up from underdevelopment and has done so through a series of five-year plans emphasizing public sector stimulants to economic growth, particularly land reform, public enterprise, public investment and subsidization, regulated markets, and strengthened infrastructure.

The extent to which the state has directed the Korean economy is related by In Joung Whang in Chapter 8, "Government Direction of the Korean Economy." The foreign aid-stimulated growth policy of the 1950s was replaced in the early 1960s by President Park's export-oriented industrialization based on a broad range of development activities directed by the government and the technocratic-bureaucratic elite. The new policy relied heavily on national economic planning and a new policy planning subculture using the national budget, public enterprise, economic regulation, and sectoral inducements to ensure compliance. Tax collection was improved, budgeting reforms were made, and financial management was overhauled. Public enterprises were established and run well by competent management. Prices were regulated and fair trade practices strengthened. The government manipulated various incentives and disincentives for the private sector to encourage investment and capital formation and provide real rates of interest. In the 1980s, the lead in economic development was shifted to a relatively small group of private entrepreneurs with a downplaying of public enterprise, economic direction, and government intervention in favor of a freer market system and economic liberalization according to the 1979 Comprehensive Measures for Economic Stabilization (CMES). These steps reduced government subsidization, redirected capital investments, and promoted higher productivity and efficiency. Though unpopular at first, the new economic policy was extensively publicized until it gained popular support. Because of the soundness of economic forecasting it worked until the end of the decade, when new economic storm clouds required further adjustment to the economy.

A key organization in the successful economic development of Korea since 1961 has been the Economic Planning Board (EPB), described by Byung Sun Choi in Chapter 9, "The Structure of the Economic Policymaking Institutions in Korea and the Strategic Role of the Economic Planning Board." Preeminent in economic policy making, the EPB has been strategically placed in selecting and changing economic policies at particular times, reflecting the visions of the technocratic elite of the country while retaining its own institutional autonomy and flexibility. Since 1963 the political head of the EPB has also been deputy prime minister and leading government spokesperson on economic affairs. Although the EPB has been only one of several economic policy agencies, it is admittedly an increasingly powerful body. Unlike other governmental agencies, the EPB has been a think tank untied to specific interest groups and able to convince the president of its broad policy perspectives. It has obtained impressive results through its hold over budget formulation. But its success has meant that it has been entrusted with more and more operational activities, thereby deflecting it from its central mission of economic planning and budgeting.

What may be in store for Korea over the next decade and what might be done to maintain a high pace of modernization is considered by In Joung Whang in Chapter 10, "The Korean Economy Toward the Year 2000." Even with slow population growth, Korea will remain one of the most densely populated countries in the world. Given the imbalance between population and national resources, problems will emerge in energy, food, education, and environment, all of which will continue to require government intervention and regulation. On the whole, prospects continue to look bright for Korea's continued development, still dependent on abundant, hardworking, and well-educated human resources, as it completes its transition to a fully modern industrialized society based on internationalization, high technology, standardization of rising living conditions, and enlarged service industries. Also expected are growing demands for welfare services, decentralization, revitalization of local autonomy, and political participation.

Korea will have to decide on several policy issues—how to achieve further modernization while minimizing further Westernization, how to preserve its cultural identity while internationalizing, how to integrate the rural and urban sectors, and how to protect the individual in the mass society. Overall, Korea will emerge regionally and internationally as a force to be reckoned with and will play a greater part in world affairs. This optimistic forecast sees some diminution in government direction of the economy compensated by expanded government activities in rural modernization, social services, research and development, policy planning, education, foreign affairs, and environmental protection. Development administration is unlikely to diminish; it will merely shift its emphasis from economic concerns to social concerns, from expanding the pie to redistributing the pieces more equitably.

In the past, the public bureaucracy had to be the primary organ of modernization simply because there was no ready alternative. According to Wan Ki Paik in Chapter 9, "Merits and Demerits of Public Administration in Korea's Modernization," that dependency has had mixed results. On the one hand, (1) pragmatic values were impressed on people and their vague notion of development was concretized into practical reality; (2) spiritual values were overtaken by technocratic, down-to-earth powers and physical values; (3) productivity (considered progressive, positive and expansive) was stressed over distribution (considered conservative, passive, and equalizing); (4) a "can-do" mentality replaced fatalism, that is, a self-resigning, stagnant, and passive mentality was transformed into an aggressive, positive, and progressive one; and (5) technological propagation improved production and promoted rationality.

On the other hand, (1) all other institutions became subordinate to the public bureaucracy, which monopolized political power and dominated decision making, and democratization was sacrificed to efficiency; (2) dependent institutions were denied opportunities to strengthen themselves and become autonomous, and state protégés were overprotected and became complacent, apathetic, inefficient, and unbalanced from a societal viewpoint; (3) cozy patron-client relations fostered *zaibatsus*, institutionalized corruption, and economic speculation among those closed out of the charmed circle; (4) unbalanced policies favoring the "haves" made for gross inequalities, regional disparities, and unnecessarily high social costs; and (5) the rush to modernization was accompanied by waste, pollution, and low-quality products—i.e., realization of ends irrespective of the costs and illegalities.

In short, the dominance of public administration in modernization has been a mixed blessing. Because the government has achieved what it has set out to do, the country can afford to encourage private initiatives in development and improve the quality of public sector performance.

As Bun Woong Kim points out in Chapter 12, "An Assessment of Government Intervention in Korean Economic Development," this conclusion has long been shared by the private sector, which has rarely welcomed the dominance of government and the public bureaucracy in plotting Korea's future, least of all when the Economic Planning Board has guessed wrong or has persisted with questionable policies.

Despite Korea's enviable growth, mistakes have been made and economic policy has not responded in time to external events. No matter how well EPB has performed, the time has come for deregulating the economy, freeing private sector initiatives, and reducing government intervention by changing from direct to indirect control. The interventionalists and statists may have been correct in the past, but now that the economy has been so successful, privatization should be seriously considered and market forces should be allowed to govern.

. . . Highly Concentrated Causing Uneven Development That Can Be Remedied . . .

A common complaint about Korea's modernization has been overcentralization and overconcentration, resulting in uneven development with disparities and distortions between the center and the periphery. To improve their prospects many people have moved to the growth centers, leaving others behind in backward, declining, and stagnant areas. Although there have been growing demands to slow down the growth of the big cities, to redirect development into new towns and areas, and to revitalize neglected regions, these have been discouraged by the highly centralized nature of government and weak local autonomy. According to Yong Duck

Jung in Chapter 13, "The Territorial Dimension of the Developing Capitalist State: Measuring and Explaining Centralization in Korea," only about one fifth of government finance and employment has been incurred at the local level. For lengthy periods local government has had no substantial powers of its own at all; thus, one cannot speak of decentralization, only of deconcentration. Korea has had an integrative prefectoral system that has complemented centralization: local officers are appointed at will by the center, local tax rates are set at the center, and decisions are handed down from the center. Such centralization cannot be explained by history or administrative rationality so much as by economic interests (the cozy partnership between the government and the *chaebol*), bureaucratic interests (retention of power), and political interests (authoritarianism). Centralization has been an indispensable condition for the maintenance of the authoritarian governing elite, and strengthening the periphery can be achieved only at the cost of weakening the center.

The key beneficiary of centralization has been the Seoul metropolitan region, which has correspondingly suffered all the problems associated with excessive population concentration. How that has impacted Seoul's municipal administration is described by Dong Hyun Kim in Chapter 14, "Financial Structure and Management: the Case of the Seoul Metropolitan Region." About one quarter of the Korean population, a steadily growing proportion, has settled in the Seoul metropolitan region. Despite attempts since 1964 to control metropolitan growth throughout the country and to develop alternative sites, the population of Seoul has doubled every decade since independence if the industrial cities, regional centers, and satellite suburbs around it are included. Urbanization has fostered the practice of public enterprises providing local utilities and services and the growth of urban expenditures. Most funding has been provided by the central government, although the bigger cities, like Seoul, have proportionately contributed more. Tighter money policies in the 1980s brought budget and financial management reforms and some privatization, especially in urban renewal. Seoul itself has been financially strapped, being unable to increase its narrow tax sources and central government subsidies to meet accelerating demands for metropolitan services. This lack has caused it to expand the size of its administrative structures by adding additional functional elements. Its form of line and functional organization has become badly outmoded and inadequate and needs drastic reorganization, as does its personnel recruitment system.

According to Dong Hyun Kim, the whole local government system needs a thorough overhaul to shift much of the load of municipal services off the center onto local authorities where they rightly belong, to reduce the number of central agencies working at cross-purposes at the local level, to improve coordination and planning, and to enhance organizational capacity. Seoul especially needs to improve its administrative performance in satisfying an ever increasing demand for public facilities, public safety, and utility services. Thus, economic development has brought urbanization that requires urban administration, not just local administration. More balanced regional development is needed and a deteriorating urban environment has to be reversed, recommendations that many Third World countries would endorse because they too experience the same problems.

The push to greater decentralization, deconcentration, and local autonomy is advocated on other grounds by Dong Hyun Kim in Chapter 15, "Decentralization and Implementation of Social Development at the Local Level in Korea." Central planning cannot achieve growth-with-equity policies designed to provide for the needs of the poor, to reduce interregional and rural-urban disparities, to provide greater access to government for disadvantaged groups, and to elicit greater popular participation in economic, social, and political processes, however well-meaning the planners. What is needed is (1) bottom-up planning based on local needs, priorities, and interests, and (2) decentralized administration—in fact, an overturning of existing arrangements in Korea. A good start has been made with the *Saemaul* (new village) movement and other local initiatives designed to meet local needs through local facilities managed locally and with local government planning, coordination, and monitoring of public service delivery.

The next step is to raise public awareness of critical issues, to encourage community participation, to mobilize local resources, and to reorganize delivery systems to allow local input. This step has already been taken in experimental projects that are community-based and encompass an integrated multi-sectoral focus area, nongovernmental organization involvement, and centrally triggered local resource mobilization strategies. But decentralization alone cannot be considered as a solution to development problems; indeed, at the outset it may compound problems by creating demands for scarce resources. However, it does strengthen local planning and management capacities, improve service delivery, and offset the shortcomings of economic planning. It does promote democratization, political participation, and responsible and responsive government. In the process of decentralizing, Korea can learn from the experience of other countries, particularly in regard to rural revitalization, management improvement, administrative reform, intergovernmental relations, and public-private partnerships.

... Through the Continuing Professional Education of Public Administrators ...

Education has always been prized in East Asia, and Korea realized that mass education would be indispensable for effective modernization. After its independence, education policy was revised in accordance with the

1949 constitutional provision that everyone had the right to education, and with the government's political objectives of nationalism, anticommunism, and national development as identified in the 1968 Charter of National Education. According to Shin Bok Kim in Chapter 16, "Educational Policy Changes in Korea: Ideology and Praxis," this instrumental view has meant that education has played a greater role in national political integration than in the development of skills and individual creativity. There has been such hunger for education that quality has been sacrificed to quantity, all facilities have been overburdened, students have fiercely competed to get into quality institutions, and parents have incurred heavy financial burdens to give their children a good education. The government has intervened to control and direct teaching instruction at all levels to guarantee universal elementary education, to equalize opportunities and ensure minimum standards, to encourage the private provision of education above elementary level, and to improve education standards. The 1985 Presidential Commission for Education Reform sparked off a series of policy initiatives that have led to proposals to reform primary and secondary education that would liberalize the whole system, reduce central controls, debureaucratize procedures, and allow greater local autonomy. Even if implemented they still do not go far enough to reduce government direction, rigid educational conformity, and mediocrity that hampers continued national development.

The education of public officials has not been spared the shortcomings of the general education system. Once it was recognized that a professional bureaucracy was needed to replace archaic forms and procedures, education for public administration has mushroomed. Its progress—beginning with the formation of the Korean Association of Public Administration in 1956 and the Graduate School of Public Administration at Seoul National University in 1959—is described by Jong Sup Jun in Chapter 17, "Korean Public Administration: Education and Research." Korean public administration, an offshoot of political science and administrative law, has traditionally prepared students for higher civil service entry examinations, and the nature of those examinations has largely determined the content of administrative studies. It has been a field for professional practice, providing much needed managerial knowledge and skills for the public sector. In this respect, it has been heavily influenced by American public administration and policy studies, beginning with the U.S. military government of Korea and continuing with the education and training of most Korean instructors in the United States, combining American theories and practices with Korean cultural circumstances. A more distinctively Korean approach came with the dynamic development administrators of the 1960s and the administrative reformers and scholarly innovators of the 1970s. Nonetheless, Korean public administration studies have had difficulty in breaking away from civil service examination preparation, conducting indigenous research, and developing theories that are specifically Korean.

These concerns are taken up by Jong Hae Yoo in Chapter 18, "The Study of Public Administration in Korea." Yoo maintains that overreliance on American public administration has brought that country's intellectual problems into Korean public administration along with the problems it already had, particularly the barriers between scholars and practitioners and the challenge presented by new technology. In Korea the pressing need is to indigenize and localize the study of public administration whose scope has been too narrow. It needs to enlarge its vision and increase its presence outside of Seoul. Yoo's complaints are substantiated by Chong Bum Lee in Chapter 19, "A Critical Evaluation of Education for Public Administration in Korea," in which he traces distinctive stages of disciplinary development—initiation (1945–1960), simple imitation (1960–1975), and adaptive imitation (1975–1989)—and the growth of university courses, government training institutes, student enrollment, and publications. Lee points out that research has been concentrated at finding means to achieve given goals rather than probing the goals themselves. It needs to be reoriented toward the articulation and organization of public opinion instead of the blind acceptance of government directions. Similarly, the curricular contents need to be shifted from an affirmation of what is to an inquiry about what might be. A new generation of younger scholars is making changes along these lines and in the next decade should push the discipline of public administration in Korea toward its final stage of development, that of creativity and maturity.

... Prepared to Innovate and Reform

Clearly, these critics of the current state of public administration in Korea are discontented not only about the teaching but also about the practice of public management. They want both pedagogical and administrative reforms. As to the latter, advice on how to proceed is given by Hahn Been Lee in Chapter 20, "Two Critical Combinations for Successful Administrative Reform." The first is a combination of appropriate reform ideas with appropriate demands for social change, and the second, the combination of competent reform agents with enlightened political leadership. Because development unleashes pent-up social energies and the public bureaucracy tends to be static and closed, it needs to be opened up through new programs and organizations, not reduced of its most reform-minded and retrenched. New programs and organizations can draw on the best administrative talent and employ new blood to create different working norms and a new-method consciousness. The way has to be prepared by innovative enclaves—islands or units of change-prone and reformist elements, secured by their proved competence and eager to reach out and make alliances with like-minded elements in and around the public bureaucracy. These islands of innovation have to link up with enlightened political leaders.

Innovative officials have to advocate and political leaders have to adopt at their own risk. This is what happened in the crucial decade between 1955 and 1965 when Korea started to move forward. Islands of innovation were found in the Bank of Korea, the Ministry of Finance, the Ministry of Reconstruction, and ROK Army financial administration. Their young task-oriented leaders were serious about reform. They linked up with the newly established professional schools in academia and the military. Their reform ideas were legitimized by the 1961 military regime and by the newly created Economic Planning Board.

The lessons for other countries that can be drawn out of this reform experience in Korea are (1) that administrative reforms must be generated from within the bureaucracy in islands of innovation, (2) that technocratically oriented reforms must be relevant to urgent social needs, (3) that the reforms must be home-grown and home-implemented, (4) that the public bureaucracy must be opened up to enable innovative administrators to surround themselves with core reform-minded staff, (5) that reforms must have strong political sponsorship, and (6) that reformers must impress on political leaders that it would be politically advantageous to adopt appropriate administrative reforms. The successes of development and reform generate much social change and bring into existence a highly educated, highly urbanized, and highly citizen-conscious society—i.e., a qualitatively different society that requires a drastically different bureaucrat-citizen relationship. Thus, the future (in Korea) requires more people-oriented administrative reforms, a more decentralized administrative system, and service delivery efficiency at least matching the performance of the private sector.

The need to move further in this direction has recently been acknowledged by the president himself. President Roh Tae Woo has proclaimed "the era of the common man" and promised democratic reforms of the overcentralized governmental system. That administrative reform and democratization go together in readdressing the biases of autocracy is discussed by Bun Woong Kim in Chapter 21, "Democratization and Administrative Reform in Korea: A New Direction." In defense of authoritarianism, Korea has suffered from both the bureaucratization of politics and the politicization of bureaucracy. The balance can be restored by further political democratization, a process already well under way. Political reform directed at political development and stability should invigorate liberalization and shift the country from crisis politics to interest politics. Administrative reform directed at decentralization, deregulation, popular participation, and greater openness should shift the country from bureaucratic authoritarianism to democratic autonomy. Economic reforms directed at free enterprise, fair competition, privatization, and economic deconcentration should enhance the quality of life and promote social equity and justice, thereby promoting economic efficiency. Government reform directed at liberalization and human rights should reduce government control and direction of public expression, education, and choice and should strengthen the rule of law and public accountability. Regulatory reform, directed at reducing the administrative state, should transfer economic power from the public to the private sector, realize economies, and foster economic efficiency. These reforms are all feasible, but they can be blocked by a public bureaucracy that has the most to lose. On the other hand, by taking the initiative the public bureaucracy could bring closer to reality the visions of In Joung Whang and Dong Hyun Kim of a democratic, socially just, and prosperous Korea.

Taking Stock

When Koreans well placed in the system reflect on their experiences, they make Korea's development successes sound simpler to achieve than they were. Some amnesia is unavoidable. Some selection is probably unavoidable too. Nobody wants to dwell on all the complicated details of everyday routine, all the doubts, meanderings, wrong turns, and back-tracking that invariably accompany all new ventures. Thus, a summary of what were momentous events in the life of a new state never tells nonparticipants what they really would like to know. Sometimes it is just as well that they are forgotten.

In the case of Korea's development administration, the contributors to this volume of readings have tried to relate the parts of the story of most interest to nonparticipants. They have not unduly glamorized: in fact, they have been overcritical, dwelling on the downside costs and casualties of rapid economic growth. Muted criticism is traditionally Korean. Because they criticize does not mean that they do not admire or support what has been done; on the contrary, they are confident that what has been accomplished is so solid it can stand up to criticism. Because their criticism is muted does not mean that they fear to be more outspoken; on the contrary, they are ready with constructive proposals to improve on what has been done and hopeful that their suggestions will be implemented. Mindful of what has been accomplished, they also point out what might have been done differently and what should now be changed for better results.

Meanwhile, history moves on. The Korea of yesterday is not the Korea of today and the Korea of today is not the Korea of tomorrow. Development administration in Korea has not yet completed its tasks. There is much to be done in political and social development. As remarkable as Korea's economic growth has been, per capita income is still below some of the other dragons and is well behind that of Japan. Poverty has not yet been conquered. The risks of export-oriented industries are being felt keenly. Political frustration mounts and expresses itself in sudden out-bursts of street violence. Seoul still draws people and experiences worse traffic jams, pollution, and ugliness despite valiant efforts to clean up its metropolitan area for the Olympic Games and to keep it clean. Development problems continue to accumulate and by all accounts the current arrangements for administrative development are already outmoded.

Three recent mileposts show how fast events bring into question prevailing administrative arrangements. In 1987, Korea dispensed with a Residential Representative of the International Monetary Fund after nearly a quarter century of technical assistance from the Fund. In 1989, Korea joined the Associate Professional Officer program of the Food and Agricultural Organization of the United Nations, donating staff to that organization, the first developing country of the seventeen member states. In 1990, after forty years, the dominant role in the military alliance between the United States and Korea was taken by Koreans. It was also in 1990 that President Roh Tae Woo caused consternation throughout the Korean peninsula for meeting with President Gorbachev of the Soviet Union, as both recognized how fast the sudden collapse of the Cold War was reshaping the political globe. In turn, the border between North and South Korea was opened a crack and it looked as though cooperation might seriously be considered for the first time since division.

Meanwhile, the economic successes of the other dragons have not left Korea's path unquestioned even within Korea, where the temporary economic pause in 1989–1990 gave much food for thought as to whether or not another change in direction might not be warranted. In short, pressures were mounting both internally and externally for a reworking of development administration in Korea. Reforms were being demanded politically, economically, socially, and administratively. Korean leaders had learned in the past that development ambitions, ideals, and plans could not be realized without appropriate development administration arrangements and competent, professional, and enterprising administrators. They had also learned that change is ceaseless and that from time to time radical reforms in institutional arrangements and managerial values are necessary. Reform has to be seen as a political asset. Will the Korean leadership of the 1990s take similar initiatives? This book reveals that it does not have to look far for expert advice.

PART
I

*Two Korean
Perspectives on Development
Administration*

CHAPTER ONE

Systematization of Knowledge on Public Administration: The Perspective of Development Administration

Hahn Been Lee

ADMINISTRATION OF PUBLIC affairs in a developing society has at least three analytically distinguishable dimensions: (1) technical, (2) programmatic, and (3) political.

The technical dimension includes the basic housekeeping functions of public authority such as maintenance of public order and safety, collection of taxes, and provision of minimum public facilities like roads and postal networks. This is the traditional dimension of public administration which exist in the public domain of any society, with different degrees of efficacy and refinement.

The programmatic dimension is related to the purposeful socioeconomic developmental requirements more peculiar to developing societies, and includes such positive programs as public education, agrarian reform and agricultural development, building of social infrastructures, promotion and development of various sectors of industry, family planning, rural and community development, housing, and urban development.

The political dimension is related to the changing role of the bureaucracy in developing societies, with increasing initiatives taken by its members in the formulation and implementation of various social and economic development programs and the consequent political interactions with other emerging elites.

"Development administration" is primarily concerned with the programmatic dimension, with related interest in the political dimension. Thus, in terms of required knowledge it must cover a broader scope than tradi-

Taken from a paper presented to the International Workshop on the Encyclopedia of Public Administration, Hochschule für Verwaltungswissenschaften, Speyer, September 1981, in *Speyerer Forschungsberichte* 22 (1981):122–134.

tional public administration, which has to operate within a more or less established sociopolitical framework. The scope has to include:

1. the broad agenda of developmental requirements of a particular society;
2. the general sequence and synchronization of the desired agenda;
3. a strategy of changes and innovations required at different stages;
4. preparation and mobilization of the various resources, particularly human resources, required to undertake requisite tasks at the appropriate time; and
5. cognizance and cultivation of political and social environment that would enable the requisite changes and innovations to take place.

In terms of intellectual analyses, such an approach implies that development administration must have at least three distinct thrusts:

a. substantive areas of development policies, plans, programs, and projects;
b. the dynamic process of introduction, implementation, and carrying through of change, innovation, and institution building; and
c. the role of bureaucrats as change agents, and their recruitment and training.

In the interest of systematizing knowledge, concepts, and vocabularies related to all of the above, we must consider three aspects. In the following sections, each of the above thrusts will receive detailed treatment.

The Substantive Areas of Development Administration

The substantive areas of development administration correspond to the agenda of development of a particular society. For a society that is at the very early stage of development, the prime business of government must include the initiation of public education and promotion of agriculture, while that for a society in the midstream of development might be the development of a higher education system and the promotion of industry. But the period of more than a generation since the end of World War II has seen a panorama of various concrete developmental experiences in many societies, and has now given students of administration adequate materials to draw from in attempts to construct some pattern of developmental agenda. Below appears a sample skeleton of developmental agenda based on the author's personal experiences and observations.

1. Initial social programs to meet rising social aspirations released by decolonization and similar political changes, such as

      a. public education,
      b. agrarian reform, and
      c. agricultural development.
  2. Economic development programs, such as
      a. development of various sectors of industry,
      b. construction of industrial infrastructures,
      c. establishment of various public corporations,
      d. family planning,
      e. human resources and technological development, and
      f. expansion of secondary, vocational, and higher education.
  3. Follow-up social development programs, such as
      a. rural and community development,
      b. urban development and redevelopment,
      c. initiation of health insurance,
      d. initial welfare programs,
      e. spread of higher education and life-long education, and
      f. expansion of social and cultural infrastructures.

The question of disciplinary boundaries inevitably arises here. Yet, inasmuch as the substantive areas provide the raw materials, development administration must address itself to these problems.

The Operational Leitmotif of Development Administration

Development administration must have some distinct operational thrusts in order to initiate and effect desired changes. As the introduction and management of change are the essence of development, the appreciation of innovation and reform becomes the leitmotif of development administration in operational terms. These are the cutting edges with which development administration addresses itself to the substantive areas mentioned above:

  1. policy formulation and planning,
  2. management of development programs and projects,
  3. conduct of administrative reforms, and
  4. institution building.

Policy Formulation and Planning

Policy formulation is the first task of development administrators. This function is inherent in the management of change. Rapid and complex changes in the environment of government constantly call for new policies. Development administrators may either conceive broad policy ideas themselves or rely on policy counsels of specialists and outsiders. In any case, their function is to propose and advocate such policy ideas to their political superiors who are responsible for making policy decisions.

Planning is closely related to policy formulation. Planning is the process of preparing a set of decisions for action in the future, directed at achieving desired goals by optimal means. Thus, like policy formulation, planning is a major instrument of managing change.

Management of Development Programs and Projects

To obtain desired results of development, policies and plans must get translated into concrete programs and projects. In the final analysis, development administrators must create changes through programs and projects and therefore marshal available resources and energize participants and organizations for the implementation of actual programs and projects.

Conduct of Administrative Reforms

Administrative reforms are the vehicle through which changes and innovations are introduced into the administrative machinery engaged in development. Administrative reforms may take different channels: reorganization, budgetary reforms, personnel reforms, new methods and procedures. They may also be based on different strategies, comprehensive or incremental. Yet the function of development administrators is to select the requisite instruments and strategies, apply them to appropriate substantive programs and projects, and accomplish the desired results.

Institution Building

New programs and reforms must be sustained in order to secure their full developmental effects. This is the task of institution building. When changes are introduced into the administrative processes, the new values and norms must become protected and diffused over time—the way by which innovations become routinized. Various internal and external factors are involved, but the element of administrative leadership is of paramount importance.

These are the key functions of development administrators. In contrast to traditional administration, in each of the processes emphasis is placed on values and goals, initiative and motivations, resource mobilization, and support cultivation.

The Role of Bureaucracy and Its Implications for Training

Inasmuch as development administration involves deliberate attempts at socioeconomic development by the government, bureaucrats, especially senior bureaucrats, play relatively active policy roles.

At the initial stage of development, the bureaucracy usually takes on a relatively passive role under political elites who are typically nationalist-minded ideologues or politicians. Under the legitimizing umbrella of the politicians, the bureaucrats—some of whom might have been tainted by earlier colonial service—carry on the basic operations of government and begin to carry out some initial developmental programs, often connected with some external assistance programs. In this process the bureaucracy gains some measure of competence as well as public exposure and some of the more ambitious members of the senior bureaucracy become oriented toward political careers. It is also at this stage that some "young blood" joins the bureaucracy.

The second stage is usually more comfortable for the bureaucrats because by this time the power elite has a mixture of original politicians and bureaucrats-turned-politicians. Similarly, the bureaucracy also becomes more mixed, with the new blood gaining numbers and experience. In this way there develops a natural rapport between the politicians and the bureaucracy. This is a crucial stage. If the power elites are enlightened and responsive to social change, favorable political development can occur. However, should the power elites be repressive, the bureaucracy could easily be influenced by their whim, producing regression and systemic decay.

The third stage of bureaucratic metamorphosis comes when various countervailing elites—political parties, universities, the press, industry, labor unions, and other social organizations—grow in strength and pose effective countervailing forces vis-à-vis the bureaucracy. The bureaucracy feels uneasy about this new situation, being jealous of the quasi-exclusive discretionary power that it had enjoyed. Particularly irritating to the bureaucracy are the new industrial elites, who are usually more affluent and wield increasing resources and powers. It is at this stage that strong and enlightened political leadership, whose function is the integration of the various competing new social elements, is most necessary.

This portrait of a changing bureaucratic role corresponding to the stage of development casts many implications regarding recruitment, training, and control of the bureaucracy.

At the initial stage, rudimentary knowledge and skills in the housekeeping functions of government are needed. At the developmental stage, more knowledge and operational skills on developmental subject matters as well as innovational motivations will be required.

At the maturing stage, however, greater sensitivity to the public and a broader perspective of the society as a whole will be necessary. At the same time, efficiency would require upgraded knowledge and skills in managing the day-to-day operations of the government. At this stage there will have to be less emphasis on innovation and more emphasis on management.

In the area of recruiting, there is hardly any need for making special efforts to groom an elite group since there is a built-in tendency in almost all developing societies for young people of ambition and ability to aspire for positions in the public bureaucracy. One caveat here is the temptation to select candidates through a narrowly focused track like law or public administration. The breadth of substantive areas of development argues for a wide avenue of entry involving all the disciplines taught in the universities and other technical institutions.

The crucial point is post-entry training. Here entrants should be oriented toward applying their intellectual and motivational energies to the substantive problems of development. At the senior levels, however, the breadth of view that is necessary for coexistence and productive interactions with elites in other spheres should be emphasized. Lateral recruitments from other sectors should also be encouraged at this level. How to train senior bureaucrats to look at the countervailing elites without a sense of threat and with equanimity is something to which public administration has paid little attention in the past. Yet a breadth of mind as well as an insight into the increasing needs for genuine service to the society under constant change is the paramount requirement for maturing bureaucracies in developing societies. How to turn a *taskmaster* into a *servant* for the public is perhaps the greatest challenge facing the discipline of development administration in the coming years.

CHAPTER TWO

Alternative Social Development Strategies for Korea in the 1990s

Dong Hyun Kim

OVER THE LAST two decades, the Republic of Korea has experienced remarkable economic change. From 1962—when the First Five-Year Development Plan was launched—until 1986, the nation's economy grew at an average annual rate of 9.4 percent. As a result of this rapid economic growth, Korea today is recognized as one of the newly industrializing countries.

This rapid economic growth did not distort the pattern of income distribution in the country. Indeed, standards of living have generally improved with this economic progress. In particular, improvements in certain indicators such as life expectancy, infant mortality rates, extent of piped water supply, and middle school entrance rates demonstrate the broad benefits of development over the period. But because social development has lagged behind economic growth in Korea, a rethinking of the concept of development in general, and the emergence of social development in particular, has been called for—especially a rethinking of the economic deterministic development models that Korea has been uncritically relying upon.

Development models, which have been predominantly based on the economic conception of growth in terms of GNP, per capita income, production, physical growth, and technological growth, have not produced satisfactory development results for Korea. First, economic development has had trouble reaching the intended rate and magnitude of growth. Second, even with the measurable amount of overall growth, it was found to germinate increasing inequality rather than balanced growth. In reality, a substantial part of development gains has been clustered at the thin upper crust of society, consisting mostly of those who control the means

Taken from Dong Hyun Kim, "Alternative Social Development Strategies for the 1990s in Korea," paper presented to the 49th National Convention of the American Society for Public Administration, Portland, Oregon, March 1988.

of production and those who are immediately connected to them. While the core that directs economic activities reaps tremendous advantages, the periphery that comprises the masses remains poor and untouched, having at best only some nominal share in the social services provided by the government. In Korea the gap between the rich and the poor widened, and problems of poverty remain unsolved.

Political development is struggling almost in vain away from authoritarianism and toward some model of democracy. Political elites are still unable to conceptualize clearly the objectives of society and/or unable to effect desirable changes. The failure to instill a true democratic society, for example, indicates the limitation of transplanting externally induced ideas or institutional changes, especially when the existing power structure stands in the way and/or the bulk of the people are not sufficiently appreciative or receptive to the need for such ideas or changes. It also indicates the inadequacy of compartmentalized economic development when it takes precedence over other aspects of development. Local social cultural systems as dynamic driving forces have been neglected or even obliterated in this process of development. The failure of the economic conception of development has led to the formulation of a broader social, cultural, and political conception of development in academic circles.

There is no agreement among scholars about the precise meaning of development. All it implies is some kind of improvement in the lives of the people in the society that is developing or has developed. Some define it narrowly to include only the aspects of economic development, while some others include in it everything pertaining to the realization of the human potential to embrace all aspects of human life—social, cultural, economic, political, etc. What should be the coverage of social development? Does it refer to anything "noneconomic," the sectoral approach to "social planning," or in fact alternative rather than supplementary foci of developmental concern? If we take society, then social development should hardly be reduced to technological or economic development only, although the former implies the latter. In the process of searching for a conceptual frame for social development, critical questions have been raised with regard to the adequacy of the existing development paradigms and their derivations, and the redefinition of development and modernization. What should be the development aims of the future: growth, change, social justice, quality of life, or all of these?

Revising the Concept of Development

The existing development paradigms and their derivations can be seen in the significant changes of the definitions of development during the past decade. Viewed from a sociological point of view, the concept of development as perceived by academia has gone through four phases.

Phase One was characterized by the capital and technical know-how elements of development, whereby society, culture, and people were considered to be passive organisms, ever adjusting to the development process and environment. It was a period of "impact" studies—the economic and technological impact upon the people, the community, institutions, and culture.

Phase Two was marked by the search for social prerequisites of economic development, as a result of the increasing disillusion with economic planning, which had failed to produce desired results. Development did not take place. Social scientists were asked to lay down social, cultural, and psychological prerequisites for development to occur. This step involved discussions of the emergence of those values, attitudes, motives, and abilities that would be favorable to the process of development. It was virtually an imposition of Western development prerequisites upon the developing societies.

Phase Three was dominated by modernization theories that were virtually imbedded in an Anglo-American model of society. It was a continuation and systematization of the second phase on a grand scale.

Phase Four was marked by the emergence of the school of underdevelopment and dependency, which emphasizes the historical factor of colonialism and imperialism as the root cause of poverty and backwardness of the Third World countries, the importance of the class factor in the process of development, and the influencing international economic order. This school of thought advocates only an ultimate solution based upon the creation of class consciousness and the bringing about of a socialist revolution.

These four orientations and their modifications still continue to evolve. Some seem to move toward a dead end; others might become more promising. Viewing social development from a disciplinary perspective, one encounters a variety of emphases. Political scientists have outlined four dimensions of political development: "equality," which includes the transition in attitude from passive subject to active citizens, greater reliance upon achievement rather than ascription, and universalitistic and impersonal rules and laws rather than particularistic ones; "capacity"—that is, the rational organization of administration, and increase in the capabilities of the political system; "differentiation," which involves structural specialization; and "integration" of roles and structure.

Sociologists view society as advancing from a simple to a complex state through a process of differentiation and adaptation. The sociology of development concerns identifying and analyzing the social, cultural, and psychological changes associated with economic development and industrialization in terms of such dimensions as social values (communally oriented values versus individualistic achievement-oriented values), social organization (extended family versus nuclear family), occupational structure, social class and social mobility, urbanization, and communications.

These represent a relatively conventional set of dimensions. Another strand of sociological theory has focused more directly on the relations between social groups and between societies, on such issues as social cohesion and social conflict, and on the capacity of society to integrate and organize the interests and pressures of different social groups.

Should social development be conceived of merely as a process of change—in structure and institutions as well as in growth or product—toward certain selected goals? Here again, the important question is, Whose desirable ends and goals? For development to be meaningful, it must regard not just change but also values. The distinction here is one between development as a normative concept and development as an empirical process of change. It is argued that development is necessarily a normative concept, and that it involves values, goals, and standards, making it possible to compare a present state against a preferred one. This interpretation immediately raises the question of whose values and goals are to be taken into account in assessing development. Planners' values or citizens' values? Market values or politically determined values?

Social Development as an Alternative Development Strategy

To what extent is it possible to draw on theoretical models in order to define the relevant categories or components for a conceptual model of social development? The difficulty is that while there is no shortage of models or partial models at the present time (be they economic or political), there is no agreement about a general model of development in general and social development in particular. Evidently, the generality, ambiguity, and implicit value judgment involved in the concept of development make it difficult to arrive at a neatly defined conceptual framework of social development. Nevertheless, viewing the strength and weaknesses of various conceptions, approaches, and aims, one cannot help but enlarge the concept of social development to one that would capture the fullness of social reality. At this point, while an appropriate social development model is still in the process of being formulated, a few assumptions and facts regarding social development need to be stated to serve as the rationale for a social development framework. They are as follows:

1. The ultimate goal of development is *people*. People are not only the resources for developmental purposes, but also simultaneously the beneficiaries of the development. Benefits should be gained both in quantitative economic terms and also in social terms, which are often qualitative in nature. Changes brought about by modernization affect people's behavior, attitudes, and values, and their relationship with one another; unless these changes can be harmonized with their traditional life style and their local cultural systems, they will be the victims rather than the

beneficiaries of the new economic and social order envisaged by the development measures.

2. Development is a process in which social progress is not only a factor, but in many important respects also an arbiter and prerequisite of economic growth. This idea is gaining acceptance among the rising generation of development theoreticians and planners, and is most commonly expressed in terms of support for an "institutional" approach to development. This approach advocates an integrated whole development theory, taking into account both economic and noneconomic social factors. These are interrelated and cannot be considered or planned independent of each other, as has been the practice until very recently.

3. In the present state of development planning, the "social aspect of development" is at worst totally discounted and at best inadequately or irrelevantly addressed. Even when "social planning" is administratively recognized as a special function, it is often interpreted largely in terms of conventional sectoral approaches to the improvement of levels of life (i.e., specific programs in health, education, and social welfare) rather than from the viewpoint of promoting a cohesive structural and institutional change. And it is seen as a function entirely subordinated to "economic" planning, which invariably constitutes the major designated concerns of development planning at the national level. In actuality, economic planning and social planning are still widely regarded as dichotomous disciplines; development is not fully appreciated as an organized process calling for unified planning in which economic and noneconomic variables are simultaneously accounted for.

Conception

From the above rationale, the following premises of social development [as composite] should be considered:

1. That people are both the resources for and the beneficiaries of developmental purposes. Without this recognition, there is a tendency to consider people only as resources for development.
2. That development is the development of people in society as active participants in the development process, determining the means and goals of development.
3. That social development as a dynamic social change process involves maintaining an equitable level—between people and institutions—for seeking opportunities and providing opportunities.
4. That changes brought about by modernization and development should be in harmony with local cultural systems in regard to the people's capability for accommodation or replacement—considering

people as a dynamic cultural asset capable of engineering changes at will, rather than as a static target of change.

5. That the presumed sequential process of development with economic determinism is inadequate—that modernization and development are not a unilinear and universal process but rather can be multi-linear and cultural/historical specific.

6. That modernity and tradition are not mutually exclusive clusters of attributes, but instead have complex relationships.

7. That the three components of social development—economic, political, and sociocultural—are interconnected. Although there are no additive relationships among the three components, there are interactions among them. The combination, the magnitude, and the patterns of these interactions constitute the uniqueness of a culture. And it is the balance between the uniqueness of the local culture and the planned development and change in the desired direction at the desired rate, that should be the goal of social development for that culture.

8. That there need not be a separate development model or theory for each particular culture, but the model should be based predominantly on specific local realities. Common variables and processes across societies might subsequently emerge.

9. That the uniqueness of the particular cultural group is related more to the intrinsic cultural nature of people, which should be understood and used to motivate development. When neglected, this uniqueness often generates obstructions to change and development.

Conclusion

Of the present situation in Korea it might be said that outward appearance seems to be good and even good-looking because of its successful growth-oriented economic development. But as long as the large majority of farmers, who have contributed significantly to this successful growth, continue to be poor and are not able to share the benefits in a much more equitable manner than in the past, Korea will suffer from heart disease. The possibility of a heart attack, with serious or even fatal results, cannot be ruled out. Korea's backbone has continued to give it repeated trouble because of the so-called vicious cycle of Korean politics; it too could be broken irreparably and fatally. At the same time, the spirit of this human body has not been high because of increasing uncertainty and declining confidence in coping with various problems.

The overall picture for Korea at the moment cannot be characterized as hopeful, although it would be wrong to perceive it as hopeless. However, this less favorable situation has been somewhat compensated for by increasing public awareness of the problems and their possible resolution.

In a very real sense, development over the past thirty years in Korea has been the development of things, not the development of institutional infrastructures and not the development of people as self-reliant, self-respecting human beings. Now Korea must shift development emphasis from capital-intensive projects oriented toward economic growth measured in terms of gross national product to improvement of the quality of life for all the people. The development emphasis should move from material structures to social institutions and from GNP to quality of life.

Thus, Korea should give the highest priority to theories of social development that will, when applied, contribute most to the development of people and people's institutions. If we have been right in our identification of these theories, when effectively applied they should generate and give direction to a process of program development and implementation that will contribute to improving the quality of life for all the people of Korea.

PART II

Korea Is Different

CHAPTER THREE

The Theory and Applicability of Democratic Elitism to Korean Public Administration

Bun Woong Kim and David S. Bell, Jr.

RECENT PUBLICATIONS IN Korean public administration point to the inapplicability of Western theories to explain the unique bureaucratic environment of this newly industrialized nation. It has become increasingly apparent that there is a need for general scientific guidelines to explain the tremendous diversity of bureaucratic development in the world today. A model that is limited by, or adheres to, classic social evolutionary theory does not have the flexibility or openness necessary to accommodate the vast amount of information we have about culturally distinctive bureaucracies in the developing nations. Alberto Guerreiro-Ramos argued for the merits of "Theory P or a possibility model" that would free us from the biases of Western culture-bound determinism: There is no strict "law of historical necessity" that compels every nation-state to evolve in the same manner or at the same tempo or to the same level of "modernity" as in the West. Each nation-state must be viewed in its historical, socioeconomic nexus "in and of itself."[1]

Thus many Korean scholars have argued that conventional Western theories are not adequate to fully explain what really transpires in the Korean administrative setting. The gap between scholars of public administration and actual practitioners seems partially linked to the fact that academicians largely refer to foreign sources of information and guidance in their professional field, while the actual administrators take counsel in the local managerial staff and in their own experience. Direct participation in their own Korean administrative system may be a way to root theorists more solidly in the realities and complexities of the Korean public bureaucracy.

Taken from Bun Woong Kim and David S. Bell, Jr., "The Theory and Applicability of Democratic Elitism to Korean Public Administration," *Asian Journal of Public Administration* 7 (1985):70–76.

The contemporary Korean bureaucracy itself, however, is a complex mixture of Korean culture patterns and public administration practices adopted from abroad. Chong Bum Lee has used "indigenization" to describe the forces affecting contemporary Korean administration. Indigenization, he states, is

> the process whereby the Western science of public administration is introduced into Korean culture and takes on a new form through interactions with the existing concepts and practices in the area of public administration as well as with overall Korean cultural patterns, which leads to changes and assimilation.[2]

Indigenization, therefore, is the process of establishing a new highly adaptive system of thought and behavior that accurately reflects the social dynamics of the indigenous culture.

Korean scholars have concluded that Korean bureaucratic change will not likely follow the developmentalist model prevalent in the West because its predominant political pattern is culturally alien to Western, democratic pluralism. However, it must be noted that the development of an indigenous theory of bureaucratic change will not obviate what Robert Dahl has labeled ". . .the dilemma of organizational autonomy and control. Satisfactory solutions—much less ideal ones—elude both theory and practice in all technologically advanced countries. . ."[3] Although the dilemma is more hidden from public view in countries governed by authoritative regimes, pressures for organizational autonomy are like coiled springs precariously restrained by the counterforce of the state and ready to unwind whenever the system is jolted.

Western scholars have argued that pluralist politics is the best model for political and administrative development in developing nations. A working definition of pluralism is a model polity diffusing sociopolitical power as widely as possible throughout the society. As an ideal, pluralism has been combined with "liberal-participatory" democracy, and as a public administrative system, it has merit as a means of achieving incremental change based on long-term stability. However, pluralist solutions may be inapplicable to the Korean decision-making arena because of the pervasiveness of an authoritarian political culture.

Since the Republic of Korea's independence in 1945, the Western pluralist model has had a far-reaching impact on the establishment of the formal institutional framework of the Korean government. Beyond the formal structures, however, the impact has been minimal, and bureaucratic elitism, perhaps more accurately stated as paralytic centripetalism, rather than democratic pluralism persists in public policy making. We may ascribe this to the lack of sociocultural preconditions of pluralism. The authoritarian political tradition of Korea does not nurture such pluralistic prerequisites as (1) viable competition among individuals, elites, or groups; (2) opportunities for individuals and organizations to gain input access to the decision-making process; (3) organizational mediation between elites and masses; (4) viable instruments of mass participation in political decisions such as elections and other media of influence and access; and (5) democratic consensus based on a "democratic creed." Korea's drift to authoritarian government, therefore, should be viewed in part as historical-cultural determinism and in part by the absence of the pluralistic prerequisites.

The most important factor in pluralism, Tocqueville believed, was widespread individual-in-group participation in politics. In fact, however, contemporary empirical studies reveal that only a small minority of citizens, mostly from the upper socioeconomic strata, participate actively in American political parties and interest groups. Even the character of the voluntary association celebrated by Tocqueville has been significantly altered by the emergence of large-scale hierarchical organizations.

Critiques of pluralist theory tend to start by noting the gaps between pluralist rhetoric and pluralist practice, and the need to revise some features of the pluralist ideal itself. C. Wright Mills launched a polemical critique against the class bias of pluralist theory. Mills argued that in the United States political power had become nationalized and concentrated in one interrelated economic, military, scientific-technical, and intellectual "power elite." Moreover, the pluralist system of decision making was significantly biased toward the concerns and priorities of international corporate capitalism.[4] Henry Kariel pointed to the oligarchical tendencies of large-scale organizations that function both as interest groups influencing governmental policy and as agencies making policy of great public consequence. In particular, he stated that pluralism under conditions of large-scale technology conflicts with the principle of constitutional democracy.[5] Theodore Lowi emphasized the failure of interest group liberalism, arguing that pluralist theory today militates against the idea of a separate government because a separate government violates the basic principle of the autonomous society; and he concluded that in the United States, the new liberal public philosophy—interest group liberalism—was corrupted by the fallacies of its primary intellectual component of pluralism.[6] William Connolly explained the bias of pluralism in the following terms.

> Pluralist politics today is one dimensional. Not only are the issues generated by competing groups constrained by established values and expectations or ideological constraints, but contemporary social structure encourages groups to organize around occupational categories while inhibiting effective political organization on the basis of other considerations. These structural constraints reinforce rather than mitigate existing ideological constraints.[7]

He added that one-dimensional pluralist politics suppressed the exploration of alternatives by proliferating issues within a narrow range of concerns.

The theoretical-empirical weakness of pluralism as a model democratic ideology may help explain its dysfunctional consequences for a developing polity. Under certain conditions pluralistic politics may even have dysfunctional effects on the rate of national development. Perhaps the cultural constraints so salient in the psychocultural characteristics of the Korean people may not support the preconditions assumed to be necessary for pluralist-democratic government. The unusually cohesive Korean political culture, based on a remarkably homogeneous society, does not condition environmental time-space for the fragmentation of power or the competitive balance of power between interest groups. The absence of natural cleavages is not consistent with an "equilibrium" model of diverse political groupings in balance.

The elite-mass class division of Korean society tends to support a political system maintained by domination and regulation, not by pluralist interest group balancing. The high degree of political centralism or authority imposes elitist-made policy upon the different strata of the masses. Other persistent ideological/ecological constraints in postwar Korean government also inhibit pluralistic prospects for political and socioeconomic development. These include (1) a narrow range of individual political freedom; (2) executive dominance of the bureaucracy, legislature, and judiciary; (3) limitations on the role and function of political parties; (4) increased role of the military in politics; (5) the security threat from North Korea; and (6) national planning for rapid economic growth. In addition, the Republic of Korea confronts universal dilemmas of nation building such as the centrifugal forces of familial ties, psychopolitical oppositionalism, and other problems caused, in part, by the influence of Western ideologies and institutions. The gradual, incremental nature of the pluralist model with its ideal of popular participation in public policy making may not facilitate political stability or socioeconomic development in Korea.

Joseph LaPalombara has argued that the concept of modernity carries with it culture-bound assumptions of Western determinism positing a unilinear evolution historically traceable to the social Darwinist model of development. He suggested that "given certain national developments a bureaucracy that does not fully conform to democratic norms may be more effective in bringing about certain kinds of change than one that does manifest such conformity."[8] Fred Riggs advanced a similar concern:

> the developmental problems of the new states should be examined in their own terms, and not as possible arenas for the importation of methods and solutions which have proved useful to other countries facing a different set of problems. It is just as fallacious to think that transitional coun-

tries can or should take over intact the latest political and administrative techniques of the most developed countries as to think that they should go through the same stages of change as were experienced in the eighteenth or nineteenth century by Western nations.[9]

The Korean bureaucratic elite, a bureaucracy that clearly does not conform to democratic forms, warrants consideration as an effective instrument in facilitating economic and social developmental objectives. There are several significant ecological changes in the social-physical environment which may help in understanding how bureaucratic elitism assists development. These ecological changes are: (1) population increases and demographic mobility; (2) the impact of the Korean War on political institutions and political consciousness; (3) the effect of economic inflation on political regimes; (4) the expansion of education, urbanization, and the size and status of the military; (5) institutional changes, that is, the growth of formal organizations, and the growth of occupational specialization; and (6) ideological changes, bringing with them a positive new view of democratic ideals. Widespread rapid ecological change has had significant effects on traditional Korean social structure, such as the proliferation of what Suzanne Keller termed "strategic elites" replacing to some extent the ruling classes of the Japanese colonial period, 1910–1945. According to Keller, the term "strategic elites" refers to a minority of individuals designated to serve a collectivity in a socially valued way. Their origin lies in the complex heterogeneity of modern societies—age, sex, ethnicity, skills, strength, and division of labor.

However, the bureaucratic elite impedes the development of democratic objectives. The new Korean elites tend to base their elitism on the assumption that the masses are not yet democratically acculturated and therefore incapable of making any viable national policy judgments. Koreans "perceive democracy and politics in close relationship to some high ideals and principles rather than to institutionalized procedures for expressing the people's will or free choice." As a consequence, public policy making is generally considered to be the exclusive domain of a few select and experienced leaders. However, it seems culturally conceivable that the present antidemocratic bureaucratic elitism might become what has been termed "democratic elitism" operating in a quasi-democratic institutional framework.

According to Joseph Schumpeter, democracy may be defined as elite competition, presuming that "the democratic method is the institutional arrangement for arriving at political decisions in which. . .individuals acquire the power to decide by means of competitive struggle for the people's vote." Thus, according to Schumpeter, ". . .democracy means only that the people have the opportunity of accepting or refusing the men who are to rule them," implying "government approved by the people" instead of "government by the people."[10]

The democratic elitist contends that elites must become the chief guardians of the system, viewing the political passivity of the people not as an element of democratic malfunctioning, but as a necessary condition to allow for the creative functioning of the elite. Therefore, the business of making important decisions and policies is that of elite domination after the masses select the elites. In Korea, a great expansion of governmental institutions has taken place during the last four decades. Nevertheless, by the early 1980s, most sectors of the Korean polity appear to be unable to perform self-governing responsibilities. In fact, it seems that Korean political culture necessitates administrative centralization and collectivism from the core or strategic elite to maintain sociopolitical stability as modernization proceeds. Thus the result is that all important decisions are made unilaterally at the highest levels, viz., presidential and ministerial, and all public employees are exhorted to work for the accomplishment of the collective objective. Jong Sup Jun states that

> implementing the developmental goals, the government has achieved a great deal by appearing to the people to act cohesively in the national interests. Once administrative orders are given from the top echelon, strict obedience is expected without questions or criticisms. Since the public employees are always told what to do, it is easier for them to follow orders rather than reasoning; in case of possible failure of administrative directives, they don't have to be blamed for their disobedience or irresponsibility.[11]

This, of course, underestimates the potential contributions of all employees below the top echelon, produces passive behavior, overemphasizes the vertical consciousness of bureaucrats, and reinforces the exclusivity of the governing elite.

The guardian beliefs of democratic elitism seem culturally compatible with the Korean polity in which key governmental policies are determined by elite preference. Whatever the desirability or feasibility of democratic elitism, the democracy of limited-participation government by competing elites and political stability may offer a theoretical option reconciling democratic ideals with Korea's bureaucratic elitist heritage. If democratic elitism were to undergo some transformation in the Korean setting it would probably not extend beyond some form of "guided democracy," which would violate many of the stated principles of the classic pluralist model of participatory democracy.

Notes

1. Alberto Guerreiro-Ramos, "Towards a Possibility Model," in Willard A. Beling and George O. Totten (eds.), *Developing Nations: Quest for a Model* (New York: Van Nostrand Reinhold, 1970), pp. 21–59.
2. Chong Bum Lee, "A Prolegomenon to the Indigenization of Public Administration," *Korean Political Science Review*, 13 (1979), p. 363.
3. Robert A. Dahl, *Dilemmas of Pluralist Democracy: Autonomy vs. Control* (New Haven, Conn.: Yale University Press, 1982), p. 3.
4. C. Wright Mills, *The Power Elite* (New York: Norton, 1969), pp. 5–25.
5. Henry S. Kariel, *The Decline of American Pluralism* (Stanford: Stanford University Pres, 1961), pp. 3–4.
6. Theodore Lowi, *The End of Liberalism* (New York: Norton, 1969), pp. 46–52.
7. William Connolly, "The Challenge to the Pluralist Theory," in William Connolly (ed.), *The Bias of Pluralism* (New York: Atherton Press, 1969), p. 17.
8. Joseph LaPalombara, "Bureaucracy and Political Development: Notes Queries, and Dilemmas," in Joseph LaPalombara (ed.), *Bureaucracy and Political Development* (Princeton, N.J.: Princeton University Press, 1963), p. 55.
9. Fred W. Riggs, "Bureaucrats and Political Development: A Paradoxical View," in LaPalombara (ed.), *Bureaucracy and Political Development*, p. 167.
10. Joseph A. Schumpeter, *Capitalism, Socialism, and Democracy* (New York: Harper & Row, 1975), p. 269.
11. Jong Sup Jun, "The Paradoxes of Development: Problems of Korea's Transformation," paper for the 1982 ASPA National Conference, March 21–25, Honolulu, p. 17.

CHAPTER FOUR

The Administrative Culture of Korea: A Comparison with China and Japan

Mahn Kee Kim

SINCE THE THREE nations of East Asia—China, Japan, and Korea —have for many centuries maintained a very close relationship among themselves not only in terms of culture but also in terms of geographical proximity, they are often recognized as a common cultural sphere, the cultural sphere of Confucianism or of *Han* (China). In fact, Korea and Japan are seen to have belonged to the same cultural sphere as China for more than 1,000 years. Nevertheless, in the case of studying the bureaucratic system or bureaucratic culture of the three nations of East Asia, scholars have tended to confine the object of their analysis to only one nation of the three. However, it is self-evident that a comparative study of more than two nations will be more meaningful.

Among scholars, there are some who seek similar basic characteristics for the three nations of East Asia and there are still others who maintain that though the three nations may seem similar to the eyes of Westerners, more dissimilarities than similarities can be found among them when a closer analysis is made.

From such a viewpoint, based on the premise that Confucianism can be a frame of reference to inquire into value orientation and personality of the members of these three nations, this study attempts to find characteristics of Koreans that clarify the similarities and dissimilarities among the three nations.

We generally tend to list Confucianism as the greatest determinant in the formation of Korean culture, particularly in the formation of traditional value orientation. But there are many determinants in Korean culture in addition to Confucianism. In this connection, Suk-choon Cho lists Con-

Taken from Mahn Kee Kim, "Administrative Culture of Korea: A Comparison with China and Japan," *Korean Social Science Journal* 10 (1983):116–133.

fucianistic, Buddhistic, and folk elements and Wan Ki Paik presents Confucianism, Buddhism, and Shamanism, while Bun Woong Kim presents Confucianism, Buddhism, and Taoism. According to Chang Tae Kum, in the formation of historical religious tradition of Korea Confucianism led the formation of culture in the upper class and Shamanism in the lower class while they were coexisting and interacting with each other.[1] While Confucianism provided Korea with principles of ruling and a normative system, folk faith based on Shamanistic practice and the primitive faith prevalent in Northeast Asia became deeply rooted among the grassroots.

In the case of China, Confucianism was not a single dominant religion. It formed a dual structure in alliance with Taoism, a similar tradition of superstition, or with Buddhism. Even though the normative consciousness of Confucianism was deeply rooted in the ordinary life of Chinese people, Taoism was the religion of the folk and Confucianism was a religion most suitable to patriarchal bureaucrats.

Thus, not only Confucianism but Buddhism, Taoism, and Shamanism greatly influenced the cultural sphere of *Han*. However, the greatest determinant of Korean administrative culture is Confucianism, which led to the formation of an upper-class culture, providing the traditional society of Korea with principles of ruling and normative systems. In other words these three nations of East Asia belong to the cultural sphere of Confucianism in politics and administration.

Yet, one should take note of the fact that while Confucianism exerted a great influence in the formation of administrative culture in these three nations, the degree of influence varied from one country to another. To start with, Confucianism became systematized in China over every corner of the country. To the Chinese people, Confucianism became something like a skin that can never be rubbed off. It has been generally recognized that though Korea introduced Confucianism from China, Korea became an honor student of Confucianism, in some aspects, more faithful to the tenets of Confucianism than the Chinese people were.

Japan presents a somewhat different picture. In Japan, Confucianism was something that never exceeded the realm of scholastic study. It provided a norm of behavior, to some extent, for the Samurai (warriors) class in the upper echelons of society, but it failed to penetrate into the ordinary life of the farmers, merchants, and artisans in the lower echelons. Again, Japan did not adopt the state-examination system for the recruitment of higher civil servants while other Confucianist nations did— Japan did not see the formation of a bureaucratic organization operated by Confucian scholars. If there was anything similar to bureaucrats in Japan, it would be the *buke* (families of samurai) who upheld the martial arts as the supreme goal of their training. Though Confucianism was taught at the *hanko* (schools in feudal territory), it was merely an elective course for one's general education and was not a required course. In other words, Confucianism was a part of general education in the period of the *buke* system and failed in penetrating deep into the life of politics and administration, as was the case in China and Korea. Of course, Japan also had Confucianist officials but they were not above the position of either secretaries or archivists. Statesmen from Samurai classes held the positions of public officials in their own hometowns for many hundreds of years and they were rarely transferred to other regions. Bureaucracy of this nature cannot be called a bureaucracy in a real sense and from such a viewpoint, it is generally accepted that true bureaucracy did not exist in Japan until the era of Meiji.

The varying degrees of influence of Confucianism in the three nations of East Asia will be examined later in this chapter. However, the ethical view of Confucianism and the general attributes of thought on politics and administration will be briefly touched upon here.

Tae-rim Yoon defines the ethical view of Confucianism as self-effacing, patriarchical, and family centered. Confucianism is said to be a political ethic that upholds and protects the authority of rulers rather than the freedom and equality of individuals. Thus, it is claimed that in a Confucian society, there only exists a hierarchial relationship—a relationship of orders from above and obedience from below.[2]

Woon-tae Kim summarizes the general attributes of the political and administrative thought of Confucianism as those of benevolent government, moral justification, hierarchical orientation, and classicism. He describes the characteristics of ethical views held by every walk of life in the society of the Yi dynasty, when Confucianism became the state religion and Confucian political culture became an indigenous element of society, as (1) tradition-orientation, (2) ascription, (3) fatalism, (4) conservatism, (5) subserviency to the stronger, and (6) affectivity.[3]

Arthur Wright has extracted the following list of approved attitudes and behavior patterns from the Analects of Confucius.

1. Submissiveness to authority—parents, elders, and superiors
2. Submissiveness to mores and norms (*li*)
3. Reverence for the past and respect for history
4. Love of traditional learning
5. Esteem for the force of example
6. Primacy of broad moral cultivation over specialized competence
7. Preference for nonviolent moral reform in state and society
8. Prudence, caution, and preference for a middle course
9. Noncompetitiveness
10. Courage and sense of responsibility for a great tradition
11. Self-respect (with some permissible self-pity) in adversity
12. Exclusiveness and fastidiousness on moral and cultural grounds
13. Punctiliousness in treatment of others.[4]

On the other hand, Shin-pyo Kang insists that the study of Korean traditional culture should start with, in the first place, grasping the basic structure of culture of the three East Asian nations.[5] Thus, he offers three basic concepts—*pao, nunch'i,* and *amae*—in explaining social actions in Korea and Japan which had been affected by Chinese culture.

The basic concept for understanding the social actions of the Chinese is called *pao. Pao* as a verb means "to repay," "to retaliate," "to respond," and "to retribute." The core of the concept *pao* lies in response and return. Chinese believe that the reciprocity of actions between man and man and between man and supernatural beings should be as certain as a cause and effect relationship. Therefore, when Chinese act, they normally anticipate a response or return. The principle of reciprocal response has been applied to all kinds of social relationships in China beginning with that between the ruler and his subjects, which was the first of the *Wu-Lun* (Five Relationships).

The basic concept for understanding social actions in Korea is *nunch'i.* The word as a noun means "a social sense," "an eye for social situations," "tact," or "savior faire." The word as a verb means "to try to read one's mind," "to study one's face," "to grasp a situation," "to spy one's motivation," or "to see how the wind blows." The word *nunch'i* is often used to describe "a deceitful tact" of the weak (subordinates) toward the strong (superiors). In this connection, Se-chol Oh says *nunch'i* is "a self-defensive tact" rather than "an eye for social situations." Jae-sok Choi sees the characteristics of Korean behavioral patterns in *nunch'i* and describes it as "*nunch'i* culture." So-called moodism defined by Bong-shik Kim as characteristic of Korean administrative culture and the "*nunch'i* culture" seem to supplement each other.[6]

The most important concept for understanding the affective patterns of Japanese is called *amae. Amae* is defined "to depend and presume another's love," or "to seek and ask for another's indulgence." Thus, *amae* can be seen as role-fulfillment of the weak for achieving "oneness in infinite harmony" on the supposition of the benevolence of others. *Amae* of such nature is related to *on*—a notion opposite to *pao* of China. In other words, such *amae* is hidden behind the sense of obligation—that *on* (a kind of favor) should be returned. An *on* is given always by a superior to an inferior and thus constitutes a Samurai ethic that stresses the hierarchical order.

Now we need to select a number of important variables for comparison with a view to grasping the characteristics of Korean administrative culture amidst the three East Asian countries.

For the purpose of reference in selecting these variables from among many, a review will be made of those alleged by many scholars to be the characteristics of Korean administrative culture.

To start, Bong-shik Kim presents authoritarianism, nepotism, "safety-first" prudence, formalism, and moodism. Wan-ki Paik points out fatalism, familism, authoritarianism, affective humanism, ritualism, and anti-materialism. Woo-kon Yoon mentions authoritarianism, personalism, and make-believe in administrative execution. Suk Choon Cho selects eight variables for examination: familism, authority-relation between public officials and citizens, sense of law, status of man in an organization, generality and specificity, honorable poverty and material temptation, ascriptive orientation vs. achievement orientation, and affectivity vs. affective neutrality.

In this study, five common variables will be discussed to throw light on the characteristics of Korean administrative culture in comparison with those of the other East Asian nations. The five variables are (1) familism—notion of public and private, (2) authoritarianism—relationship between public officials and citizens, (3) sense of law—legal consciousness, (4) mental hierarchies—status of man in the organization, and (5) ritualism—formalism.

Familism

It is well known that family (blood) relationships have been traditionally stressed in all of the three nations of East Asia. However, there has been some difference in its strength among the three nations.

In the light of the influence of an extended family or of patriarchy, the general consensus among some scholars has been that family relation is strongest in China and weakest in Japan, and Korea is situated in the middle. In China, where the tradition of the large extended family has been firmly rooted, it was said that great wealth could not afford to be handed down for three generations, however great that wealth might be, because those related in blood to a successful family of the main tree and those in the relation of masters and servants depend on and devour it. Such a mutual-help practice within the same family clan is similar in Korea. In Japan, on the contrary, under a feudal system, the primary loyalty was extended not only to the family but to the feudal lord to some extent, and this has brought about a big difference in behavior patterns in administration from those of China and Korea. In other words, among the three nations of East Asia, Japan has most strongly distinguished public interest from private interest, placing public interest first.

Opinions differ among scholars as to whether China or Korea has a stronger influence of familism. While Moritani Masanori holds that familism in Korea has been quite strong but less so than in China, Yong-woon Kim maintains that family ties and blood consciousness of Koreans are far stronger than those of Chinese or Japanese.[7] Despite some discrepancies of opinions among scholars, it is commonly held that the strength of family consciousness is about the same in Korea and China, and that of Japan is relatively weaker.

However, Hae-jong Chon takes a contrasting view, focusing his attention on the aspect of "blood lineage." In his view, historically Japanese have held blood lineage most important.[8] In China, because of the state examination system for recruiting public officials, a change of regime was possible and frequent. Plain soldiers could become generals and even a humble man could become an emperor. Since the state examination did not set a limit in qualifications as to class, blood lineage did not count for much. In Korea, the change of dynasties was not so frequent as in China and in the Yi dynasty, the *yangban* (aristocrats) system developed in favor of blood lineage. There was still a high level of mobility among classes, yet family lineage was highly regarded since it was a society of hierarchial order. As has been pointed out earlier, not only the social status but the social position was hereditary in Japan because of its highly hierarchical structure. Since there was no system to control the tendency arising from blood lineage and familism, it is generally pointed out that the modern style of bureaucracy in the real sense was not developed in Japan.

However, there are some points we have to note in discussing the strong blood consciousness of Japanese. The view on blood ties in China and Korea is far different from that of Japan. First, the scope of blood ties in Japan is very narrow, circling around parents and siblings, and at the broadest extending only to uncles and cousins. Second, the important constituents of a family were not natural persons within the blood lineage but tangible and intangible assets or traditions that form the background history and facade of the family.

Such peculiarity in blood lineage in Japan is said to have been associated with the fact that unlike in China or Korea, Confucianism could not penetrate into the realm of daily life, limiting itself within the realm of scholastic study, and that the entities of the *han* (a feudal region) wielded a powerful influence in Japan. A *han* was a local feudal system established in the Tokugawa period. It was an extended form of a family system, providing momentum for a decentralized form of bureaucracy even in its imperfect form. As the *han* system was stabilized, the blood consciousness was weakened and limited in scope and the axis of groups shifted to *han*. And the collective consciousness deriving from the *han* system seems to have been handed down to the government and business organizations of Japan today.

In comparisons of social characteristics of Japan and Korea, Korea has been described as that of the family-oriented society or of extended-family-oriented society centering around "filial piety" while Japan has been noted as a nuclear(small) family-oriented society based on "loyalty." The collective tendency and selfless attitude of arduous labor are quite apparent in public and business administration in Japan. Thus, Japanese are rated as quite functional and well performing as members of a group. The collective tendency is also strong in Korea. In this sense, Korea is closer to Japan than to China. However, in Korea, such a collective orientation carries a different pattern from that of Japan. While the collective consciousness of Japanese centers around small groups, that of Koreans is oriented toward families, relatives, and other consanguine groups.

China traditionally promoted paternalism as the basis of the social structure, but paternalism did not exist in Japan. In contrast, *munjung* (family clan) in Korea is similar to "consanguine group" or "clan" of China in the same vein of a typical paternal group. In Japan, where there is no paternal system, the field in which an individual belongs (such as one's office or the village) carries great importance since it becomes an index of belongingness to a collectivity. Thus, a Japanese tends to stick to his group once he is assigned to that group, from a desire to attain stability, reinforcing the sense of belongingness. In most cases, a Japanese serves out his years at one working place until the age for mandatory retirement, a tendency that is also observed in the case of government officials.

In comparison, human relations in Korea are far more flexible and fluid. In Korea, blood ties including that of the paternal consanguine relationship work in favor of one's activity and one's social status. Furthermore, in Korea, one can mobilize the aid of ties with people from the same hometown, with school alumni, or with business partners. Thus, it seems that the influence of nepotism in the realm of public administration in Korea appears to be stronger than in Japan.

Koreans and Japanese alike use the word *hakbŏl* (in Korean) and *gakubatsu* (in Japanese, "school alumni relationship"). However, the meaning of this word differs widely between the two countries. According to the *New Dictionary of Korean Language, hakbŏl* is defined as (1) one's status and prestige deriving from one's schooling background and (2) factions formed around scholastic pursuit. The word in Japan is mainly used in the definition of (2) and the word is more widely used in Korea in the definition of (1). In other words, while the Japanese apply the meaning of this word to a sphere of influence, not of an individual, in Korea the word is used to denote one's educational background or social status. Most prime ministers of Japan are graduates of Tokyo University. Thus, it is said that, however excellent one may be, even by passing the higher state examination for public officials, a student can give up hope of advancement in public officialdom if he is not from Tokyo University. Elders and seniors of school alumni strive to recruit brilliant graduates from the same school to their organizations or offices so as to perpetuate the influence of the school alumni group. On the contrary, there is in Korea the word *munbol* (family clan group) which cannot be found in Japan. Even though Korean society has undergone striking changes since World War II, the influence of family clan groups seems to be preserved intact in various organizations or in social relationships in Korea, and no one can deny that the influence of familism and nepotism is still rampant in Korea.

In the light of the foregoing discussion, it seems proper to say that, while the structural analysis based on vertical relationships is relevant in analyzing the characteristics of social structure in Japan, it is more proper to submerge the vertical relationship within the frame of consanguine relationship in Korea—in other words, analysis of social structure in Korea will be done more accurately through the analysis of the vertical relationship that flows along the path of consanguine lineage.

Authoritarianism

Almost without exception, scholars studying Korean administrative culture refer to an authoritarian character of Koreans saying that this characteristic has been derived from a tenet of Confucianism. In other words, it is that Confucianism sees all human relations in the light of a vertical relationship and that upper classes always wield authority and lower classes always obey authority.

Because in Japan Confucianism has been weaker, whenever public bureaucrats try to formulate any plans or regulations for the purpose of control based on their certain policy perspective, they are bound immediately to run into stiff opposition from private sectors on the pretext of "excessive" authoritarianism or of bureaucratic control. In this connection, some also say that most higher civil servants in Japan today (department or bureau chiefs) are seized with an obsession that they are being persecuted. Seen from the outside, Japanese bureaucrats may seem to have huge power but it is said, in fact, they do not at all feel that they can wield such an influence or power.

Then, what is the case in Korea?

Though China and Korea are both Confucianist countries, the ideal in Korea has been oriented around the *yangban* (aristocrat) family clan and the ideal in China has been centered around the "gentry" family clan. The main concern of the gentry in China has been focused on the maintenance of order rather than the possession of power. The gentry in China did not care whether they were in government service and did not show much interest in forming communities for the maintenance of their interests and privileges. On the other hand, in Korea, the *yangban* had to be closely associated with power groups in order to preserve their privileges as *yangban*. The *yangban* classes in the Yi dynasty had endeavored to organize a community of their own in order to protect their status and they were intent upon enjoying the privileges as individuals vis-à-vis other members of the society. Thus, bureaucrats were strictly distinguished from others. People at large could not assert their rights against public organizations and they had no other choice but obedience. Government was always superior vis-à-vis any private organizations. Public policy had to be set by bureaucrats alone and private policy had to follow.

It seems that the exercise of public authority has been more powerful in Korea than in Japan and China. Yet the level of equality consciousness among people has been higher among Koreans than among Japanese. Kim Yong-woon maintains that while hierarchical relationships were predominant in Japan, equality consciousness was deeply rooted among people in Korea. If Japanese believed that "superiors are the same as heaven," Koreans firmly believed that "man is heaven and heaven is man." In this sense, the culture of Japan can be called a vertical culture while that of Korea is horizontal. Again, the history of Japan has been one of rulers and Korean that of the people.

Up until the modern age, people in both Japan and Korea were severely exploited by public authority. However, when such exploitation reached a point of unbearable extremity, Japanese farmers appealed to authority, even sacrificing the lives of the masterminds of revolt, while Korean farmers begged good-willed measures from the king, staging sit-in demonstrations in front of the royal court. In this sense, Koreans seem to have been treated far more "democratically" than their Japanese counterparts, at least in terms of institutional practices.

According to Pyoung-choon Hahm, it is not their authoritarian mentality that causes Koreans to fail to appreciate the importance of a "loyal" political position. It is their dislike of every form of tension, strain, conflict, challenge, confrontation, aggressiveness, combativeness, and so on.[9] In other words, Koreans prefer that rulers control themselves, survey what people want, and reflect such findings in their governing of the country rather than that the people themselves control the power of the rulers by building up their own power base. Seen in such light, it seems to be too hasty to draw a conclusion that Korea's administrative culture is far more authoritarian than that of Japan or China.

Sense of Law

Confucianism seems to have stressed, traditionally, "rule of virtue" (benevolent government) more than "rule of law." The political ideals of Confucianism upheld the realization in politics of ethics in line with the rules of courtesy (li) and the rules of heaven. For this purpose, it set "rule by virtue" through "personal cultivation" as a precondition.

What, then, are the similarities in legal culture among the three nations of East Asia with the same background of Confucianist culture?

In China, the legal sense seems to have been weak in daily life including economic activities. Historically, there did not exist any lawyers in the Western sense. This can be attributed to a tradition that "strong-willed kings may break the state law," but at the same time it can be also attributed to the fact that the Chinese were indifferent to procedural laws for litigation. China did not develop such legal consciousness as the natural law of Rome or the statutatory laws embodied from the natural law of Rome. Even in litigations in China, it is said that "rule of appropriateness" was more respected than "rule of legal provisions."

Korea, like China, did not experience the rise of lawyers or the development of natural law or statutory law. Reliance on the rule of appropriateness based on human affectivity in litigation at the court was also similar to that in China. In Korea, punishment meted out for violations of law was often criticized as being too harsh or as being an outcome of ignorance of the related circumstantial relationship involving the violation and a less strict application of law was rated as a better administration of justice. In handing down a verdict or conducting negotiations, Koreans did not examine each provision of law but preferred to resort to extra-legal human affectivity. Koreans show a negative response to a move to limit the scope of discretionary judgement, which aims to embody the Confucianist morality placing the "rule of man" before the "rule of law." Even though the rule of law is observed in the course of time and the limitation on discretionary latitude may be tolerated on the surface, it has hardly been internalized.

Thus seen, the Koreans' sense of law is more or less in the line of "rule of man" while that of the Japanese is of "rule of law." There is a saying in Korea, "a man can live on without the intervention of laws." In contrast, the Japanese "cannot live on without the provisions of law." That is, the particular sense of law held by the Japanese stipulates that an observance of law should precede the individual sense of morality of each person. Thus seen, the Japanese seem to comply with the legal sense of the Romans or with the ideals of Max Weber more than do the Koreans or Chinese.

Yet Suk Choon Cho maintains that the law-observing spirit of Koreans is high in comparison to any other nation. Since law has been employed as a *modus vivendi* by rulers throughout the ages of the Yi dynasty and of Japanese domination, Korean people tend to see law more as a threatening and frightening entity. Thus, it is often seen in public offices that while legal knowledge is respected, the observance of law is strictly encouraged in the public sector, and superiors in high positions demand more strict observance of law from their inferiors, they themselves violate the law and they also demand more strict observance of the law from people.

Mental Hierarchies

Hierarchical orientation has been a part of the general attributes of political thought of Confucianism, as has been pointed out earlier. It was a natural outcome of Confucianism which upholds ethics, cause, and realistic order of society and which derives from the hierarchical trend of the feudal system that seeks stability and harmony of the primary social groups in the hierarchical system of vertical order.

According to Suk Choon Cho, a dominant value governing bureaucratic behavior in Korea is that of hierarchical order, which tends to be regarded as the natural form of human relations. Confucianism was instrumental in the formation of this view of the bureaucracy. Egalitarian norms introduced after World War II have not brought a significant change in the traditional behavior patterns of bureaucrats.

In regard to China and Japan, it is said that hierarchical order is stronger in Japan than in China. That is, in Japan, the criterion of hierarchical order functions stronger in social life. In China the merits of individuals or individual achievements always precede the hierarchical order though a hierarchical order for age and status is observed as a courtesy for the sake of social order.

In Japan, subordinates observe the hierarchical order even when they air their opinions. When they do not, they tend to be criticized as violating the hierarchical order or as revolting against superiors. As such, in Japan, mental hierarchies work strongly not only in terms of superficial behavior but also in terms of airing opinions. In China, subordinates show their respect for their superiors—for instance, placing themselves a few steps behind superiors—but when an important issue arises subordinates are said to boldly air their opinions in front of their superiors.

Then what is the difference in mental hierarchies between Koreans and Japanese?

Yong-woon Kim describes Japanese society as vertical and Korean society as horizontal. Mental hierarchies in Japan and Korea are well expressed in honorifics of discriminatory wordage in their languages. There are more than ten words in Japanese, compared to two or three in Korean, to indicate the first person singular. There is a feminine gender in the Japanese language while in Korean there is none. In Japan, those from a lowly class cannot exert their influence even if they become rich. In Korea, there is strict discrimination between high and low classes. However, despite such surface differentiation, there exists a consciousness expressed in a Korean saying, "Even a butcher from a lowly class can be in a high class if he throws away his butcher knife." Nowadays, Koreans believe that one can be in a high class if one is rich enough.

While differentiation in social hierarchies was quite strict and mobility in social status was almost impossible in Japan during the feudal system under the rule of warrior (Samurai) classes, such a differentiation in classes was less conspicuous in Korea and China and there was some social mobility in social classes. Common people in Japan, since they could not extricate themselves from the yokes of such rigid structure of social hierarchies, developed a strong orientation toward the achievement of their individual goals and attained the blooming of folk culture, folk taste, and folk entertainment. In China and Korea, social mobility was possible through the state examination system and by means of the change of rulers, and they developed a strong tendency of aspiring to higher status.

In regard to the status of individuals within a given organization (or group), less restriction has been imposed on individuals in a group in Korea than in Japan. While the individual has tended to be subordinated within a group in Japan, the individual in Korea has been able to enjoy more freedom and receive less group restriction.

Ritualism and Formalism

According to Max Weber, while Westerners tend to regulate their own behaviors based on internal awakening deriving from individualism and based on their own sense of responsibility, East Asians tend to be influenced by ritualism and formalism in line with a large number of conventions and customs.[10] Woon-tae Kim also points to ritualism and formalism as a part of general attributes of Confucianist political thought. Formalism starts from the discourse on courtesy in systematizing Confucianist ethical order. Since courtesy is the comprehensive basis of all social behavior and social order, anything not allowed by courtesy cannot be recognized legitimately. In this sense, formalism is said to be a tendency to guard the criterion or form in meting out social legitimacy.[11]

The political ideal of China is "the rule of courtesy." Generally, the Chinese are known to highly regard "face" (*mentzu*), and such a tendency may be taken as ritualism or formalism since *mentzu* upholds the side of cause (justification). Some scholars point to the defects of traditional Chinese bureaucracy in explaining do-nothingism and the lack of initiative. Marshall Dimock points out that, influenced in part by the Chinese tradition, the Japanese bureaucrats also developed solidly established ways of thinking and working that involved much red tape, set procedures, and form for form's sake, and resulted in a blurring of responsibility and a deadening of initiatives.[12]

Nevertheless, the mental structure of Japanese can be said to be far more pragmatic than that of Chinese; Japanese have a high sense of realistic perception for the sake of *modus vivendi* and can separate cause and interest. The principle of "separation of politics and economy" or the co-existence of the emperor system and the democratic political institutions bespeak the basic pattern of Japanese culture based on dual structure. In the political and administrative ideologies, while China was based on "the rule of courtesy," Japan regarded academism, art, and culture as something separate from politics.

Then what is the difference between the value orientations of Japanese and Koreans? Generally, the value sense of Koreans based on the principle of cause seems to be closer to that of Chinese. Historically Korea has sided with China, and in the application of the tenets of Confucianism Koreans were more thorough-going than the Chinese, who originated Confucianism.

In feudal times in Japan, the strongest among many feudal lords held hegemony at a given time, also in the realm of thought and religions. The Japanese selected the most influential ideas and with some revisions made them their own. In Korea, scholars in the time of the Yi dynasty never deviated from the traditions of confucianism or the doctrines of *Chu-tzu*.

Yong-woon Kim holds that the primary reason why the value orientation of Japanese based on efficiency-first, which can be described as the national characteristic of Japan, came to be established may be that Japanese did not need to uphold their own tradition or ethnic culture by dint of the geographical position of Japan as an island country. In other words, they did not have to fear threats from outside. In contrast, Korea is situated on the fringe of a continent and Koreans had to confirm their own identity all the time. They were seized with an obsession that they would otherwise be absorbed into the continent. Such psychological burdens on the minds of Koreans are said to have been reflected, after all, in Koreans' propensity to hold to "cause."

It is such mental traits of Koreans clinging to "cause" and traditions that have led to their ritualistic or formalistic administration. And this, in effect, has resulted in the loss of much pragmatism in implementation.

Notes

1. Suk Choon Cho, *Korean Public Administration* (Seoul: Pakyŏng-sa, 1980), p. 134; Wan Ki Paik, "Administrative Behavior in Korea," in Woon-tae Kim *et al.*, *Politics of Korea* (Seoul: Pakyŏng-sa, 1976), p. 433; Bun Woong Kim, "Korea: Political Culture, Administration, and Democratic Elitism," Ph.D. dissertation, Claremont Graduate School, 1976, p.23.
2. Tae-rim Yoon, *Personality of Korean* (Seoul: Hyŏndae Kyoyukch'ongsŏ, 1977), pp. 145–172.
3. Woon-tae Kim, *History of Public Administration in Yi Dynasty*, rev. ed. (Seoul: Pakyŏng-sa, 1981), pp. 44–53, 57.
4. Arthur F. Wright, "Value, Roles and Personalities," in A. F. Wright and Denis Twitchett (eds.), *Confucian Personalities* (Stanford: Stanford University Press, 1962), p. 8.
5. Shin-pyo Kang, "Toward a New Understanding of the Culture of the East Asians: Chinese, Korean and Japanese," *Journal of East and West Studies*, 3-1 (19750, pp. 40–41.
6. Se-chol Ol, "Koreans: Social Psychology in Depth," *Wŏlgan Chosŏn*, 2-1 (Jan. 1981), p. 163; Jae-sok Choi, *Social Character of Korean* (Seoul: Kaemun-sa, 1979), p. 21; Bon-shik Kim, "Characteristics of Korean Bureaucracy," in Kun-shik Yoon *et al.*, *Contemporary Politics and Bureaucracy* (Seoul: Taewang, 1976), p. 482.
7. Moritani Masanori, *Japan, China, and Korean—Comparison of Industrial Technologies: An Approach for the Study of Comparative Technology*, trans. Sang-yong Kim,

(Seoul: Kyŏngyong Monhwawŏn, 1980), p. 35; Yong-woon Kim, *Japanese and Korean Swords and Brushes* (Seoul: Ppurigip'ŭnnamu, 1981), p. 12.

8. Hae-Jong Chon, "Japan, Japanese, and Japanese Culture," in Bac-ho Hahn *et al.*, *Anatomy of Contemporary Japan* (Seoul: Han'gil-sa, 1978), pp. 286–287.

9. Pyong-choon Hahm, "Toward a New Theory of Korean Politics: A Reexamination of Traditional Factors," in E. R. Wright (ed.), *Korean Politics in Transition* (Seattle and London: University of Washington Press, 1975), p. 153.

10. Max Weber, *The Religion of China*, trans. Hans H. Gerth (New York: Free Press, 1951), pp. 226–249.

11. Woon-tae Kim, *History of Public Administration in Yi Dynasty*, p. 49.

12. Marshall Dimock, *The Japanese Technocracy* (New York and Tokyo: Walter/Weatherhill, 1968), p. 45.

PART
III

The Nature of
Korean Leadership

CHAPTER FIVE

The Formation of the Governing Elites in Korean Society

Wan Ki Paik

THE ANALYSIS AND interpretation of the "elite" phenomena can be considered as most important in the developing countries, for the decision on who is likely to be the governing elite is most likely to determine the direction, speed, and content of development. Numerous students of the social sciences in Korean society have paid much attention to the problems of Korean elite recruitment.

The elite factor is considered to be very important as an independent as well as a dependent variable in social sciences. First, as a dependent variable the recruitment pattern and establishment of the elite can be an accurate indicator for showing how the power of the society is structured and distributed. In addition, the recruitment problem of the elite not only represents the dominating value system of the society but also shows the continuity and discontinuity of the value system. The recruitment of the elite goes further to enable us to predict and measure the degree of representativeness of the various departments of the society, the stratification structure, the changeability of political roles, and the transformation of economic and industrial structures.

Now the role of the elite factor as an independent variable is also very important. This factor as an independent variable determines the kinds and contents of policies, accelerates or retards the speed of change, and influences the stability and changeability of the political system. Also, how the elite component is recruited and of whom it is composed could certainly produce tensions or instability among the various circles in the society. This concept of the elite factor as an independent as well as a dependent variable leads us to conclude that the elite factor is an important conceptual structure in understanding social, political, and economic phenomena.

Taken from Wan Ki Paik, "The Formation of the Governing Elites in Korean Society," *Korean Social Science Journal* 9 (1982): 49–65.

There are various kinds of elites—for instance, political, economic, managerial, military, administrative, and intellectual elites. This article will deal with only the governing elites composed of political and administrative personnel. The concept of the political elite here will be restricted to those who occupied ministerial posts in the government from 1948 to 1980, excluding the elites in the top echelon of the political parties and interest groups. Administrative elites mean those who occupied posts higher than the third grade in the Korean civil service system during the same period. The main reason to deal exclusively with these governing elites is that they determined almost all kinds of values in Korean society. Here we assert that Korean society has been a politics-oriented society in the sense that the weights and roles of political and administrative elites were incomparably higher than any others.

The Society of the Monolithic Power Structure and the Elites

Korean society has been historically characterized by a monolithic power structure in the sense that all kinds of power were centralized into the hands of one person. This power structure has surprisingly been reinforced while otherwise the society has been modernized and differentiated. We usually like to indicate that the power structure has come to be pluralistic and dispersed as the monarchical political system and the caste system have been abolished and the society has been professionally specialized and differentiated. This is not actually the case in Korean society. Korea might rather be the reverse of the historical development trends. We have witnessed many changes and much modernization in various aspects of the society during the last three or four decades, but the only change in the monolithic power structure during these periods is that it has been strengthened.

Even in the period of the Yi dynasty, the power structure had a moderately pluralistic character through the share of the power among the leading figures. In other words, the king's power became weakened as control was shared by some of the powerful subjects. All the more, the king's power was severely restricted by various institutions and regulations. Therefore, no kings were able to arbitrarily wield their power except the kings Yŏnsan-Kun and Kwanghae-Kun. Although the kings existed, the power was not monopolized by them but was divided among the powerful courtiers.

It was an irony, however, that the power structure became even more centralized as Syngman Rhee was elected as the first president under the democratic political system in 1948. Rhee was a typical charismatic leader who attempted to monopolize all political power. His charismatic character claimed the concentration of the power around him as its center. Because of this, the democratic political system did not contribute to making the political power pluralistic, but rather came to justify a dictatorial political leader through an imitation of democratic procedures. Thus, political power became monolithic as the political leader, even though elected by the people, claimed charismatic leadership that in fact resembled dictatorship. An elite system formed under dictatorial conditions is characterized by subordination, submission, and passiveness.

This dictatorial leader recruited only those who were subservient to him as the governing elites, intentionally avoiding those people who were self-assertive and popular, that is, those considered to be the main sources of possible uprisings to break down the virtually one-man system. A political leader characterized by charisma, self-righteousness, and dogmatic ideas is certain to regard the elites as his subordinate circle or attendants. Hence, only the people who unilaterally and unconditionally followed the charismatic leader were recruited to be governing elites. This kind of elite system is bound to lack continuity and representativeness. In addition, the elite recruited on the basis of the leader's personal trusteeship were immediately dropped from the elite group if they came to lose that trusteeship. It was also natural for the elite group personally attached to the leader to disappear at the same time that the leader fell from power.

It is apparent that Syngman Rhee's first cabinet selection greatly disappointed the Korean people. In composing his cabinet, he deliberately excluded such well-known figures as Ku Kim, Sŏng-su Kim, So-ang Cho, and Pyŏng-ro Kim. These men were highly regarded by the people for their patriotic, intellectual, cultural, and educational achievements, but were considered by Rhee to be troublemakers. The persons he sought in filling the cabinet posts were not the ones enjoying popularity but the ones he could easily handle and manipulate. His intention of avoiding the popular figures was shown from the start in his designation of the first prime minister, Yun-yŏng Yi. Yi had indeed been a minister in a church, and had become vice-president of the minor political party *Chosŏn Minju-Dang*. He had no political support base in South Korea, as he came from the northern part of Korea. Almost no one had even heard of him.

Accordingly the first Korean Assembly refused to ratify him as prime minister. Syngman Rhee then designated Pŏm-sŏk Yi, another unexpected nomination, for the post of prime minister. Seung-jo Hahn commented on Syngman Rhee's elite recruitment as follows:

> Syngman Rhee recruited elites and appointed them to the posts of minister and other important positions on the bases of personal confidence, intimacy, and affective relationship, ignoring the factors of education, training, experience, qualifications, capacities and political purposes. He just appointed his trustful followers to the high governmental posts as the king did in the monarchical system and considered neither rationality nor democratic responsibility in the recruitment of the roles.[1]

Obviously, the criteria for recruiting elites of Syngman Rhee were not the upgrading of system capacities and the building-up of legitimacy, but the personal confidence, devoted attendance, loyalty to him, role expectation as his hands and feet, and the advantages and usefulness for extending his regime. He never hesitated to jettison even a person once intimately tied with him if the person came to be regarded as someone of no value or, particularly, a threatening figure, and then reemploy that same person if he came to be reevaluated as being of some use. This kind of recruitment of the elite naturally derived from Rhee's philosophy of one-man rule and continued to exist for twelve years until his regime finally collapsed.

This pattern of recruitment of an elite was not confined to the composition of the cabinet, but extended to the composition of the governing bodies in the political party *Chayu-Dang,* which he created as an expedient for oppressing the forces of the opposition party. The appointment of Ki-bung Rhee to the post of chairman of the Central Committee in the party was a good example. This man claimed the total loyalty of the party for himself by appointing trustful retainers to the key posts of the party.

This kind of monolithic power structure and one-man rule system continued and came to be even more consolidated in Park Chung-Hee's regime. Park, however, paid considerable attention to the problems of national solidarity, representativeness, legitimacy, and professional qualification in composing his first cabinet. The designation of Tu-sŏn Choe for the post of prime minister was a good example of that attention. Choe had been for a long time the president of *Dong-A Ilbo*—one of the most powerful newspaper publishers—which was regarded as representing anti-governmental forces, and Park tried to put on a show of national consolidation through his appointment. Park also appointed a number of civilian experts to ministerial posts for the sake of eliminating the "smell" of a military cabinet.

Despite his initial endeavor to remove the crude characteristic of a military cabinet, however, Park's power structure continued to be more and more centralized than Rhee's previous regime. For the entire period of his eighteen years in power, he wielded almost absolute power, never restricted by any constitutional limitations, and built the efficiency-oriented structure of elites considered to be a necessary instrument for achieving indefinitely prolonged power. Park needed elites more concerned with the implementation of policies than with their formation: the kind of "elite" system he wanted was an instrumental one. In other words, he liked administration-oriented elites, not politics-oriented elites. The system of an elite which smacked of political character was hateful and troublesome to him. The ruling elites formed in this kind of political process were always subordinate to the political leader. The relationship between the political leader and the elites was characterized by domination and submission.

To make matters worse, the political leaders desperately attempted to hold power throughout their lives. Syngman Rhee and Park Chung-Hee were thus altogether typical models of the dictatorial personality. Both of them tried every possible means to extend their powers beyond their regular terms, even directing the revision of the constitution. It is beyond doubt that the political power monopolized by two separate political leaders over several decades came to lose its legitimacy: elite groups created by this kind of dictatorial leaders can never be deeply rooted in the people's minds, and hence have no appeal and little power over them. The establishment of an "elite" system having stability and continuity could no more be anticipated in Korean society than in any other. In any case, there could be no continuity and mutual allowance between the elite groups in a society where one corps of elites is totally replaced and eliminated by another quite different elite group through undemocratic and revolutionary measures.

The characteristics of the system of elites in a society with a resultant monolithic power structure, one where a political leader seized and pursued lifelong power through the monopolization of the political, economic, and other power sources, are as follows:

First, the governing elites alone decide and allocate all the major kinds of values in the society. No organizations or other groups were permitted to challenge or act against this elite group—and not allowed even to exist if they stood against those in power. Of course, there were quite a number of groups that pretended to criticize this elite group and acted as the ornament necessary for what passes for democracy at its best. Their challenge or criticism was not substantial but formalistic. This group of apparent elites looked powerful or somewhat effective, but in fact even its foundation of existence was very weak because its legitimacy and representativeness were always suspected by the people. As the prolongation of the power came to weaken the apparent legitimacy and authority of the political leader as well as the elite group, this group would of course be uprooted with the collapse of the leader.

We must thus assent that the peaceful change of power is essential for the prevention of instability and collapse. If a political leader seeks to make permanent his political power, he and his power elites can expect a miserable future. The elite group will be corrupt, spoiled, and will decay if the power is not changed. Power per se needs a certain period of rest; if it is endlessly pursued without a rest, it will not be able to escape facing a miserable collapse. The respite of power inevitably means the peaceful change of power.

Second, internal conflict—a power struggle for hegemony—and disruption would necessarily occur in the elite group. In the dictatorial system a unified single elite alone will exist and the counterelite will go underground. Meanwhile, without the existence of an opposition group, there will be no competition between the elite groups in and outside the government. A group will usually be able to strengthen its solidarity and hold together when it is surrounded by various challenging forces; if the group has no opposition, it usually suffers internal divisions or splits. The internal split in the elite previously cited did not occur as a challenge against the leader, but rather as the question of who would win the leader's personal confidence and occupy the center of the power around him. Social changes and development usually proceed with stability and continuity in a society where the pluralistic political elites openly compete with each other for the acquisition of power. On the other hand, when only one elite group exists, the changes or developments occur in the form of discontinuity or interruption in the replacement process of the elites. Any policies or programs pursued in a dictatorial political system supported by a single elite group, if it comes to fall, are likely to be totally rejected by the new emerging elites. Again, a society usually becomes dynamic and equilibrated when various elite groups exist and openly compete for the accomplishment of their political goals, while the society where only one elite group exists with the possibility of creating internal ruptures is full of dangers, including that of monotony.

Third, the ruling elite did not possess any kind of autonomy or self-assertion since it acted only as the tool or the limb of the leader. As will always happen, this elite shared the fate of the leader who created it, its characteristics being passiveness, subordination, and heteronomy. This elite group thus showed no unique or particular character since it was always identified with the leader. It was not concerned with policy making; instead it was totally devoted to serving and implementing the leader's will. It was not conceivable for the elite to stand against the leader. If one member of the elite did not follow his leader's unilateral directions, he was either not allowed to stay in the elite group or, if he stayed in the group, he became simply a nominal figure. It is beyond question that such an elite group is very far from the will of the people.

The Closed Character of Elite Recruitment

One of the most important parts of the theory of the elite is whether the openness of the elite recruitment is guaranteed. This is the problem of elite circulation: the openness of the elite recruitment is the precondition to guarantee their circulation.

In general, the base of elite recruitment in a traditional society would be very narrow or almost closed, being based on ascriptive criteria such as blood, aristocracy, and the possession of land. Later, as the society becomes more industrialized and democratic, the base of recruitment widens and becomes universal. In a word, the ascriptism is replaced by the achievement criterion in recruitment. It can hardly be denied, of course, that wealth, education, and religion are still among the important factors in being a member of the elite even in a democratic society. These factors are not decisive or absolute, however, but just conducive to becoming an elite. The first requirement to become an elite in a democratic society is still the individual's capacity.

One of the most important criteria for elite recruitment in a democratic society is representativeness. In other words, whether the elite group represents a majority of the people is the big question. The elite is usually considered to represent a certain group, which may be a geographical area, an occupational group, or an ethnic group.

The representativeness is guaranteed through the opportunity for articulating the interests of the groups concerned. These groups attempt to protect their interests through political representativeness. Here, the elected elites or even the appointed elites come to be justified through representativeness of the group concerned. In other words, if the governing elite lacks the representativeness, its legitimacy or justification is weakened. And if the geographical areas or occupational groups are over- or underrepresented in the elite recruitment, tensions or strains come to exist between the groups, and the elite system is likely to lose stability. The stability of the elite system therefore depends heavily upon representativeness. In this sense, the system of the elite is required to possess geographical, occupational, and even symbolic representation. A lack of representativeness inevitably brings about conflicts, tensions, and antagonisms between the groups and eventually the destruction of the nation-building effort.

The ascriptive conditions for becoming a member of an elite have disappeared through the abolishment of the aristocratic or caste system in Korean society. Any capable person can in theory be recruited as an elite. Despite the disappearance of the traditional factors, however, there have been controversies about the representativeness of the Korean "elite" system. It has been quite often indicated, for instance, that some geographical areas or universities were overrepresented while certain other areas were underrepresented. These two factors—geographical and educational—have been very sensitive in Korean society. Let us first consider geographical representativeness. The cabinet members and administrative elites will be considered separately in a discussion of this regional factor.

In Rhee's regime, Seoul was overrepresented with its 40 members (32.3 percent), followed by the Kyŏngsang, Ch'ungch'ŏng, and Kyŏnggi areas. Meanwhile Chŏlla province was underrepresented for its population. In short, most cabinet members were from the Seoul and Ki-Ho areas in Rhee's regime. The situation changed in Chang's regime. Chŏlla province became the most overrepresented area, with its 10 cabinet members (27.8 percent). The overrepresentation of Chŏlla province could be explained by the fact that many leaders of the opposition party who fought against Rhee's dictatorial regime came from this region.

Park also changed the pattern of recruitment of the elite. The over-representation of Kyŏngsang province led to cynical comments that Park recruited many elites from his native place. So many elites came from the Kyŏngsang area during Park's time that his regime was called the "Kyŏngsang-Do" regime. Kyŏngsang province produced as many as 79 cabinet members (27.5 percent). In fact, this region had also produced many cabinet members in the previous two regimes, but it was indeed highly overrepresented during Park's elite recruitment.

Let us now turn to the recruitment problem of administrative elites. The provincial areas of Kyŏngsang, Seoul, and Ch'ungch'ŏng were over-represented while the areas of Chŏlla, Kyŏnggi, and Kangwŏn were un-derrepresented. The Kyŏngsang area especially continued to be highly overrepresented through the years. This kind of overrepresentation could be explained for the same reasons as that of the cabinet members.

The regional or geographical area has historically had very important implications in the problems of power structure or value allocation in Ko-rean society. That is why Korean people have been so sensitive to the ge-ographical representativeness of the elite. Regionalism has been always raised as one of the most sensitive political matters in every presidential election or assembly election in Korean history. People eagerly desired that their regional areas produce presidents, members, assembly ministers, and higher administrative officials. This kind of aspiration for having many governing elites from their regional areas is entirely understandable be-cause these elites, full of loyalty to their native places, determine the values and even allocate the budget distribution in the society. The administra-tive elites have not been simply functionaries who execute others' orders but the creators as well as distributors of the societal values.

In this sense, the regional representativeness of the governing elites should be emphasized for the sake of elevating the legitimacy of the elite, keeping the people in harmony, and balancing development among regions. Especially if the elites recruited from a certain place comprise a core group among the whole, the legitimacy of the elites as well as their power comes to be weakened. This kind of elite system is certain to be-come the target of complaint from the underrepresented areas, thereby creating tensions and antagonism between the regions. In this sense, the regional quota system in the preliminary examination for the *Mun'gwa*—the terminal degree—in the Yi dynasty deserves to be reassessed.

Let us now consider the university connection as another factor of representativeness (almost all members of the elite attended a university). For instance, only two of the 52 cabinet members under Syngman Rhee had not received university education. The dominance of highly educated elites was extreme in Park's regime as well: only four of 89 cabinet members in Park's initial composition of the cabinet (1963–1970) had not attended a university. According to a statistical report published in *Cho-Son Ilbo* on July 22, 1980, 97 percent of the total administrative elites (higher than third grade) had received a university education. Thus, higher education has been considered to be an inevitable course to becoming a member of the elite in Korean society.

In addition, in Korean society, what mattered in the relationship between education and the elite has been not whether an individual received a university education, but *which* university he attended. The representativeness of the school or university has had a significant meaning because the university connection has been one of the objects of attention in Korean society. Graduates of Seoul National University increasingly came to dominate the bureaucratic society. They took 36.8 percent of the total administrative posts in the period 1948–1967, and came to occupy 42.9 percent in 1980. This percentage of occupation would be predicted to go up for a while. What was conspicuous in the educational background was that the percentage of the graduates of universities other than Seoul National, Korea, and Yonsei rapidly increased from 17.5 percent in the period 1948–1967 to 40.1 percent in 1980. Another outstanding fact was that the percentage of people educated in foreign countries decreased from 30.0 percent to 3.9 percent.

It is worth noting in comparison that monopolization of the higher positions in the government by a single university has been more conspicuous in Japan. According to statistical data of the Japanese Central Committee of Personnel Affairs, 63.2 percent of the total administrative elites employed in the 20 departments of the central government graduated from Tokyo University. This sort of monopolization by a single university has been indicated to be the same in the case of Oxford and Cambridge in Great Britain. However, this is not the case in the United States. The total of high administrative officials produced by the "big thirty" universities there in one year was no more than 41.7 percent of the total. The largest number of high officials produced by a single university occupied no more than 3.4 percent of the total.

The figures for monopolization of administrative posts by the elite universities vary from country to country. The occupation of 40 percent of the total high officials by Seoul National University alone could be controversial in terms of overrepresentation. It might be justified by such a fact that only those who have shown an intellectual capacity by passing the high civil service examination could reach a high administrative position. The overrepresentation by a single university, however, not only fosters a sense of overprivilege, but also prevents the society from being pluralistic and hence deepens the social stratification. In any case, the society is not so simple that it can be represented by a single university alone. All the more, the administrative position is not always one that requires a high level of expertise or brain power that only highly educated persons can handle. In this sense, the representativeness of the elite should be enlarged through consideration of the regional area and educational background as well as the qualification and capacity in the employment and promotion system. Distributing representation among graduates from various educational institutions might diminish efficiency, but it would improve representation and equity, and thereby democracy itself.

The Replacement Process of the Elite

The closed character of the elite system is in direct relationship with the replacement process, in that the replacement of the elite does not usually occur in the closed system of elite recruitment.

The replacement process of the elite can have two parts. One is the process of replacing the elites by nonelites and the other is the replacement of the elites in power by other elites outside power. Both of them are absolutely necessary for the sake of the maintenance of the system of an elite itself. The collapse of the closed system that denies the circulation or replacement has often proved to be only a matter of time. In a word, the closed system usually ends without giving a continuance to the other, opposing elite group. The closed elite system without the experience of circulation will normally inbreed corruption, decay, and stagnation, while the nonelite groups proceed to grow up as massive organizations. In other words, such undesirable forces as stagnation and putrefaction begin to set in within the established elite class while the superior quality accumulates in the nonelite class. Vilfredo Pareto properly indicated that revolution usually broke out when the various types of corruption were heaped up in the closed elite class while the superior quality and capacity were stored up in the lower strata.[2] This result directly implies that the circulation and replacement of the elite are necessary to maintain the stability and equilibrium of a society.

The replacement of the elite can be discussed in various terms. It can be dealt with in terms of age, social background, and degree of expertise. More significant in Korean society, however, has been the replacement of the governing elites by military elites and the absence of peaceful replacement of the elites.

The absolute majority of the cabinet members of the Commission of Military Revolution and Military Government have come from the military since the military coup of May 16, 1961. At that time, the proportion of military men to the total number of cabinet members was 68 percent, or 29 of 43 members. This was not surprising at all with a military regime. All the more, in the case of the first cabinet of the Military Revolution

Commission the total number of cabinet posts occupied by the military reached 80 percent, or 13 of 16 members. In comparison, the first cabinet led by Park's Republican Party included only 5 military men of 18 cabinet members. Thus, although the percentage occupied by the military came to be drastically reduced to 28 percent, it was still much higher than those of Rhee's or Chang's regimes. Further, even though the percentage of military men in the cabinet dropped suddenly, nobody thought that military government was terminated. Indeed, the emergence of the military elites as the elites in power has brought about many social impacts and implications for Korean society.

The military class has been treated as traditionally and historically inferior to the class of literary men, and has been gravely discriminated against by the civilian officials. The esteem granted the literary man and the disdain for the military man were in the extreme in the Yi dynasty. In Japan and Western Europe, in contrast, the knight class acted as the main force to initiate social development. The prestige and social respect given to this class were remarkable. It is interesting to consider that the society where the military used to rule the literary has turned out to be the society where the military are ruled by the literary, while the society where the literary ruled the military has conversely become the one where the literary has come to be ruled by the military.

We may be able to indicate some plausible reasons why the military has emerged as the dominant elite in underdeveloped societies. The group that possesses and controls the military and physical forces is likely to emerge as the power group in a society where political order or authority is situated in the vortex of crisis. In other words the military comes to infiltrate the political world when that world is out of order. Indeed, the military has become modernized more than any other organizations or groups in the society and has been equipped with both scientific spirit and technology. These military elites have traveled to the developed countries to learn advanced technologies and management skills and have acted as the forerunner to initiate a modernization program after they came back to the home country. These military elites have always had the possibility of being switched into the governing elites, given the advantage of their management skills as well as the chaotic situation of a given society.

The conversion of the military elites into the governing elites in Korean society has been caused by such various factors as the repercussion against the literati-oriented society, the political instability, and the modernization of the military. In other words, the intervention of the military into the political world has been called for by historical as well as actual situations.

The emergence of the military elites since the military coup has produced many impacts and changes. First, the structure of social stratification has been to a large extent transformed. Prior to the coup the governing elites used to come mainly from the upper class such as the landowner or *Yang-ban* class, but thereafter many elites came to be recruited from the lower class. In other words, the base of elite recruitment came to be widened by making the way of becoming an elite open to the lower class. The thought that anyone could be a member of the elite if he was able was almost revolutionary to a society espousing the traditional closed-thought pattern.

Second, the elites born in Kyŏngsang province have arisen as the core of the power elites since Park's military coup. The number of elites born in this region has been rapidly and continually increased. The elites born in Seoul, Kyŏnggi and Ch'ungch'ŏng had constituted the principal axis of power elites in Syngman Rhee's government, but this group was replaced by elites born in Kyŏngsang province in Park's regime. The strong predominance of elites from this province in the political and administrative fields was matched in the fields of business, military, and in the intellectual class. In short, the Kyŏngsang-Do elite system has come to be established in Korean society since Park's regime. In Korean society, where regional biases have been deeply rooted in the minds of people for a long time, this kind of regional maldistribution of the elites could surely cause unrest and criticism for its violation of principles of equitable representation.

Third, management-oriented elites with an emphasis on efficiency and prompt action have been fostered rather than legitimacy-oriented elites with a high regard for political ethics or representativeness. In Syngman Rhee's government, there had been cases of men being recruited into the cabinet who had fought for Korean independence or who enjoyed respect and popularity through out the nation. In Park's government, however, there were few such cases of recruitment into the cabinet of any nonexpert, even those who were well known. Therefore, the elite system in Park's regime came to be characterized by expertise and specific skills rather than general and wide experience and knowledge. What they pursued and emphasized were not permanent and universal values, but those of visibility and expediency. They paid much more attention to the economic values of wealth and short-term income than to the political and human values of democracy and individual freedom. The highest priority being placed on economic values led directly to the predominance of economic experts in the cabinet. In addition, the value of morals and ethics which had traditionally been highly regarded in Korean society came to be diminished as the physical or pragmatic qualities such as economic, scientific, and military skills began to be emphasized as core components of power. It was not surprising, in such a situation, to see that the most welcome elites were managerial people equipped with scientific and technical expertise.

Fourth, the governing elites were totally under the direction of the top leader—the president. The elite groups simply acted as the administrative tool of the leader: they were never expected to counteract the will of the leader. Such a thing as autonomy of the elite group could never be dreamed of. If they had conflicts with each other in initiating or deciding policies or programs, they could not solve them for themselves through mutual adjustment or compromise, but had to resort to the judgment of the leader. The power structure of the elite was thus thoroughly centralized and monolithic. Therefore, while seemingly stern and solid, this power structure always had many weak points in substance.

We have thus far discussed the social implications of the emergence of military elites as the governing elite in Korean society. We now turn to the problems of the peaceful replacement of the elites. We in Korea have never in fact experienced peaceful coexistent replacement between the elites in and outside government. The elites driven out by the new groups came to be uprooted by the absence of a peaceful replacement process. The elites faced either triumph or downfall because the zero-sum game alone existed between the elite groups. They did not know how to co-exist peacefully with each other, but "to kill or be killed." No replacement of the elites in the strict sense existed in this all-or-nothing situation. The replacement process in a system of elites ideally contains a continuity between those in and outside the power. A collapse of the elite obviously means discontinuity, and the replacement of elites in Korean society has generally meant the disappearance of the previous group. The elites driven out were filled with feelings of deprivation toward the new group and, furthermore, could not escape from the position of being the accused.

In sum, what has existed between the collapsed elites and the newly emerging elites has been negation, exclusion, and animosity. They have never experienced a due process in changing their position. This was why we had not been able to expect any continuity of policy in Korean society. In such a society, two or more competitive elite groups could not live together in peace, but could only compete subversively for power.

Elite groups characterized by openness, fairness, and universality could not develop in a society of one-man rule. If the elite group in power does not compete openly and honestly with the outside elite groups for any objective, the former are inevitably led to closed procedures, stagnation, and corruption. Korean experience has indicated that the absence of competitiveness among the elite groups was ultimately disastrous for the nation and its people and for the elites themselves. It was thus clear that we could expect the development of better policies and programs and the emergence of government truly in the service of the people only if open competition is allowed between groups of elites.

The Desirability of a Pluralistic System

We have insisted on the importance of competition between the elites with their differing points of view. The pluralistic aspect of the system of elites is also very important. By this is meant the functional pluralism of the elites. This functional pluralism automatically exists as the society is specialized and differentiated, but the point of emphasis here is that the functional elite should have the authority to make important decisions and solve big problems in its own field. In practice, even if the society was differentiated, and functional elites correspondingly emerged in each functional field, the power elite in government decided all of the major and fundamental issues in every field, while the body of functional elites was mainly concerned with handling minor problems.

It can be said that Korean society has produced a number of professional elites in each field as it became functionally specialized and differentiated over the last forty years. This kind of pluralism had no autonomy, but only a superficial formality. The power elite in government has historically as well as traditionally made every important decision in Korean society, dominating and directing the other elites. The scope of action of the functional elites was confined to the minor areas permitted by the governing elites. The functional group desperately contrived to flatter those governing because even their existence and their developments were threatened if they came to be a target of the governing elites. This was thus not a pluralistic state, but a domination-subordination state between the elite groups: only the subjugation of the functional elite to the governing elites has existed in Korean society.

When the power elites in government come to dominate the functional elites such as business, professional, intellectual, educational, and the like, all social and economic problems become political problems, requiring political power to get the problems solved. In such cases, rationality and objectivity in the process of decision making in any functional area can hardly be anticipated because the power elites infiltrate their subjective or dogmatic values into the question while claiming their leadership over the functional areas. The result is that every important decision is made on the basis of the often subjective values of the power elites.

The domination of the governing elites over the functional areas is not supposed to be interfered with by any outsiders, a situation certain to be highly detrimental to the whole society. This monolithic domination of the power elites not only makes the society full of tensions, conflicts, intrigues, conspiracies, and heteronomies, but also prevents the society from growing with diversity and uniqueness by imposing a uniformity on the societal development. The self-adjusting function of an economy could hardly be anticipated in a society where politics decides the economy. The economic world is not so simple that it can be decided by the political or administrative elites; it needs its own autonomy to decide its problems. Economic elites by themselves can rationally solve the economic problems; the same is true of the other functional areas. This is not at all to say that every functional elite group should have its own independent activity, being completely separated from each other, but that the functional elite should have its own autonomy to solve its problems, in concert with other functional elites.

In a society where the pluralism of elites is established and guaranteed, the overall development is likely to accelerate, while the hateful feelings and the distrusts toward the power elites will be greatly diminished. Further, the pluralism of elites will not only enable energies to be easily and effectively mobilized for a developmental goal in each functional area, but will also make the social structure more level, thereby sowing the seeds of democracy.

Concluding Remark

As we saw at the beginning of this chapter, any society, developed or developing, is likely to be governed by an elite group. If we accept the proposition of the rule of the elite, we always hope that the elite will keep a desirable character.

The members of the elite are desired to be intellectual, legitimate, representative, and pluralistic, but this is often not the case. The Korean system of the elite has been strongly characterized by the qualities of being closed and exclusive for the last forty years. Since then, we have not had a peaceful replacement or change between the elites in and outside the government. In addition, the elite system has lacked the representative character in terms of regional area and university connection, which are very sensitive in Korean society. It is undeniable that a drastically uneven representation can make the society unstable, set the people at variance, and eventually go far toward breaking down the national structure. Desirable features to seek in a system of elites such as circulation, representativeness, professionality, competitiveness, openness, and pluralism can never be overemphasized in the acceptance of government by the elite.

Notes

1.   Seung-Jo Hahn, "Recruitment Patter of Korean Political Elites," in *The History of April Revolution* (Seoul: Sŏnggonsa, 1960), p. 18.
2.   Vilfredo Pareto, *The Mind and Society* (San Diego: Harcourt Brace Jovanovich, 1935), p. 431.

CHAPTER SIX

Crisis, Regime Change, and Development: A Quantitative Analysis of South Korean Political Transformation, 1945–1987

Suk Joon Kim

A LEADING MEMBER of the newly industrializing countries (NICs), South Korea has achieved rapid economic development during the last two decades. With three other Asian NICs—Taiwan, Hong Kong, and Singapore—Korean economic performance has deservedly been called an "economic miracle" by Westerners. In contrast to its economic achievement, however, Korea has experienced serious political underdevelopment, with five regime changes in this period. Most Koreans have experienced sociopolitical sacrifice either in exchange for the economic miracle or just because of its militarism.

Employing a comparative perspective on a world scale, some indicators show this contradiction clearly. Taking the world as a whole, Korea's per capita GNP of US$105, which ranked 100th among 135 in 1965, rose to US$2,180 in 1985 ranking 39th among 126. However, its political rights index and civil rights index have worsened from 3.9 and 4.6 in 1960, to 4.9 and 5.6 in 1975, to 5 and 6 in 1984, moving its ranks from 40th and 60th in 1960, to 60.5th and 94.5th among 135 in 1975, to 92.5th and 127th among 168 in 1984.

Regarding the economic miracle, neoclassical economists argue that the "correct choice" of export-led development strategy based on a comparative advantage of cheap labor has largely contributed to extraordinary eco-

Taken from Suk Joon Kim, "Crisis, Change, and Development: A Quantitative Analysis of South Korean Political Transformation, 1945–1987," *The Korean Journal of Policy Sciences* 2 (1987):67–87.

nomic performance, while statists assert that a "strong state" maximizing state autonomy is the major variable for economic development. Both economists and statists try to explain economic development, but neglect Korea's political underdevelopment.

Concerning this paradoxical outcome of economic development and regime change, only limited theories, such as the bureaucratic authoritarian (BA) model and dependent development among others, try to account for it. O'Donnell's BA model, which relates the rise of authoritarianism to an economic strategy of "deepening," has been applied to analyze the Korean Yushin system of the 1970s. Some characteristics of the Yushin system similar to those found in the BA regimes of Brazil, Argentina, and Chile are: (1) politicoeconomic exclusion of the popular sector, and (2) emphasis of technological rationality, efficiency, and social stability.

Despite these similarities in political consequences, the fundamental factors that differentiate the Korean case from the BA model are (1) the manner of incorporation into the international capital system, (2) the strong state and stunted populism, (3) the preparatory period prior to the invitation of a BA regime, and (4) the state's dominant position in the triple alliance. In detail, first, the deepening hypothesis is inappropriate in the Korean case, because the deepening of the Korean economy began in the mid-1970s and was the consequence rather than the cause of a BA regime. The Yushin regime was not justified by an economic crisis; instead, President Park Chung-Hee justified Yushin on the pretext of continuing economic development and the national reunification.

Second, although there was more significant popular political activism in 1971 than earlier, there were no serious antiunion or antileftist fears among the military, the upper and middle classes, and the state bureaucrats. Instead, external factors, such as North Korean military threats and the Nixon doctrine, facilitated security fears among the ruling class. Third, Korea had established a strong state long before the rise of the Yushin regime and the Korean case does not support the strong state hypothesis of the BA model. Fourth, the Korean state has dominated other ruling coalition partners, such as local business and foreign capital, since 1962. Thus, no BA coup coalition that can press for a regime change existed on the eve of a BA regime rise in Korea. The economic determinism and functionalism of the BA model are also theoretical weaknesses.

Furthermore, Peter Evans' "dependent development" model, which assumes that "the alliance of transnational, state, and local capital" can produce development under a dependent situation, has been applied to explain Korean development after 1963. Since the BA model is considered a bureaucratic instrument of "dependent development," the criticisms made above are also relevant to the "dependent development" model when it is applied to Korea. In addition, geopolitical security interest relations between Korea and the United States have characterized the fundamental framework of the "triple alliance" of the Korean state, local business, and foreign capital. The United States preferred a stable strong state in Korea. The strong Korean state not only dominated domestic business but also controlled U.S. multinational corporations (MNCs) that were involved in the Korean industrialization process. Political repression was largely due to political stability and security reasons rather than the economic interests of the MNCs. Furthermore, popular exclusion has had a long history in Korea and cannot be seen as causally linked to the problem of dependent development. The Korean state has controlled the activities of MNCs and local businesses by controlling all foreign direct investments until 1979. It was possible because Korean involvement in the capitalist world system was different from that, for example, of Latin America. Third, the Korean state preferred foreign loans to foreign direct investment and pursued foreign loans as an instrument of "strategic dependency" since U.S. decisions of military reduction and withdrawal in 1970s. Their logic is "foreign loan=foreign security support" since large-loan lenders will be anxious to maintain Korean security to keep their economic interests.

Although both the BA model and the dependent development theory can partially apply, their limitations need significant revision in using them for the Korean case, 1945–1987. Thus this chapter develops an alternative framework, namely, that of the neomercantile security state. This position argues that Korea's contradictory development is mainly a consequence of the rise of a neomercantile security state, which itself is a result of a series of crises and regime changes. Unlike other Asian NICs, Korea has experienced several crises that eventually changed the existing regimes in its initial state-building process during 1945–1987. Crisis is defined as a situation, rather than a variable, which is caused mainly by the discongruity between state and society, both domestic and international. When the state possesses the capacity to manage the demands of society, the gap between state and society will be minimized and the state will manage social demands within the existing state structure. However, when the capacity of the state is not capable of this demand management, then crisis ensues and either the society presses the state to alter its structure or the state represses social demands. Major types of political crises are identity crises, legitimacy crises, distribution crises, and penetration crises. Economic crises include import substitution industrialization (ISI) crises, and export-led industrialization (ELI) crises, which was mainly derived from development strategy that changes the economic interests of existing social class in its distribution process. In many cases, economic crisis is expressed as political activity.

Thus, major indicators of crisis are: (1) political protests including strikes, (2) riots, (3) armed attack, (4) death from internal violence, and (5) economic downturn. Crisis situations occur mainly as a result of pressures from class inequalities, the world system, previous state action, or their interplay. Among the states of the world, the Korean case has demonstrated a high possibility for crisis. Indicators of the Korean crisis show that protest demonstrations ranked 13th among 124 countries; while riots, armed attack, and death from internal violence ranked 11th, 49.5th, and 41st among 130, 133, and 127, respectively.

Major crises in Korea have been (1) postwar identity crisis in the initial state-building process (1945–1948), (2) legitimation crisis and ISI crisis (1960), (3) penetration crisis (1961), (4) legitimation crisis and distribution crisis (1971–1972), and (5) legitimation crisis and ELI crisis (1979–1980). Major actors of crises have conditioned the nature of regime change and its developmental strategy. A political regime is the norms, rules, and institutions that link state and society, that is, that link ruling class and popular social classes. Political regime change is the change in norms, rules, and institutions that results from the conflict among classes, the state, and the world system over defining, making, and revising those norms, rules, and institutions. Rather than a simple notion of democratic or authoritarian regimes, this study classifies political regime into four conceptual types according to state goal and state institution. Regime change occurs when a change in the balance of power of actors leads to the intensification of politicoeconomic crisis.

Because institution building and regime change are a continuous historical process, major indicators of regime change can be: (1) irregular executive transfer, (2) executive adjustments, and (3) government sanctions. Government change in Korea has been very frequent, ranking 10th, 9th, and 21st among 57, 133, and 137 countries respectively, according to these indicators. Major regime changes in Korea are marked by the rise of the First through the Fifth Regimes in 1948, 1960, 1961, 1972, and 1980.

The basic research questions posed in this chapter are: (1) How does crisis relate to regime change? How do world system, social class, and state interplay in a crisis situation and influence regime change? and (3) What is the impact of regime change on state capacities of development?

This study hypothesizes first, that different types of interplay among world system, social class, and state produce different patterns of regime change in relation to its economic and security capacities, and second, that the nature of the state and regime will produce different patterns of Korean development—the higher economic capacity of a state will produce rapid economic development, while the higher security capacity of a state will promote political underdevelopment. Quantitative methods can be applied to verify these hypotheses.

The Conceptual Framework of the Neomercantile Security State: the Nature of the State and Regime Change

The Neomercantile Security State and Four Types of State Institutionalization

States can be classified by two major criteria of state institutionalization: state ideology and state bureaucracy. Although each state pursues interrelated and multiple goals including political, military, economic, and welfare, the emphasis in each is slightly different. Although it is easy to oversimplify, each state can be categorized into two broad groups according to its orientation toward the pursuit of power: (1) the political power-seeking state, and (2) the economic power-seeking state, in both domestic and international arenas. In general, most countries mainly pursued political power in the international system during the Cold War period. Political ideologies were the most important variable in international relations among states. Since détente, however, economic power has become attractive to the "late-late industrializers," some of whom now have become the NICs.

Major indicators to identify state's goal-seeking behavior are: statements, slogans, political behavior, and the official goals of state elites and their relation with other state elites. These can be categorized into liberalism, conservatism, and mercantilism, for example. The percentage of economic issues mentioned in the presidential addresses of presidents Syngman Rhee and Park Chung-Hee differed significantly—38 percent and 50 percent, respectively—while their citing of political issues was 32 percent and 15 percent, respectively. Between Korean regimes, the emphasis on economic issues increased significantly over time, focusing on the pursuit of more economic power.

From a comparative perspective, major indicators of political power seeking (and Korean rank/number of all countries in 1965, for example) are: the number of memberships in international organizations (89/122) and diplomatic representation (diplomats sent and received, missions abroad; 58.5/119); while indicators of economic power seeking are foreign trade (as percentage of GNP), foreign aid and loans (12/113), and concentration of export commodities (88.5/101). A lower rank in the concentration of exports means higher economic power. Rank of a country can be compared with that of other countries to clarify the nature of the state. The Korean state in 1965 shows a high economic power-seeking orientation. Its indicators of power seeking are significantly above average for the world as a whole, while indicators of political power seeking are below the average.

In addition to goal-seeking behavior, states also reorganize their state structures. State institutions are virtually static and difficult to change. Increasing environmental pressure, however, stimulates the reorganization of the state bureaucracy and its relationship with domestic and foreign actors. Although the state has multifunctional institutions responding to multiple demands emanating from the environment, various state institutions can be grouped into two categories: (1) the security-oriented state, and (2) the welfare-oriented state.

Major indicators for security-orientation (and the shift in the Korean state's rank from 1965 to 1975 in whole world/number of countries) are: military manpower (total per thousand, working age population; from 8/121 to 6/140), defense expenditure (as percentage of GNP; 39/121 to 33.5/142), ratio of military-turned-ministers (from 6 percent in 1950, and 6 percent in 1960, to 48 percent in 1965, to 39 percent in 1975, to 35 percent in 1985), and ratio of exmilitary officers in top state bureaucracy (5 percent in 1950, 3 percent in 1960, 33 percent in 1965, 16 percent in 1975, and 22 percent in 1985). Indicators of welfare orientation are public health expenditure (as percentage of GNP; 121.5/126 in 1975), and education expenditure (as percentage of GNP; 100/130 in 1975). For comparative purposes, ranking nations can be used to identify its nature. Korea has been an extremely security-oriented state in the world state system.

According to these two criteria of state institutionalization, each state can be classified into one of four cells of a matrix:

Four Types of State Institutionalization

		Center of State Bureaucracy	
		Security-centered	*Welfare-centered*
State Goal	*Political Power*	Political security state	Political welfare state
and Ideology	*Economic Power*	Mercantile security state	Neomercantile welfare state

1. The political security state (PSS) is a state pursuing political power by strengthening or restoring both internal (i.e., police) and external (i.e., military) security-oriented state institutions. By the mid-1950s, the Korean regime under Syngman Rhee and the Taiwanese Kuomintang (KMT) government belonged to this type of state. More broadly, the PSS includes most of the authoritarian states of the Third World countries in Southeast Asia, Africa, Central America, Latin America (except NICs), and the Communist countries.

2. The neomercantile security state (NMSS) seeks more economic power by utilizing a security-centered state bureaucracy that controls economy-related state institutions. Regarding economic affairs, technocrats and economy-oriented state machinery can have significant "autonomy" to achieve more economic power, but security-related institutions still remain more powerful in state operations in general. Both Korea since Park Chung-Hee (1961–1980) and Taiwan under the KMT (since the late 1950s) are

model cases of this NMSS. The NMSS includes those states seeking economic growth in Latin American and East European NICs.

3. The political welfare state (PWS) intends to keep more political power by maintaining welfare-centered state structure. The PWS is found in many western European welfare states and the North American states of the United States and Canada. Korea under Myon Chang (1960–1961) tried to shift from the PSS toward the PWS immediately after the April Revolution, but the military coup of Park Chung-Hee in May 1961 prevented Chang's efforts from achieving success.

4. The neomercantile welfare state (NMWS) pursues more economic power by using a welfare and economic performance-centered state bureaucracy. Korea under Doo-Hwang Chun (1980–1989) tried to shift from NMSS to NMWS, but it did not happen because of its fundamentally militaristic nature. Because there had been no significant change in the ruling coalition and state institutions for welfare affairs on one hand, and the reorientation of security-oriented state institutions on the other, regime change could not occur. Although the Chun regime had officially adopted welfare and justice as major goals, the nature of the state itself did not change. Good examples of the NMWS are West Germany and Japan. Both states were not allowed to rebuild security organizations and, instead, restructured their state bureaucracies to be economic and welfare centered in the postwar period. As "late-industrializers," both states achieved tremendous economic, political, and welfare performances with this type of state institutionalization.

State Institutional Change: Regime Change

The status shift of each state occurs, though with difficulty, when the factors of state institutionalization are changed. When there is a significant gap between state and society—that is, a crisis situation—both sides try to reduce the incongruity between them. When the societal forces, both domestic and international, are stronger than those of state power, the state should reflect social pressure by either reorienting its ideology, reorganizing its institutions, or both. A revolutionary situation, such as the Korean April Student Revolution in 1960, is a good example of this case. During and after a revolution from below, social forces can fundamentally reorganize state structure and its relation to society. However, when the state possesses power stronger than that of the social forces, it can reduce the incongruity between state and society by controlling and restructuring social forces. Examples are illustrated in Korea by the three coups of 1961, 1972, and 1980.

Under a crisis situation, the major variables that affect the shift of a state's status are class struggle, the world system, and state action. The first variable is class struggle, that is, a significant conflict between the ruling class and antiruling social forces due to crises in governmental performance, such as economic performance failure, crisis in political legitimacy, and critical problems in distributional justice. Class struggle is more influential to regime change in a strong society than it is in a weak society. When a society is weak, the political role of the military is crucial in the power struggle between ruling class and antiruling coalitions, as exemplified by the April Revolution of Korea in 1960 and the People's Revolution of the Philippines in 1986.

The second variable is a critical change in the world system itself and its linkage to the domestic state. The changed nature of the international system from a "military-political world" in the postwar period to a "trading world" is very sensitive to those "semi-sovereign states" like Korea and Taiwan. Korean relations with the U.S. have gradually shifted from "dominant security dependence" in the 1940s and 1950s toward the economic security "interdependence" in the 1980s. International crises, such as war, severe external threats (i.e., military competition of South Korea and Taiwan with North Korea and China, respectively), and oil crises are included in this category.

According to the third variable, the previous state action itself can challenge the existing state structure and result in regime change. State action is made under the influence of social class and world system pressures, but the state also can rearrange society and its relation to it. Education reform under the American military government (AMG) enhanced student power in Korea, initiating the Student Revolution in 1960, while land reform under the AMG and the Rhee regime facilitated its social situation by destroying a previously strong landlord class. The rapid military build-up under Rhee produced a potentially omnipotent military power in Korea which initiated three continuous military coups.

In summary, throughout the interplay of the world system, class struggle, and state action, the Korean state shifted from the political security state under the AMG and the Rhee regime through Chang's political welfare state to the neomercantile security state since the Park regime. The current struggle for democracy in Korea has been an effort to move toward the neomercantile welfare state in the 1980s.

Conclusion

A series of crises in Korea induced regime changes that conditioned the nature of subsequent regimes. Under a crisis situation, the pattern of interplay of three actors—the world system, social class, and the state—conditioned the regime that followed. Crisis occurs because of the gap between state and society. Given Korea's nature as a security state, the gap was reduced by the state's repression by security institutions—except in the case of the April Revolution. The world security system played a key role in the rise of the Syngman Rhee's security regime under the identity crisis, while social class played a crucial role in its fall and the rise of the Chang regime under ISI and legitimation crises. Since then, the military as a major state institution has played a key role in both political and economic arenas by establishing a neomercantile security state.

Korea's contradictory development is the consequence of its becoming a NMSS rather than its being an example of the BA model, dependent development, or statist theories: its enhanced economic capacity produced an economic miracle, while its security capacity facilitated political underdevelopment. Unless it changes its nature, it will continue this contradictory development. And, in order to change its nature, it must experience a significant shift in either state ideology and policy or state institutions. The Korean people's struggle in the 1980s and 1990s is a political struggle not just for democracy, but for the shift of the state from NMSS to NMWS, in order to produce both economic and political development. Under this NMWS, Korea will be able to achieve welfare with more equal distribution. The shift of the state's nature includes changes in its ruling coalition, development strategy, ideology, state capacities, focus of its state institutions, its role in society, and its linkages to both domestic societal actors and foreign actors.

Instead of one-way repression by the state, which distorts structures of both the state and society, the gap should be reduced by the interaction from both sides due to their changing relations with each other and with the world system. Recently growing social classes will soon play a key role in Korean political economy because their strength among the three actors continuously grows more rapidly than the other two, that is, the state and the world system.

CHAPTER SEVEN

Korean Democracy and the Limits of Political Engineering

Jung Suk Youn

LIBERAL DEMOCRACY IN Korea seems, on the surface at least, to lack native roots; its development in Korea has been singularly brief; and its origins were both involuntary and imposed. However, this unqualified characterization of the antecedents of liberal democracy in Korea is incomplete and seriously inadequate for assessing the current trends in the process of democratic development. More than constitutions and formal political institutions must be taken into account. The following arguments are rather important and relevant.

Conceptually, the development of a political system that allows for oppositions, rivalry, or competition between government and its opponents is an important aspect of democratization, though democratization and the development of public opposition are not identical. Furthermore, a high level of socioeconomic development not only favors the transformation of a hegemonic regime into a polyarchy but also helps to maintain a polyarchy. The argument as it stands is, to be sure, overly simple. It proposes also that an advanced economy automatically generates many of the conditions required for a pluralistic social order, and that as a pluralistic social order evolves, at least in an elementary form, some of its members make demands for participating in decisions by means more appropriate to a competitive than to a hegemonic political system.

Even if an advanced economy creates some of the conditions required for a pluralistic social order, it does not necessarily create all the conditions required. As we have already received a few criticisms on the current Korean political development from foreign observers, we realize that the fit between economic "level" and political systems is loose. What has been experienced during the last decade is the fact that as a government

Taken from Jung Suk Youn, "Korean Democracy and the Limits of Political Engineering," *Progress in Democracy: The Pacific Basin Experience.* Seoul: The Ilhae Institute, 1989, pp. 143–161.

with hegemonic systems moves to high levels of economic development, a centrally dominated social order is increasingly difficult to maintain; that is, economic development itself generates the conditions of a pluralistic social order.

As Robert Dahl aptly hypothesizes, the democratic development of the political system varies with regard to the rapid economic growth in a country.[1] Korean experience persuasively tells us that the monopoly over socioeconomic sanctions enjoyed by the hegemonic leaders is undermined by the very success of their economy; the more they succeed in transforming the economy, the more they are threatened with political failure. If the political leaders allow their monopoly over socioeconomic sanctions to fragment and yet seek to retain their political hegemony by exploiting their monopoly over violence, then they confront the enormous limitations, costs, and inefficiencies of violence, coercion, and compulsion in managing an advanced society where incentives and complex behavior are needed that cannot be manipulated by threats of violence. Therefore, we look for a pluralistic social order in which a political system will develop into democratic processes. We call it "pluralism" in social order.

Pluralism is a wonderful concept. It seems to go along with a number of other concepts that political scientists consider "good," such as democracy, constitutionalism, freedom, independence, and in the secular idiom, "every one doing his/her own thing." The concepts can be realized in many ways, the meanings of which are not necessarily contradictory. Some of the basic components of pluralism may include the existence of relatively autonomous and voluntary institutions, associations, organizations, and groups between the individual and the state. It is widely accepted that these intermediate structures are legitimate and indeed essential to the functioning of constitutional democracies. Thus, pluralism assumes the legitimacy of social conflict but posits that multiple memberships in voluntary groups and associations result in crosscutting cleavages that mute conflict and promote consensus. Pluralism is the opposite of a hegemonic political system in which individuals are authoritatively mobilized into structures that tie them directly into the state power system.

Implicit in pluralism is the assumption that individuals and groups compete freely in the political marketplace and that the outcome of the policy process is the result of the parallelogram of forces involved in politics. Elections are at the very least a way of keeping score. That is, elections permit the weighing of the political strengths of various groups and, in a rough and imprecise manner, the relating of mass opinions to the policy outputs of politics.

However, critics in Korea have pointed out some unarticulated and generally unexamined consequences of the functioning of pluralistic systems. Pluralism is a facade behind which the dominant elites manipulate the political process. Advantages and disadvantages are not randomly distributed in the free play of political competition; as a result, some groups are systematically excluded from effective participation in the political process while others compete at a grave disadvantage. The weak, the poor, and the socially marginal are unable to take advantage of the claimed possibilities of pluralism for the furtherance of their interests.

In this chapter, I will examine other unanticipated consequences of pluralism: these are (1) that an effectively mobilized, pluralistic political system may be so highly fragmented and immobile that the dominant elites lack incentives to provide effective government for coping with societal problems; (2) that the interests of the rulers and the interests of the society may be mutually incompatible; and (3) that there may be no simple institutional remedy for this state of affairs in the short run.

This chapter looks at Korea rather than pluralism. My concern is understanding the reason for what conventional wisdom labels the ineffectiveness of the Korean government. But a great deal can be learned about pluralism in the course of talking about Korea. For it is my contention that the lack of effectiveness of the Korean governmental system can be attributed to the extreme pluralism of the society, the existence of high electoral mobilization, and the importance of institutions that intervene between the citizen and the governing authorities.

Democracy in Korea

The institutional structure of the Korean government is a familiar one. It is a presidential system with a unicameral legislature—the National Assembly. The president of the republic, the head of state, is currently elected by an electoral college, composed of over five thousand representatives of the local constituencies. The president has somewhat more power than in the French Fifth Republic. The president appoints the prime minister and cabinet ministers, but the prime minister must obtain a confidence vote from the National Assembly convening immediately after his appointment. There is also a constitutional court in Korea that has rendered several important controversial decisions; without acquiring the prestige of the U.S. Supreme Court, it nevertheless has played an innovative role in the system.

Discussions of the problems of Korean democracy sometimes begin and end with the problems of civilian supremacy and a stable government. Up to a point this is quite proper, but the problem of civilian supremacy must be traced back further—to the elite circulation and the electoral bases of the party system. Since the development of Korean politics has been brought about while Korea has fought for survival against Communist threats, the dominant power source and the elites were naturally from the military community. Those who had a higher education during the 1940s had to join the Japanese army. Later they became a major leadership group within the Korean military circle during the Korean War and thereafter. Among these leadership groups, the most nationalistic leaders took the initiative for the renovation of government and finally took part in a military coup d'état in 1961. Afterward, young and able military officers joined the government as ministers and National Assembly members, and the military culture and discipline began to dominate the party apparatus and government operations. The fall of the Park Chung-Hee regime in 1979 again allowed military intervention in Korean politics, which does not necessarily mean military leadership vying for power.

For the last three decades or so, the presidents and cabinet ministers, including the prime ministers, were recruited out of the military, which wielded strong power to run the country. The formation of political parties by the government groups was naturally based on the structure of the officer groups in the military intelligence corps or military police forces. More recently, in 1980, the Democratic Justice Party was organized by military intelligence officers and by civilian officers associated with the former Korean CIA. Surrounding those groups of leaders, some former opposition party members, businessmen, university professors, and former government officials were asked to join the new party.

A change of previous regime, as for example after the assassination of the late president Park Chung-Hee, has always brought about a drastic change of leadership groups in Korea. This led to the formation of new parties with new leadership for both ruling and opposition forces in 1981.

Parties and Elections

Korean parties are not represented by a simple left-right spatial model. Koreans do not view politics as stretching from the Communist Party on the left to the ultranationalist or neofacists on the right, a habit probably acquired through the historical experiences of the Korean War. No Communist activities have been allowed in Korean politics since the war broke out. A strong anti-Communist tendency prevails in Korean politics.

Of course, there are, however, far more dimensions to Korean politics today than can be ascribed to conservatism after the Korean War. But for an overwhelming majority of the electorate, these dimensions coincide rather well with the overall conservatism. By and large, Korean conservatives are distinctly divided into four major camps.

1. The Democratic Justice Party (DJP), newly formed in 1980, which won support through a reformist policy after President Park's assassination.
2. A grouping of former majority party members under the Park regime (Park's party, the Democratic Republican Party, was dissolved in 1979, but some of its members established a new Korea National Party in 1981).

3. Vestiges mainly of Korea's first majority party, the Korean Democratic Party founded in 1947: the members currently competing with the governing party were recruited from the party rank and from the opposition during the last three decades. Their party name is now the Reunification Democratic Party (RDP), which separated from the mainstream opposition New Korea Democratic Party (NKDP) in 1987.
4. The Socialist party, the Social Democratic Party (SDP).

In the general elections for the National Assembly in 1985, although the government party gained only 35.25 percent of the total votes, it occupied 47.28 percent of the constituency seats in the National Assembly. The composition of the National Assembly is primarily based on the popular vote, but the share of the national constituency seats is determined on the basis of the proportion of constituency seats held by each party. The party with the most seats in the National Assembly will occupy two-thirds of the national constituency seats. Thus 61 out of the 92 national constituency seats are allocated to the party that won the most seats in the election. The rationale behind this modified proportional representation system is to maintain the stability of the parliamentary majority.

But the second feature is that there are three opposition parties, whose total support in 1985 was over 58.1 percent of the total. In the Korean electoral system, each constituency can elect two assemblymen, but the voter has only a single ballot to be cast at the poll. With this peculiar representation system—a two-member district with a single-ballot system—the party system in Korea tends to be multiparty, with the opposition parties in a very competitive situation in the election campaigns.

A fundamental complication of party politics in Korea is that Korean parties are not monolithic blocs. Each party is divided into factions based upon policies, ideologies, personal ambitions, and socioeconomic groupings. For example, the Democratic Justice Party is an uneasy alliance of notables with a clientelistic following, organization-based career party officials, business-oriented conservatives, agricultural-rural groups, some left ideologues, and trade unionists. In a sense, the DJP contains a substantial segment of the left-right continuum, but its leaders were predominantly military and administration officials before they entered politics. Therefore, for liberals within the party the great enthusiasm always generated at the prospect of a civilian and progressive government is soon replaced by the realization that hopes of reform are giving way to inclusion of civilians in the patronage system at the top of the party leadership. The importance of the new patronage and clientelistic ties that came with public office will lead to an intense struggle for personal advantage within the DJP.

For many years, the dependence of the government parties, the Democratic Republican (1963–1979) and Democratic Justice (1981–1987), on military leadership made an alliance with liberals unthinkable. The liberal conservatives who gathered around the opposition parties, the New Korea Democratic (1985–1987), Democratic Korea (1981–1987), and a newly formed Reunification Democratic (1987–), began to acquire an increasing organizational independence from each other in the last decade. The tension is lingering between the opposition's commitment to reform and its defense of the constitutional order.

When the New Democratic Party began its campaign for the democratization of Korean politics in 1986, its left wing and extreme activists broke away and formed the Reunification Democratic Party, a party that remained in close alliance with the Council on Democratization Promotion. At the time this chapter was written (1989), the tension had not been reduced between the government party and the opposition on the constitutional reform and democratization issues. As for the constitutional reformists, they look forward to bringing about civilian supremacy within the government through the liberalization of political processes in Korea.

The Basis of Stability and Instability

The Korean situation just described is hardly the ideal type of pluralistic system envisaged by conventional wisdom. Yet it is my contention that it is the strongly pluralistic nature of Korean society combined with the high level of electoral mobilization and institutionalization of political support that is responsible for this seeming instability. Proponents of pluralism generally point to the support for the system generated by citizens' participation in the making of decisions that affect them. Critics of pluralism emphasize its imperfect nature. Korea in many respects combines the worst of both worlds. It is highly pluralistic, but it is the intermediate institutions rather than the political system that receive the loyalties of the citizenry. The high levels of mobilization and institutionalization eliminate the flexibility in electoral politics that make change not only possible but rewarding for political entrepreneurs.

The Institutionalized Tradition

Students of Korean politics emphasize the existence of different subcultures, the importance of ideological differences, and the critical role of the social networks in which people find themselves. These social networks are in part subcultures; as they also involve ideological differences, the various explanations of the basis of pluralism in Korea are not mutually incompatible. Most Koreans are born into a political tradition that has an ideological expression, particularly support of the regime or withdrawal from it, that receives support from some social groups more than others, that involves citizens in interaction with others sharing the same social network, and that limits political access largely to contact with others within the political tradition.

The criticism that those of low political resources are not able to compete in a pluralistic society is in part met in Korea by the importance of institutions such as the Reunification Democratic Party, the Council on Democratization Promotion, and their affiliated organizations. Both of these are able to provide channels of influence or at least of communication to the very weakest and most marginal of individuals.

The dominant institutions of Korean society, including political parties and the central government, are largely bureaucratic. There is still a strong tendency to consider bureaucratic position as a form of property to be exploited in a clientelistic fashion for personal gain. Korean institutions are more clientelistic in their functioning than is generally expected in bureaucratic organizations. Korea is probably still more ascriptive and clientelistic in the distribution of rewards than the advanced industrial societies with which it is frequently compared. Because of these numerous bureaucratic institutions (and the state machinery would have to be listed as one of the most important of the institutional actors in the political system), Korean society and polity are both hierarchically organized. One makes a career or one exercises influence by carefully cultivating ties with those above and below one in the hierarchy so that the hierarchies themselves are simultaneously modern bureaucracies and patron-client networks. Thus, emphasizing ideological and cultural themes is to ignore the ubiquity of these face-to-face ties throughout Korean society. For most individuals, political power is simply a means of rewarding one's friends and punishing one's enemies. Therefore, it is highly probable that the pattern of interest group activities in Korea falls short of that expected in a truly pluralistic society.

In a way, it may be true that because the government bureaucracy treats people of all socioeconomic conditions, the government determines which of the many claimants will be granted access. Thus, its opponents are generally disbarred from direct and continuing interactions with most of the decision-making apparatus. That is why the opening to the liberals and the inclusion of the reformists have been such important events in recent Korean politics. Yet it is also understandable why the New Korea Democrats should have quickly become a part of the patronage system, for there were rewards and no immediate drawback after the 1985 general elections: one of the weaknesses of the Korean system is that it has no effective means of electoral rewards and punishment. The electoral arrangements do not effectively provide for either; there is very little change from one election to another.

The Policy Process and Status Quo

In fact, in Korea there is virtually no relationship between the electoral game and the policy-making game. The former merely determines what the strength of the forces in parliament will be. Politics emerge from the political process within a governing party, from the struggle of factions and personalities for position and influence. It is hard to relate electoral inputs to policy output. It has been widely demonstrated that the Korean party system reflects the deep divisions within the Korean electorate. It is not necessary to go into the data here, but the differences between a governing party and the opposition are very great on most of the major themes of policies, including socioeconomic questions, democratization processes, the orientation of Korea in international affairs, and particularly in relation to national unification policies. Yet these differences exist at the mass level as well as the elite level.

However, I reject the view that politics is simply a reflection of social forces. It is a sociological illusion that politics is a dependent variable, and that the motive force of change in society is to be found only in the line-up of social forces. Politics, politicians, and policies all make a difference. Applying these assumptions to the analysis of Korean politics, I do not conclude that social conflict in Korea makes change impossible. But in order to remain in power, present Korean policymakers are reluctant to alter the status quo by more than the minimum necessary.

The groups that support the current Democratic Justice government are not likely to benefit as much from change as other groups in society. This is not to deny that benefits might accrue to all Koreans by a more effective utilization of resources. Nor is it to suggest that many groups that support the Democratic Justice Party are not likely to benefit from a general redistribution of wealth and power. But among the most visible and powerful supporters of the Democratic Justice Party are groups that benefit most from the status quo. The supporters of the Democratic Justice Party are the establishment and are relatively satisfied with things as they are. They are by and large intelligent people who are knowledgeable about the major trends in industrial society, and it must seem obvious to them that evolutionary trends are not working to their advantage.

The most obvious example is what change entails for the university campus. The students can hope to benefit very little from change. A major complaint brought by the university students against elites of Korea is their failure to bring about a thorough secularization of politics. Given the close ties between the present political elites within the Democratic Justice Party and the university, it would be extremely surprising if the DJP should lead a movement toward secularization. Indeed, it is surprising that it has accommodated as well as it has to the secular trends of industrial society. On some issues it is clear that the elites are more accommodating than the rank and file of the Democratic Justice Party. And it seems to be a characteristic of dominant parties that they rely heavily upon the support of groups that do not demand too much of them, thereby simplifying their problems of choice, especially concerning redistribution.

If we turn to the Democratic Justice political elites themselves rather than to their supporters, we still find few reasons to expect rapid change.

Lacking a majority and searching for marginal electoral advantages vis-à-vis other parties, the party must court particular groups and individuals. Moreover, individual leaders must compete with other leaders for influence in the party and for preference votes in elections. Hence the party depends heavily on patronage and clientelistic networks. The resources of government are used to secure votes, not by means of a favorable public reaction to intelligent policies effectively administered but rather by specific benefits obtained by particular individuals as a result of particular government activities. Thus the cost-benefit calculus is based as much on individuals as on socioeconomic categories and broad policies.

Each minister operates his ministry as a personal fiefdom that is to be used to further his own strength within the party and that of his faction, and, of course, the strength of the Democratic Justice Party within the electorate as a whole. Governmental largesse is available only to the government party supporters in good standing and to those recommended by them. The hierarchy of the party organization is deeply involved in this highly personalized clientelistic network. Governmental services are provided in return for votes or monetary payoffs or often both. Public expenditures—whether new industrial plants, road construction, or new educational programs—are dispensed according to criteria that are much more heavily political than would likely be the case in other advanced industrial democracies. None of this of course is unique to Korea. What is different is the degree to which these criteria permeate decision making at all levels and the absence of control over the system, the inability to punish those who step over the limits of tolerable activities.

The opening to the liberals broadened the bases of groups participating in the system; it did not alter the system itself. But it has at the same time greatly complicated decision making, for it has widened the range of interests that must be accommodated. Since policy making emerges from the interplay of personal and factional interests within the ruling coalition as well as from the demands and needs of supporting groups, it is difficult for the system to act decisively.

The Korean political system lacks flexibility because it is a pluralistic system that is extremely highly mobilized. It shares with other pluralistic systems the existence of alternatives and the independence of intermediary organizations and associations between the individual and the state. But with a very high electoral turnout there is almost no change from one election to another. In most pluralistic systems there exists a reserve of floating voters who can be mobilized for particular elections when certain issues become sufficiently salient. And even if there is minimal switching from one party to another, the surge of voters into and out of the electorate makes possible a genuine shift. In a society in which almost everyone is mobilized, a policy of minimal change and maximum exploitation of incremental and marginal differences seems to be the policy best calculated to lead to continued political success for the elites of the dominant parties.

Political Engineering

If we assume that a political system is more than a simple reflection of its social and economic environment, then politics itself must make an independent impact. And if politics makes a difference, we must face the classic question, "What is to be done?" What can be done in the way of changing political structure, legal norms, and behavioral patterns in order to alter the functioning of the system? Political engineering is used to facilitate the achievement of desired ends. There are undoubtedly as many desired end states for Korean politics as there are ideological positions, and perhaps far more than that. However, our concern is very modest and hence easy to specify. We want to know what are the most likely possible changes in the short run rather than what is most desirable in the long run. Thus this discussion will be limited to proposals for change that are seriously considered by observers of the Korean political scene.

As my criteria for evaluating what needs to be changed, I posit a modest set of goals. I will look at proposals for change that promise to bring about greater coherence in the determination of policy and greater effectiveness in its execution. This change has to be based upon the success in democratizing the political process and in restoring civilian supremacy. However, without attempting to specify what specific substantive changes should be facilitated by alterations in the structure, I would suggest that any changes should make it provide the government with an increased capacity for carrying out its policies. I will briefly review several of the proposals being seriously considered in Korea, starting with those that would incorporate the largest number of changes.

The Authoritarian Solution

The authoritarian solution has few advocates among students of Korean politics. I begin with it because it has been too widely discussed during the Park regime to be discounted. And there have been enough unexplained incidents involving the Korean army, police and intelligence services, as well as hints of high governmental involvement in dubious intrigues, to make this a plausible solution again. The extreme pluralism and high levels of mobilization of Korean society of which we have already spoken make any authoritarian solution less likely. But an authoritarian solution could be either of the right or of the left. An authoritarian Communist "takeover" seems highly unlikely in contemporary Korea because of the anticommunism of the army and of the police. However, authoritarianism of a military and bureaucratic nature would encounter far less institutional opposition than would that of the left. In both cases it would be easier to take power than to exercise it.

Authoritarian restructuring of the political system would indeed be political engineering on the grand scale. However, as such restructuring would likely be carried out by the same forces that dominate the present political system, there is little reason to believe that an authoritarian regime in Korea would function effectively. A strong state might reduce labor slowdowns and rationalize some practices, with a seemingly rapid improvement in public services as a result. But the effects would probably be short-lived, unless drastic alterations were made in the structure.

Consociational Democracy

Many highly pluralist political systems have evolved patterns of mutual accommodation that have come to be labeled consociational democracy in the literature of political science. This is a pattern under which elites mobilize masses within particular subcultures or social categories, accept the rules of the game, and bargain among themselves to protect their own subcultures and to further those mutual goals upon which they are able to secure agreement. Examples of consociational democracies include the Netherlands, Austria, and Switzerland. It is often pointed out that the protagonists in these systems have at times in the past been extremely bitter enemies, and that it was the overriding need for national survival combined with the inability of any single segment or subculture to dominate the others that led to the growth of consociational democracy.

At first glance it is somewhat strange to think of Korea as a potential consociational democracy. However, the German socialists of the nineteenth century were quite alienated, yet eventually they sought accommodation with the system. As the Korean liberals might as easily follow the same path, the possibility of Korea's evolving in the consociational direction cannot be rejected out of hand. The opposition and extraregime forces have been increasingly cooperative, and they have deeply involved themselves in the political system at many levels and in many ways. Furthermore, the opposition leaders are among the strongest defenders of republican institutions.

The fear is widely felt and sometimes articulated that liberals in power would take revenge against the right-wing leaders. However, it is the nature of consociational democracies that no single political force has a monopoly of power. If present trends continue, the consociational solution may be the most likely one for the long run. The trouble is that it is impossible to specify what the long run is. The opposition wants to enter the government now; most of the DJP is opposed. The grand coalition, the "historic compromise," seemed, in 1989, an unlikely outcome. Moreover, many observers predicted that this experiment would result in an authoritarian solution of the liberals or the governing leader, which came to pass in 1990.

A Coalition of the Liberals

Closely related to the consociational democracy solution, which would involve a coalition of most of the parties and especially the large ones, is the possibility of a coalition of the opposition parties. This is not presently an impossibility, for all of the opponents together, from the NKDP to the RDP, receive more than 50 percent of the vote. A liberal coalition would be especially appealing if the DJP were to fail to accommodate a liberal shift in the electorate. Moreover, in that case a split in the DJP would become more likely, as its liberal wing might despair of the future of that party and opt for extensive reforms carried out on a pragmatic basis by a liberal coalition. But this coalition would be even more frightening to traditional groups than the consociational one, and hence would be more likely to generate a preemptive authoritarian response from the right.

A New National Electoral Law

Manipulation of electoral laws is an obvious form of political engineering. Few alterations can have the dramatic impact of a change in the method of elections. In particular, the shift from single member districts to proportional representation (including 2–6 member districts) and vice versa is likely to produce substantial alteration in the distribution of seats in the legislature.

The debate over proportional representation has a long history. Hermens attributed many of the evils of the twentieth century to it and argued that single-member district systems could have prevented the rise of national socialism and fascism in Europe. Duverger has also posited a relationship between single-member districts and two-party systems. Rae has dispassionately examined the consequences of electoral laws. Many critics, including Sartori, have pointed out the inadequacies of assuming a simple relationship between electoral systems and party systems.[2]

Many single-member district systems and seemingly two-party systems, including the British, Canadian, and American, have at various times had several political parties. And, while the single-member district system may reduce the competition within a particular district to two sides, it does not and cannot assure that it is the same two parties that compete in all districts. Furthermore, there are many polities in which the existence of only two parties would put an intolerable burden on the system: many people think that this was the case with Korea, as a two-party system would almost certainly have pitted Democratic Republicans against New Democrats during the Park regime. Few think that these two would function as Labourites and Conservatives in Britain or Republicans and

Democrats in the United States. Would either give up power graciously to the other?

There are good reasons why so few people advocate changing the Korean electoral system. The main one stems from the equation of democracy with proportional representation in Korea and the historical reasons for this belief.

More of the Same

Political survival is undoubtedly the key phrase in this entire discussion. The present Korean constitutional system may not generate extreme and vocal support from the citizenry; indeed, precisely the opposite is true. But it is the system that divides Korea least. It is, however, the citizenry who ask for the constitutional reform from the indirect presidential election to the direct one. So far, the political leaders from both the governing and opposition parties are likely to reach an agreement on the constitutional reform issues soon.

Political leaders will certainly continue to exploit the system in every way that they can. As they are interested in survival, leaders from all of the major parties have until the present time always drawn back from steps that would be totally destructive.

Crisis itself has a role in the functioning of the system, for it is only through crisis that the political elites are able to generate agreement on important programs. Crisis is itself part of the decision-making process. Things that can be postponed will be postponed. When decisions must be made, they are generally made—or at least they have been up until the present.

All Korean elites are concerned with their own survival. Most are equally concerned with survival of their party and the traditions that it represents. For most of them, that survival is linked to the survival of the present republic: thus, even if their primary loyalties may be to the intermediate structures rather than to the constitutional order itself, most elites would have little to gain from dramatic changes in the structure of the political system. Those in a position to make changes are ones who benefit most from the present system. They are likely to favor only those minimum changes that will preserve it. Crisis demonstrates to them that certain changes are necessary. Others are likely to be postponed.

Korean elites have been reasonably successful in dealing with domestic conflict, but there are aspects of politics that are outside of their control, such as those stemming from international balance of payments difficulties. The resulting crises are the ones most likely to generate substantial internal changes, for they are thrust upon the country in a manner that makes it impossible to ignore them.

As long as the Democratic Justice and Reunification Democratic parties continue to support the constitutional order, it is likely to survive. What impact economic crises could have on their determination to do so cannot be predicted. Nor can the eventual impact of continued violence be anticipated. It is difficult to foresee who would benefit from electoral changes. And it is difficult to see who could bring them about, given the high levels of electoral mobilization and the near absence of a floating vote. Although the present era must someday end, the current elites have demonstrated remarkable staying power.

Postscript

The course of Korea's political development was changed in June 1987 when popular uprisings forced President Doo-Hwang Chun to promulgate a new and more democratic constitution. At the direct presidential election in December 1987, Chun's chosen successor, Roh Tae-woo, was elected with less than 40 percent of the popular vote because his major opponents, Young-Sam Kim of the RDP and Dae-Jung Kim of the Party for Peace and Democracy (PPD), failed to unite their parties. In the general election for the National Assembly held in April 1988, the ruling party, the DJP, failed to win a majority against the three major opposition parties (PPD, RPD, and the New Democratic Republican Party) for the first time in Korea's history. It had to form short-term alliances with one or more of the opposition parties to get legislation passed, often as not unsuccessfully. Roh had encouraged political assaults on the *chaebol*, or big business. The four largest groups—Samsung, Hyundai, Lucky-Goldstar, and Daewoo—accounted for about half the GNP and seven trading companies accounted for almost 40 percent of the country's exports, whose temporary setback in 1989 did not help matters.

Then came dramatic political developments. The chairman of the DJP, Jyun-kyu Park, was forced to resign at the end of the year when he revealed what in fact was soon to come to pass—namely, that the four-party system would be reduced to a two-party system to enable the traditional ruling party to resume full authority, with President Roh dissolving the old DJP to reside over a new political alignment. In January 1990, all three conservative parties—the DJP, the RDP led by Young-Sam Kim, and the NDRP led by Jong-Phil Kim—were dissolved at a hastily organized national convention. On February 9 an inaugural convention of the new Democratic Liberal Party (DLP), which bears a strong likeness to Japan's ruling Liberal Democratic Party, under the joint leadership of Roh, Young-Sam Kim, and Jong-Phil Kim, was held. Its secretary general was to come from the DJP, its floor leader from the RDP, and its chief policymaker from the NDRP. Thus, the new DLP would have a two-thirds majority over the PPD and a new opposition party, the Korean Democratic Party (KDP), which was formed by dissident RDP and NDRP members but was too small to form a floor-negotiating body. The DLP was expected to push for a parliamentary system under Roh's heir apparent, Young-Sam Kim.

The merger of the conservative parties isolated the PPD's Dae-jung Kim, who in 1971 had narrowly lost the presidency to Park. The government was expected to take bold action to tackle the country's problems. It did so by strengthening the *chaebol*—cracking down on labor and other dissidents and adjusting economic policies. President Roh had at last rid himself of the DJP, which he had inherited from the unpopular Doo-Hwang Chung. At the same time he had made partners out of his former critics: Jong-Phil Kim, once prime minister under President Park, resumed as an influential (and conservative) leader in the new party, particularly when one of his former NDRP colleagues became the DLP's chief policymaker.

An independent assemblyman Chul Lee commented that "the three parties merged without asking the intention of their party members and without considering the will of the general public;" he thought that the merger was a "political fraud masterminded jointly by a military regime fearful of losing its control and two opposition parties lured by the promise of political power." Indeed, many people who had voted for the opposition parties were greatly disappointed that their parties had joined the government and ruling party. The opposition PPD denied the government's claim that the new two-party system reflected the maturing of Korean politics. The sudden and unexpected loss of the middle ground meant that there were fewer institutional channels for less radical dissenters, although the rival factions in the DLP would make unity difficult on particular issues.

The country's politics would continue to be stormy, although now the government at least had more legitimacy and civil liberty had been advanced. The government would also be freer to impose reforms from above and speed democratization if it were so minded. Indeed, one of its boldest initiatives was immediately to open a dialogue with the Soviet Union and to normalize relations with Eastern Europe, something that had been unthinkable a few years earlier. Within the DLP, Young-sam Kim did not take kindly to this step, while outside the government, at by-elections in April 1990, the new party did not fare well.

Since 1987, politics is more in the open, despite the secret nature of the formation of a new conservative ruling party. Political participation does not need to be underground or violent. Confrontation does not have to be extreme, although the two-party system does solidify opposition. Nonetheless, civic participation is still weak and the grassroots still has little say in how things are done and in curbing elite manipulations. One consequence of the merger has been a perception of increased polarization between the favored regions and the unfavored regions, particularly Dae-jung Kim's Chŏlla province and its long-standing resentment of the more elitist regions such as Kyongsang province, home of Young-sam Kim. In the future, however, a greater rivalry is likely to emerge between the

Seoul region and the rest of the country. The elites will continue to exploit every opportunity to maintain their superior position, and it will take a traumatic national event to displace them.

Notes

1. Robert A. Dahl, *Polyarchy: Participation and Opposition* (New Haven, Conn.: Yale University Press, 1971), p. 1.
2. F. A. Hermens, *Europe Between Democracy and Anarchy* (Notre Dame, Ind.: University of Notre Dame Press, 1958); Maurice Duvergier, *Political Parties* (London: Methuen, 1954); Douglas Rae, *The Political Consequences of Electoral Law* (New Haven, Conn.: Yale University Press, 1967); Giovanni Sartori, *Parties and Party Systems: A Framework of Analysis* (Cambridge: Cambridge University Press).

PART
IV

*The Government and
Economic Development*

CHAPTER EIGHT

Government Direction of the Korean Economy

In Joung Whang

REGARDLESS OF POLITICAL ideology, governments the world over engage in the mobilization and allocation of resources, stabilization of the economy, and promotion of technological innovation. Korea has been no exception with its introduction of economic planning to stimulate national development. The strategy adopted was export-oriented industrialization based on a broad range of critical development activities such as the establishment of physical infrastructure, consolidation of industrial parks, human resource training, research and development in science and technology, a legal and administrative framework for industrial promotion, and incentives for export-oriented industries. Government direction of the economy has been more successful than the previous foreign-aid stimulated growth of the 1950s.

Economic Development: 1960–1979

Korea entered the twentieth century unprepared for self-reliant development, plagued by poor leadership and external interference. During the first half of this century, Korea struggled through a loss of sovereignty and colonial exploitation (1910–1945) by a neighboring country. As a result, the new Korea, which was born after the end of World War II, required a judicious restructuring of its institutions as part of nation-building efforts. This prerequisite for development went unrecognized, however, and impatient attempts to build democratic institutions resulted in not only political confusion, but also economic disruption and social disorder. The four-year turmoil (1945–1949) afforded little opportunity for laying the

Taken from "The Role of Government in Economic Development in Korea During the Sixties and Seventies," Occasional Paper, Korea Development Institute, 1986; and "Korea's Economic Management for Structural Adjustment in the 1980s," presented at the World Bank, Washington D.C., June 1986.

foundations of a new nation. The Korean War (1950–1953) similarly delayed national development: in addition to enormous losses of lives and assets, the national economy became greatly damaged by wartime distortions. In this respect, not until the early 1950s did the nation begin to mobilize its potential for modernization. A series of self-reliant development efforts for nation building were made in the 1950s and on. They included the massive educational drive and the land reform of 1949–1952. From the early 1960s, in particular, the government became strongly committed to economic development and modernization.

Leadership Commitment

Government direction of the economy largely depended on the commitment of political leadership, which was often reflected in presidential speeches. Park Chung-Hee was more strongly committed in the 1960s to industrialization than his predecessor Syngman Rhee in the 1950s. Park used vivid political symbols to muster public support, terms such as "national modernization," "economic planning," and "administrative reform" as compared to Rhee's doctrine expressed by "anticommunism," "antipathy toward Japan," and "patriotism." Rhee viewed economic development as part of economic recovery and an extension of economic stabilization. He depended on foreign aid, considering economic planning as a tool of a Communist regime and foreign loans as an infringement of national sovereignty. He remembered that a loan from Japan in the waning years of the Chosun dynasty had led to eventual colonization. In contrast, Park urged that economic development was essential for national modernization. A self-supporting economy could not be achieved by foreign aid alone. Planning was needed to attract foreign loans to aid industrialization.

In regard to government bureaucracy, Rhee perceived the whole Korean society as a family and the president as the "father of the nation" (*Koukbu*), with officials as hardworking, patriotic servants. In contrast, Park, an authoritarian military reformer, regarded the bureaucracy as an action instrument to carry out his political objectives. He stressed the need for administrative reforms, anticorruption measures, and rationalization and emphasized "administration by identification." He frequently visited industrial sites for project identification and he often attended opening ceremonies. He personally monitored export performance and received detailed monthly reports on the status of the economy. His strong commitment to economic development motivated the bureaucracy to formulate realistic plans and the administrative elite to put utmost effort into the successful implementation of planned targets.

Organization of Economic Planning

In 1961, Park established the Economic Planning Board (EPB) for economic planning, national budgeting, foreign capital management, and statistics.

In 1963, the minister of the EPB was designated deputy prime minister. Also in 1961, an Office of Planning and Coordination was established under the prime minister to evaluate and monitor project and program performance, and planning and management units were set up under the vice minister in every ministry to superintend and monitor tasks. Although at first coordination between planning and budgeting was not smooth, after 1966 middle-level executives were exchanged between the two bureaus so that planning officials learned about financial feasibility and budgeting officials became familiar with project implementation. To infuse the bureaucracy with rational values and development philosophy, about 10 percent of senior administrators in economic ministries were directly recruited from the military and academia in the early 1960s. Later, senior administrators were promoted or transferred from within the bureaucracy, particularly from the EPB, which became the primary source of elite formation. With them came the EPB's planning values such as future orientation, innovation, planning techniques, and research capabilities, which stimulated participation in planning and implementation consistent with national planning.

Policy Planning Subculture

The executive branch dominated decision making and policy execution, further centralized by Park's leadership style and the organizational structure for planning, budgeting, and information. The government quickly prescribed solutions to problems, constantly monitored their progress, and adjusted policies as necessary. In other words, the Korean approach was a process of trial and error. This pragmatism allowed a wide choice among all available instruments without any ideological bias and permitted the government to apply specific policies to a limited number of clients. Although such particularism helped solve problems, it fueled corruption whenever bureaucrats misused their discretion.

In the first economic development plan, the idea of a mixed economy was defined in terms of "guided capitalism" in which "the principle of free enterprise and respect for the freedom and initiative of private enterprise will be observed, but in which the government will either directly participate in or indirectly render guidance to the basic industries and other important fields." In the second plan, "guided capitalism" was dropped to emphasize the private sector and the principles of a market economy. Nonetheless, the government stated it would intervene in the economy when necessary to maintain economic efficiency. In the third plan, references to the government's role were deleted although it was clear that it would be primarily planning by direction.

Intervention Mechanisms

Four major instruments were employed to implement economic planning, namely, the national budget, public enterprise, regulation, and inducements. At first, after an ambitious increase in government spending in the early 1960s brought budget deficits and inflation, government spending was drastically reduced (from 21.6 percent of GNP in 1962 to 13.0 percent in 1964). Thereafter, resumption of growth in government spending was gradual and consistent, with revenue increases in the range of 18 to 21 percent of GNP. Spending on social and economic services rose sharply to over 10 percent of GNP, at the expense of general services and defense, with economic services outstripping social services. The government moved from net dissaver to net saver after 1964, and fixed investment through the government sector doubled (from 3.5 percent of GNP in 1963–1965) thereafter. As government consumption remained at between 9 percent and 11 percent of GNP, government savings and investment contributed significantly to economic growth. Nondefense spending rose from the cutback low of 9.5 percent of GNP in 1964 to 16 percent during the 1970s.

The efficient use of the budge in resource mobilization was largely attributable to improved tax collection with the establishment in 1966 of the Office of National Tax Administration, which protected tax collection from political interference. In addition to tax audits, tighter supervision, and public campaigns, the Tax Office adopted a system of tax collection targets or quotas by geographic area and tax items and awards or penalties for exceeding or falling short of the targets. Efforts were made to establish a Program Budgeting System in 1962 and a Planning-Programming-Budgeting System in 1968 and more rational budgeting procedures were instituted.

Besides the budget, the government owned many industries in the form of state-owned enterprises (SOEs), enough to constitute the leading sector in the national economy. Furthermore, SOEs grew substantially more rapidly than the economy as a whole (from 52 in 1963 to 108 in 1972), and rose from 7 percent of the GDP to 9 percent. Their purpose was to engage in basic industries or public infrastructure activities that required capital-intensive technology, to undertake large-scale business operations, and to support import-substituting industries to improve the trade balance. They were also created to cope with market failures involving entrepreneurial inadequacies, the imperfect capital market, shortage of market information, and unwillingness of the private sector to bear risk. Whereas they may have been slightly less efficient than private Korean firms, they were generally more cost-efficient than SOEs elsewhere. Their performance was largely attributable to nonpecuniary incentives, as most of their executives were military or business appointees. Thus, good economic performance was due to the general competence of the labor force, strong leadership, and efficient administration.

The Korean government also used its power and authority to directly influence the private sector. The Price Control Act of 1961 introduced a price ceiling system for five essential commodities and, under inflationary pressure, later applied it to thirteen others. The Public Utility Rates Review Committee controlled the prices for public utilities, so that in 1963 about 53 percent of total economic transactions were directly under government price control. Because price control was not effective or efficient, it was gradually abolished after 1964 and replaced by cooperative pricing determined by agreements with producers. The executive branch tried to insist on fair trade practices, but the legislature defeated its attempts until the enactment of the Price Stabilization and Fair Trade Act of 1975. This was later revised as the Anti-Monopoly and Fair Trade Act of 1980, whose objectives were to control the abuse of monopolistic or oligopolistic power, ensure free competition, and protect consumers.

Indirect taxation replaced direct taxation and became the major source of government revenues, especially with increases in gasoline taxes and the introduction of a value-added tax system in 1977. Greater dependency on indirect taxation also reflected limited government efforts to improve income redistribution. The government did apply various tax incentives and disincentives such as a preferential depreciation system, subsidies, tax exemptions, and differential commodity tax rates to discourage consumption of luxury commodities. In 1968 a real estate speculation control tax was introduced. In spite of these measures, government played only a limited role in domestic capital formation because of a limited tax base at the early stages of development and the rigidity of budgetary outlays for defense, education, and other legally determined expenditures.

In the early 1960s, because interest rates were held artificially low, businesses were overdependent on bank funds and indulged in speculation. An interest realization program was implemented in the late 1960s to increase interest rates; although it temporarily discouraged production, it normalized financial institutions. Despite higher interest rates throughout the 1970s, because these still did not allow the banks to absorb excess money supply, inflation and speculation resumed. Although monetary policies were ineffective in resource mobilization, they did promote efficient allocation of resources into desirable (export-oriented) industries. The government also had trouble with foreign exchange rates, fixed too low when foreign exchange requirements were met by foreign aid in the 1950s. Once demand for foreign exchange rose, a free-floating system was introduced in 1965 to reflect real market forces. But the government failed to heed market forces in the late 1970s and delayed devaluation until 1980. Meantime, the government had to provide to export industries other forms of tax and financial incentives that distorted their financial structures.

From Planning to a Market Economy: 1979–1990

While the government's role in economic growth was quite impressive, the major portion occurred in the private rather than public sector. Between 1960 and 1980, the lead was assumed by an experienced group of private entrepreneurs well seasoned in introducing new products, adopting efficient processes, and penetrating new markets. The relationship between government and business underwent fundamental changes to improve the international competitiveness of exports. Instead of preferential loan packages, efforts were made in the late 1970s to encourage technological innovation through research and development. The shift in the government's role was a necessary response to the changing international economic situation in which export markets were becoming more restrictive because of increased protectionism and more inaccessible overseas resources. The Korean government sought to shrink the public sector in order to strengthen market mechanisms that would enable the private sector to play a more dominant role in the economy.

The economy had grown in size and sophistication to the point that the government could dispense with some planning. Henceforth, private initiative was to be fostered by normalizing market functions and minimizing government intervention. In shifting the pattern of state intervention, the government continued to use financial instruments but relinquished direct control in favor of indirect control of the economy. This step called for the liberalization of financial institutions, including increased autonomy for banking institutions, internationalization of the capital market, and promotion of direct foreign investment. What unmistakably marked the turning point was the announcement on April 17, 1979, of the Comprehensive Measures for Economic Stabilization (CMES), which had as its far-reaching goal no less than restructuring the economy to enable the country to make full use of its potential for continued high growth. This goal required a dramatic change in the philosophy as well as the mode of government direction of the economy.

The CMES had three main components. It involved a gradual reduction of fiscal and monetary incentives for export promotion and agricultural subsidies, a reduction in rural housing loans, and a realignment of investment schemes for heavy and chemical industries, none of which could have been contemplated ten years before. It was not popular among vested bureaucratic and business interests or considerable segments of the population. But the government was determined to proceed and later was gratified by its results in terms of economic stabilization, sustained economic growth, recovery of international competitiveness in industrial products, and improvement in the balance of payments.

Organizational Context of Policy Planning

Besides the economic planning organization that had been established in the early 1960s, various other specialized policy research institutes had been sponsored by the government to strengthen public policy planning. They included the Korea Development Institute (KDI) under the EPB, the

Korea Institute for Industrial Economics and Technology (KIET) under the Ministry of Trade and Industry (MTI), the Korea Research Institute for Human Settlements (KRIHS) under the Ministry of Construction, the Korea Rural Economic Institute (KREI) under the Ministry of Agriculture and Fisheries, the Korea Institute of Population and Health (KIPH), the Korea Women Development Institute (KWDI) under the Ministry of Health and Social Affairs, and the Korea Education Development Institute (KEDI) under the Ministry of Education. In the field of science and technology, many other research institutes were fully sponsored by the Korean government.

With respect to the five-year development plans, the EPB took the initial step by preparing and issuing preliminary guidelines in terms of major policy targets and directions, together with macroeconomic projections for both the international and the domestic environment of the economy during the plan period and thereafter. At that stage, the intellectual interaction between EPB technocrats and economists of government-sponsored research institutes was crucial. Individual ministries then formulated their own sectoral plans in accordance with the guidelines. In these, extensive use of a number of working committees drawn from government ministries, industrial associations, financial institutions, universities, and research institutes was made. The preliminary guidelines and the individual sectoral plans were then consolidated and presented at a series of public policy forums conducted at KDI and other relevant research institutes. Many experts and representatives from business organizations, labor unions, and consumer groups were invited to make their comments and express their views on the draft plan. Finally, the EPB, with the help of policy research institutes and individual ministries, formulated the consolidated draft plan. This was reviewed first by the Plan Working Committee, consisting of vice ministers of economic affairs, and then by the Plan Deliberation Committee, which was comprised of the prime minister and other cabinet members; eventually it was sent for approval to the president.

To implement the mid-term plan, the government used annual rolling Economic Management Plans (1) to translate the policy targets and strategies embodied in the five-year development plans into specific, annual action programs, and (2) to make policy adjustments by revising policy directions and the list of projects to be implemented in line with unforeseen changes in the domestic and internal economic environment. The Economic Management Plan was also intended to review and evaluate performance in the preceding year and to provide guidelines for the government's annual budget. It was further expected to indicate the stance of the government policy toward the private sector.

Every year, the EPB circulated the initial draft of the Economic Management Plan, derived from the five-year plan, to all ministries and agencies for their use in annual policy planning and budget estimates. This initial draft served as a preliminary step—just before the budget cycle started—

to enable the EPB's annual budget guidelines to be circulated to government ministries and agencies immediately after the draft plan. After the approval of the government budget by the National Assembly, the EPB finalized the Economic Management Plan.

In the case of both five-year plans and annual plans, the government worked closely with the National Assembly and the government party before the finalization of major decisions by the top executive. The individual standing committees of the National Assembly voiced their views of these plans through hearing sessions and/or policy inquiry sessions. Party–Government Consultative Committee meetings were regularly held in order to mutually share critical information and to build a consensus.

Procedures for Economic Policy Making

Economic policy proposals were usually initiated by the respective ministries concerned with policy issues. These policy proposals were reviewed with other ministries relating to the policy matter before their submission to the cabinet and the president for final decisions. In this process of review and coordination of policy proposals, two institutional mechanisms were involved: (1) the Economic Ministers Consultation Meeting, through which informal or semiformal discussions for coordination were arranged; and (2) the Economic Ministers Consultation Meeting, which was a formal setting to satisfy legal requirements for the formalization of policy proposals to be submitted to the cabinet. In support of the latter mechanism, an Economic Vice Ministers Meeting was also held.

Policy proposals prepared by a ministry were seldom available to the public for discussion and did not reflect public opinion. They were processed secretly or only among a small number of elite officials. In particular, emergency policy proposals tended to be prepared quickly by a small group of confidants. In other words, the policy-making process was streamlined, with little consultation with related ministries and private organizations. Even in the case of special working committees organized by a ministry, the participation of private experts and the general public in policy debate was limited. Some committees worked as rubber stamps to approve whatever was proposed.

This "top-down" approach was rooted in the paternalistic tradition of Korean society and also in the prevailing nature of the authoritarian system of the government bureaucracy, particularly after the military coup d'état of 1961. The concentration of decision-making power allowed the government bureaucracy to make speedy decisions and also to flexibly adjust the direction of ongoing policies.

In the case of the CMES of 1979, senior officials in EPB and KDI played the key role in policy formulation and change. A group of EPB technocrats studying the structural vulnerability of the Korean economy recognized that a dramatic shift of policy was needed if projections for 1991 were to be realized. In 1978 they circulated an internal study report, which was then elaborated upon by some 44 staff reports prepared by the economic policy bodies before the CMES was adopted by cabinet and endorsed by President Park. The president actually had a choice presented to him through other independent studies, but all indicated that the Korean economy was faced with serious problems. He indicated the outlines for the CMES whose details were fleshed out by EPB technocrats, a critical mass of competent and innovation-minded professionals essential for far-reaching policy reform.

At first, CMES did not get off to a good start, given political, business, and bureaucratic resistance. Furthermore, President Park, overconfident about past economic achievements, was not convinced enough to push strongly for it—not when it meant admitting previous investment mistakes. The timing also turned out to be unfortunate as it coincided with the second energy crisis, poor harvests, and then the assassination of Park. In 1980, the economy actually declined for the first time in a quarter of a century. But President Doo-Hwang Chun, who took over in September 1980, was strongly committed, as was the National Guardian Council before the Fifth Republic was formally established a year later. He appointed the chief architect of CMES to be his economic advisor and he continually monitored its progress, as did ministers who had supported it from the beginning. Although they understood the policy implications of CMES, they went along with the technocrats who had tended to concentrate deliberately on economic rationality, ignore the political realities of opposition and resistance to the policy change, and expect presidential approval and enforcement to obviate the need for consensus building. In the end, they were proved right. Although opportunities were provided for interested and affected parties to make their views known and to participate in performance appraisal, they were formalistic and substantially limited.

Implementation of Economic Policy Change

Besides strong political commitment, the implementation of CMES relied primarily on mechanisms for intragovernment coordination and the mobilization of external support. Although the mechanisms for intragovernment coordination had been well developed in regard to economic planning implementation for twenty or so years, internal opposition to CMES gave EPB some headaches and caused it to improve interministerial consultations and communication. EPB mobilized World Bank support for CMES and internally instigated public information, education, and communication (IEC) programs to reinforce the new policy. The IEC programs (*Kyung-jae Kyo-Yuck*, or "economic education") were addressed not only to government officials at all levels but also to the general public beyond the usual business channels. EPB knew that opposition to CMES was fragmented and would eventually be overcome. Nonetheless, this time it did seek consensus for the new policy through slide shows and other audio-visual materials required in every training institute both public and private, widely circulated to many different groups of employees, and later presented to military forces and households. Indeed, EPB launched an extensive publicity blitz to explain, justify, and raise support for CMES. The result was gratifying in that, weaned off government supports and protection, the public stepped up productivity. The receptivity of the public was aided by the high general level of education. People were ready to follow rational behavior and the right policy for their own interests and for the country in the long run.

The Korean economy kicked into higher gear in the 1980s and the state became one of the four dragons. Prices were stabilized. Industrially, Korea became extremely competitive. The balance of payments improved. Technology was upgraded and labor productivity was increased. The partnership among political leadership, reform-minded bureaucrats, and leading business entrepreneurs had worked. But, when new problems arose in the late 1980s and another structural adjustment appeared necessary, there was no guarantee that it would work once again.

CHAPTER NINE

The Structure of the Economic Policy-making Institution in Korea and the Strategic Role of the Economic Planning Board

Byung Sun Choi

OVER THE PAST three decades, the institutional structure of the Korean state has been subject to frequent changes. The transition in government and the politicoeconomic order each government represented, in particular, have brought a substantial change in the pattern of interactions among the state institutions. Again, along with the institution of the new Constitution, which represents a significant step toward a more democratic governance in Korea, the issue of bringing the state institutions in line with the spirit of the new Constitution seems to be gaining a renewed interest.

Needless to say, the foremost concern in reorganizing the state institutions is how to democratize their internal decision-making process and policy networks with the major societal groups and other legitimate policy-making bodies such as the National Assembly and the political parties. As important as the concern for democratizing the state institutions is, the chapter argues how to preserve the strategic developmental role that the Korean state has attained and is expected to continue to assume in a new and increasingly democratized policy environment. This legitimate concern seems particularly important for the case of reorganizing the economic policy-making institutions that have come to acquire distinct competences in the process of promoting economic development for almost three decades.

Taken from Byung Sun Choi, "The Structure of the Economic Policy-Making Institutions in Korea and the Strategic Role of the Economic Planning Board (EPB)," *The Korean Journal of Policy Studies* 2 (1987):1–25.

Characterizing the Pattern of Interactions Among the Economic Policy-making Institutions

Despite considerable interest, both at home and abroad, in the role of the Korean state in the process of economic development, existing studies on the structure and the workings of the economic policy-making institutions in Korea lack the sophistication of comparable studies of such states as Japan or the European industrial democracies. Some viewed the economic policy-making process in Korea as "top-down," that is, a high concentration of decision-making power at the top. Stressing the Korean government's tendency to take unreasonably drastic economic policy measures and reverse them with relative ease, others tried to direct attention to the high degree of centralization of economic decision making in Korea.

Although there is some validity to characterizing the process of economic decision making in Korea as such, common in these views is the conception of the Korean state as "monolithic." This conception has tended to obstruct a more complete understanding of the central coordinating role of the Economic Planning Board (EPB), the peculiar constellation of economic bureaucracies in Korea, the nature of interministerial relationships, and the pattern of conflict resolution among principal actors and economic agencies.

The Peculiar Configuration of the Economic Policy-making Institutions in Korea

At the heart of economic policy making in Korea is the "central" coordination by the deputy prime minister, who also serves as the Minister of the Economic Planning Board. The deputy prime minister is the president's top economic advisor, the principal government spokesperson on the economic policy, and the economic policy team leader. An investigation of how and why the EPB, which was created later than other economic ministries and which has been autonomous in the sense that it has not been closely identified with any major societal groups, has come to play a dominant role illuminates the peculiarity of the economic policy-making process in Korea.

The EPB was created in July 1961, immediately after the military coup led by the late president Park Chung-Hee. The establishment of the EPB symbolized the military government's resolve to give top priority to economic development and its commitment to a systematic and sustained pursuit of long-term economic development plans. It took over comprehensive development planning functions and foreign cooperation activities from the Ministry of Construction, which had been established only one month earlier by the military junta. (The Ministry of Construction was created from the Ministry of Reconstruction, 1955–1961.) It received a new Korean name of more progressive connotation, but its internal organization was only slightly modified. The EPB also absorbed the Bureau of Budget from the Ministry of Home Affairs to facilitate comprehensive planning and to ensure effective execution of development programs.

Although the EPB was equipped with both planning functions (for setting investment priorities) and budget functions (for allocating budget resources, the most important investment resources at the earlier stage of economic development), it was faced with many difficulties as the adverse effects of instituting the long-term economic development plan—notably, rising inflation due to high budget deficits to finance public investment programs—mounted. Under these circumstances, the EPB pressed for further strengthening of its mandate and its preeminence in the economic policy-making machinery. To signify the seriousness of the regime's planning efforts, the military government elevated the head of the EPB to the rank of deputy prime minister in December 1963.

The change did not go as far as to elevate the status of the EPB minister among economic ministers, but it endowed the deputy prime minister with a formal authority to coordinate a wide range of economic policies for effective execution of economic development plans. Other economic ministers were required to have prior consultation with the deputy prime minister when they wanted to initiate major policy proposals. But when their policy proposals did not involve budget expenditures, other economic ministers tended not to undergo the prior consultation process. Although the purpose of creating the title of deputy prime minister and endowing the EPB minister with the new title was to facilitate economic policy coordination, it also potentially increased interministerial conflicts between the EPB and other ministries in competition for policy leadership.

Based on a secure political mandate and its superior capacities to collect and analyze economy-wide information, the EPB has evolved into the leading developmental institution in Korea. The EPB has proved itself an effective economic agency, giving a coherence to a wide variety of developmental policies undertaken by other economic ministries. The EPB's demonstrably successful economic policy management in the earlier period had led the president to give an even broader mandate to the EPB and to hold the deputy prime minister responsible for the overall economy's performance.

The growing, open-ended, political mandate of the EPB and its ever-growing mission have in turn led the EPB to take many policy initiatives and preemptive moves in a broad range of policy areas normally under the jurisdictions of other economic ministries. Often in alliance with the Blue House (the President's Executive Office) economic secretariat, the EPB has propounded new policy ideas, initiated new policy proposals, and pressured other economic ministries to take the subsequent necessary steps.

The EPB's tendency to cut into domains of other economic agencies frequently entailed jurisdictional conflicts over policy leadership. The EPB's attempts at accelerating financial sector liberalization and import liberalization in the 1980s, for example, intensified jurisdictional conflicts between the EPB and the Ministries of Finance (MOF), Commerce and Industry (MCI), and Agriculture and Fisheries, which resisted such economic policy reforms. To a considerable degree, jurisdictional conflicts have been deliberately encouraged by presidents. As long as the EPB has tended to be at arm's length with business and other societal interest groups, the presidents could effectively ensure their important policy decisions against the parochial interests that other economic ministries tended to represent.

Mechanisms of Conflict Resolution

The asymmetry in institutional mandates, resources, and capacities between the EPB and other economic ministries responsible for implementing policies has led these agencies increasingly to engage in mutual adjustment. The pattern of resolving conflicts between the agencies has taken many forms. Most important, the EPB has tried to strengthen its policy leadership and the nexus between its policy initiatives and other economic ministries' subsequent policy actions by creating many formal policy coordination forums such as the Economic Ministers' Consultation Meeting (EMCM) and the Industrial Policy Deliberation Council (IPDC) chaired by the deputy prime minister. The EPB has sought to maintain its traditional means of control: planning and budgeting. The EPB's many attempts at strengthening policy review by introducing new budgeting systems—such as the planning programming budgeting system (PPBS) and, to a limited extent, zero-based budgeting—and by instituting annual economic management plans were the manifestations of the EPB's continuous struggle for preeminence over economic policy making.

The pattern of resolving conflicts has also depended crucially on the institutional capacities of other economic ministries responsible for implementing development programs. Some agencies such as the MCI have demonstrated their capability to infuse their concerns into the policy initiatives taken by the EPB or jointly by the EPB and the Blue House. From the perspective of the EPB planners, such institutional resistance was not necessarily a problem. Paradoxically, other ministries' capacities to mitigate the radical appearance of the policy initiatives taken by the EPB tended to accord the EPB planners greater freedom in initiating policies, particularly when the EPB took new and bold initiatives, as was the case with economic liberalization in the late 1970s and early 1980s.

Explaining the Relative Power of the Economic Policy-making Institutions

State-Society Linkages and Institutional Flexibility

What characteristics of the EPB have permitted it to assume a preeminent place in economic policy making in Korea? How different is the EPB's institutional structure from that of other government agencies? How does it influence interaction among governmental institutions and officials, and between the state and society?

The first factor that influences the relative strength of state institutions in the process of economic policy change is the nature of their linkages with society. Unlike other government agencies, the EPB is relatively autonomous from any particular groups in society. This institutional autonomy permits the EPB to maintain a broader economic policy perspective, to provide relatively objective analysis (as opposed to ostensibly partisan analysis as usually done by other ministries), and therefore to render a unique service to the president and to the nation. Without the constraint of parochial institutional interests, the EPB can make "less biased" statements about where the national and public interest lie, and can suggest where the economy should be headed.

The institutional autonomy of the EPB should not be construed as indicating its total independence from societal groups. What should be emphasized here is the indirect and arm's-length relationship of the EPB with societal groups. Two facts contribute to this relationship. First, a broad political mandate of promoting economic development, which has historically been lodged in the EPB, has led the EPB to consider flexibility as important in order to discharge its institutional mission. To increase and protect its institutional flexibility, the EPB has kept societal interest groups at arm's length and has resisted being identified closely with any of them. Second, as its major developmental tasks change in the process of rapid economic growth, the EPB's relation to societal groups shifted. In the process of promoting rapid economic growth in the 1960s and the early 1970s, the EPB took a position protecting the interests of low income classes and small and medium-sized enterprises. In turn, the shifting positions of the EPB deprived it of the basis of constructing an enduring relationship with any major groups of society.

In stark contrast, many operating state agencies in Korea have major groups of society as their constituents: the MCI serves the interests of business, the Ministry of Agriculture and Fisheries the farm community, the Ministry of Labor the labor groups, and so on. These ministries' linkage with their easily identified constituent groups are strong for two reasons. First, the absence or weakness of other linkages tended to reinforce the interdependent relationship between these government agencies and their constituent groups. As a result, government agencies play a crucial role as intermediaries for major societal groups, such as *chaebol* (big business groups), labor, and medium- and small-sized enterprises. Even *chaebol*, which the public believes politically powerful, exerts its influence through government agencies.

A second factor that has strengthened the interrelationship between these agencies and their constituents is strategic: In the politicized market economy, a relatively small change in sectoral policy (e.g., import protection measures) makes a big difference in consequences for the private (as opposed to social) profitability of many economic activities. Therefore, clientele groups have a keen interest in keeping a close relationship with governmental agencies to protect their interests. On the governmental side, as long as their constituent industries embody their institutional goals and visions of legitimate actions, government agencies have every incentive to foster the growth of their constituents.

The difference in the state-society linkage between the EPB and other state agencies has important implications for the ways in which policy preferences and options of societal groups are formed; the process through which societal groups' conflicting policy preferences and options are weighed against each other; and the way in which administrative means to carry out policy decisions are selected.

By virtue of its institutional autonomy, the EPB can enjoy a high degree of flexibility, compared to other state agencies. The public presumes that what the EPB proposes for the economy is in the broad national interest. It is in this capacity that the EPB could authoritatively set long-term economic policy agenda. It is also in this capacity that the EPB could use nationwide economic education programs to build support for its economic stabilization and liberalization policies in the 1980s.

Different Scope of Institutional Mission

The second factor that influences the relative power of state agencies is the different scope and dimension of mission of the EPB and other state agencies in fulfilling the visions of central decisionmakers. The EPB has come to have a broader political mandate than does any other economic institution in Korea. The EPB not only embodies a certain vision of the need for coordination of economic development policies but also has certain capacities to effect that coordination.

Since it was created in 1961 by the military government of Park Chung-Hee as an institution undertaking systematic pursuit of long-term economic development plans, the EPB has continuously expanded its strategic roles. Equipped with planning and budgeting functions, the EPB has proved itself an effective economic agency giving coherence to a wide variety of developmental policies undertaken by other economic ministries. The title of the deputy prime minister given to the EPB minister, the deputy prime minister's formal authority that was brought with the title, and the deputy prime minister's demonstrably successful coordination of sectoral policies in the earlier period of economic development led the president to centralize ever greater power in the EPB, give a broader mandate to the EPB over time, and hold the EPB responsible for the overall economy's performance.

Since its inception, concern for inflation has become the hallmark of the EPB. Although inflation influences all sectors of the economy, inflation has been only a minor consideration for many other economic ministries. Identifying policy options and weighing their consequences, these ministries have been less concerned with the effects of their policy preferences on other sectors in the economy than with fostering growth of their constituent industries.

Consider the process that led to the adoption of the import liberalization policy in the late 1970s. It illustrates how the institutional vision of central decisionmakers influences the relative strength of policy preferences and the options that governmental institutions take, and how economic policymakers' perceptions of these visions are influenced by their institutions' political mandate and mission. In the late 1970s, in the face of rising inflation that tended to aggravate the challenges to the *Yushin* (heavy industrialization) regime, different institutional players developed different policy perspectives. President Park believed unflinchingly that despite the escalating inflation rapid economic growth would sustain the legitimacy of his regime. Encouraged by his strong commitment to sectoral policies, including heavy industrialization and many rural projects, many operating ministries continued to pursue parochial sectoral interests, exacerbating the tensions of the *Yushin* regime. Concerned about escalating inflation, the EPB advocated an import liberalization policy. Why did the EPB respond differently?

With its broader economic policy perspective and strong analytical capacities, the EPB realized the significance of escalating inflation. Being autonomous from any societal groups, the EPB had little reason to be constrained by the existing economic policy, which frustrated its efforts to curb inflation. The EPB's predicament was that inflation was regarded only as the EPB's problem.

Under these circumstances, how did the EPB manage to make its policy prescription prevail? The EPB's strategy was the make inflation the president's problem. Lacking any direct connection with any disaffected groups in society and lacking direct control over other economic ministries, the only way in which the EPB could make its proposal prevail was to persuade the president and then bring his influence to bear in inducing other economic ministries to go along with the EPB.

In persuading the president, the EPB argued that the adoption of the import liberalization policy not only would help reduce inflationary pressures in the economy, but also would provide a better economic environment for accelerating the heavy industrialization and other sectoral programs that were persistently on top of the president's policy agenda. The EPB further sought to induce the desired behavior of other ministries indirectly by influencing their clientele groups, such as export industries suffering from high inflation. The EPB used the press to provoke consumer reactions and public opinion calling for some fundamental antiinflation measures and brought their pressure to bear on other ministries reluctant to cooperate with it. The EPB also made statements about where the national economic interest lay, thereby defining the parameters within which other ministries could protect their constituent groups.

These strategic actions of the EPB show both that the institutional autonomy and flexibility of the EPB made a difference in shaping policy preferences and options, and that the EPB's broader scope of institutional mission in fulfilling the visions of central decisionmakers led EPB leaders to have not only broader policy perspectives but also strategic managerial orientation, which provided a unique service to the president. As the above example illustrates, EPB leaders consciously managed their political mandate (at least in the past) by always trying to make the EPB look like the nexus of discussions about overall economic policy and by steering clear of executive responsibilities.

Furthermore, the EPB's organizational culture has been strong and congruent with many of its responsibilities, such as forecasting, budgeting, planning, and presidential advising. These responsibilities gave EPB staff access to much information, various sources of indirect influence, and resources to monitor continuously external, macroeconomic, and microeconomic conditions. Moreover, the EPB's prestige attracted high-quality minds with impressive credentials.

Nonetheless, the EPB's high degree of political attuning exhibited some problems. In the early 1970s, when the *Yushin* policy was instituted, for example, the EPB quickly adapted itself to the president's macropolitical strategy and his vision of economic development (and defense-related industrial development) in Korea's political order. The EPB could hardly have challenged the president's macropolitical strategy, reflected in the defense-related heavy industrialization, as it was couched in terms of national security and strategic response to other external threats (e.g., rising protectionism abroad) to the future of the Korean economy.

In contrast, in the late 1970s, the EPB sought to influence the president's policy choice by stressing the need to adopt an important liberalization policy. But even the EPB's insistence on import liberalization did not produce the desired result. The major change in economic policy to control inflation was made only several months before the assassination of President Park, when he really came to grips with the serious political consequences of escalating inflation, reshuffled the cabinet, and gave the newly appointed deputy prime minister a clear mandate to devise comprehensive policy measures to combat inflation. In the 1980s, with the transition in government, the EPB has consolidated its policy prescriptions for a more market-driven politicoeconomic system, which have been reflected in its continued pursuit of economic stabilization and liberalization policies and a strong enforcement of the antimonopoly and fair-trade regulations.

The EPB's influence in presidential decision making started to rise during the late 1970s. Since the early 1980s, the EPB's preeminence has become even clearer, as it actively sought to infuse its policy preferences for a more market-driven economic system with the new political leaders who came to power with little knowledge and experience in economics.

Macropolitical Change and the EPB

The transition in government in 1980, following the assassination of President Park, seems to challenge the institutional analysis made thus far that stressed the strategic actions of the EPB in selecting and promoting particular economic policies at particular stages. One can argue, for example, that the demise of the unpopular *Yushin* regime, the transition to a new government, and the rise of new political leaders may have dictated a major policy change in the 1980s. Such a view is not warranted. Although there was a big change in the political scene, the economic policy changes initiated under the previous political regime maintained a remarkable continuity in the 1980s. How can we explain this?

In explaining major economic policy change, state-centric models suggest that policy legacies and economic crisis are important factors in increasing the state autonomy to overcome these challenges. These models focus on the ways in which a government can increase its capacities to effect its distinctive policy preferences. In my view, these models are useful in understanding how the state can narrow policy choices, but we still need additional variables to understand why a specific course of economic policy change was chosen and by whom. To explain this, I argue that we have to examine divergent policy preferences among state institutions and state officials, which the state-centric models tend to ignore.

Although the bureaucratic politics model addresses this concern, I have also found it unsatisfactory as a framework for explaining Korean economic policy reform in the 1980s. Its many organizing concepts (such as players in positions, parochial perceptions, political goals and institutional interests, faces of issues, and action channels) provide useful guidance to probe why different players take different positions and actions. But this model neglects the overwhelming importance and constraining effects of the political regime's macropolitical objectives on the position that principal players take and the possibility of changing the variables that the bureaucratic models implicitly assume as given. The preeminent position of the EPB vis-à-vis other economic ministries in the economic policy-making machinery in Korea further limited its application to this particular case.

Despite the transition in government and the change in the new military regime's macropolitical strategy, why did the new political regime choose to continue the economic policy that had been advocated by the EPB in the late years of the previous government? First, the president relied heavily on the EPB as an institution to carry out economic policy reform. Why did he decide to do so?

A crucial factor that influenced the president's selection of the EPB as the institution to carry out the economic policy reform was the EPB's institutional autonomy. The task of correcting the policy legacies of the previous government could not be entrusted with the economic ministries that were a part of these legacies. Over two decades, ministries such as the MCI and the MOF had deeply intervened in the economy. Of course, the EPB had not been an exception. But, in contrast to these ministries, the indirect nature of the EPB's intervention, its institutional autonomy, and its consequent flexibility permitted it more easily to break out of these legacies. The key role played by Jae-Ik Kim, the first economic secretary to the president, as a link between the president and the EPB also contributed to the preeminence of the EPB. In a sense, the macropolitical change increased the value of the EPB's distinctive institutional assets— institutional autonomy and flexibility—rather than dictating a specific set of economic policies.

The second reason for the continuity of the EPB's economic policy reform was the rise of liberal economists in several key economic policy-making positions. When a transition in government takes place, new officials inevitably come in. A more important question is why and how certain similar-minded people came to hold the center of the economic policy-making machinery. Two facts stand out: (1) Hyon Hwak Shin, the last deputy prime minister who served President Park, brought in advocates of economic stabilization and liberalization within the EPB and promoted this group, who had constituted a minority section within the EPB, to higher ranks. Deputy prime minister Shin, a bureaucrat-turned-politician, clearly understood that his mandate was to fight inflation. He knew that his party rallied behind him. By virtue of his political career, he knew how to protect the EPB's policy prescriptions from major societal pressure groups (big businesses and agriculture, for example) by mobilizing support from the environment. He wanted people who could offer him strategic analysis. (2) Because he was leading advocate of economic stabilization and liberalization in the EPB, Jae-Ik Kim had been sent to the Special Committee for National Security (SCNSM) in May 1980 to serve as its Economic Subcommittee chairman. Ever since he served General Doo-Hwang Chun, chairman of the SCNSM's Standing Committee, he was the most trusted economic advisor for the president. Later, as the first economic secretary to President Chun, he exerted a great influence over presidential appointments.

Structuring Interactive Roles Among Institutions and Institutional Actors

Defending the EPB's Distinctive Competence and "Institutional Integrity"

In the preceding section, we have identified as the distinctive identity of the EPB its institutional autonomy and the consequent flexibility, its broad scope of mission in fulfilling the visions of central decisionmakers, and the strategic managerial orientation of EPB leaders.

Particularly since the transition in government in 1980, the EPB has anxiously embraced new roles and ever strengthened its economic policy coordinating role. I question the wisdom of centralizing ever greater power in the EPB, particularly its embracing of operating functions.

In my view, the president and the leaders of the EPB may have learned the wrong lessons from the EPB's achievement of great influence in recent years. Rather than seeing the EPB's growing influence as the result of its strategic analyses, good management of its internal and external environment, and its distinctive competence, they may have seen the EPB as generally competent with respect to anything having to do with economic planning and policy making.

Some evidence can be adduced in support of this argument.

Example 1. The secretariat of the International Economic Policy Council (IEPC), which was established in January 1983 as a separate wing of the EPB to effectively coordinate foreign economic policies, represents a good example. The most immediate impetus toward creating the IEPC came with the need to coordinate many foreign economic cooperation issues that were generated by President Doo-Hwang Chun's state visits to many countries. Since about 1984, the IEPC secretariat has taken on functions of negotiating with foreign governments' representatives regarding trade disputes and of promoting foreign direct investments. In the course of negotiations in 1985 with the United States regarding opening the Korean market in many areas—including both trade and service industries—public discontent and protests, interministerial disputes, and political pressure from the ruling Democratic Justice Party against the IEPC's relatively accommodating approach continued to build. Under this pressure, the newly appointed deputy prime minister dissolved the IEPC with the president's approval and restored external negotiating functions to the relevant ministries in early 1986.

Example 2. The creation and operation of the Industrial Policy Deliberation Council (IPDC), chaired by the deputy prime minister, have also been problematic, although it served as a major vehicle through which the EPB has accelerated economic liberalization process. The creation of the IPDC in 1982 was a clear expression of the EPB's attempt to consolidate its industrial policy leadership within the FPB. The proposed "Industrial Assistance Law," which provided for the establishment of the IEPC, was opposed vehemently by the MOF and the MCI because they saw this legislation as an evisceration of their legitimate institutional mission and functions. Under strong resistance by these ministries, the EPB's legislative initiative was aborted. After an intense turf struggle between the EPB and these ministries, the MCI finalized the "Industry Development Law" and the MOF amended the "Law Regarding the Reduction and Exemption of Taxes" on their own.

Example 3.   The creation of the Fair Trade Committee and the Office of Fair Trade, the committee's staff organization, within the EPB is another example. With the transition in government in 1980, antimonopoly and fair trade regulation had become an economic banner of the "just" society that the new political leadership espoused. The Antimonopoly and Fair Trade Law of 1981 signified new government resolve to regulate *chaebol* groups' monopolistic market practices and to prevent high concentration of economic power. The EPB has actively consolidated fair trade enforcement as its new, important institutional mission. It had been controversial whether the committee should be put under the deputy prime minister. At the public hearings on the Fair Trade Law, all participants argued that the committee should be established as an independent body under the president or the prime minister to ensure its implementation. The EPB insisted on having the committee within the EPB as a deliberative, standing committee, and won the day. The EPB argued that the government had no experience of fair trade enforcement and that the committee would allow the EPB to secure consistency in seeking industrial structural adjustment.

These examples indicate that the EPB attempts to concentrate ever greater power, a tendency that ought to be curbed. The EPB's distinctive competence is not consistent with these operational activities. Increased interministerial jurisdictional conflicts aside, they have tended to impair the EPB's institutional integrity. The EPB's new operating functions, such as negotiations with foreign governments and antimonopoly and fair trade regulations, seem to have damaged the EPB's distinctive identity. The EPB has been criticized for its accommodating approach toward foreign demands to open Korean markets and for its lukewarm approach toward big businesses in fair trade enforcement. Although it is hard to substantiate such public charges, they are nonetheless important signals indicating that the EPB's distinctive identity and public image suffers. To preserve the EPB's distinctive competence and valued functions, it would be better not to overload the EPB or to give the EPB such operating and administrative functions as negotiating with foreign governments and enforcing antimonopoly regulations, which tend to deflect its central mission.

CHAPTER TEN

The Korean Economy Toward the Year 2000

In Joung Whang

THE KOREAN ECONOMY has been one of the most rapidly growing economies in the world. Since the launching of its First Five-Year Economic Development Plan (1962–1966), Korea has achieved rapid and sustained economic growth and development. During the last three decades, for instance, the country's Gross National Product (GNP) has grown at an annual rate of 8.4 percent in real terms and per capita GNP also increased drastically. As a consequence, despite its lack of significant natural resources and excessive defense burden, Korea has transformed itself from a largely agrarian, subsistence economy into a newly industrializing economy. Furthermore, in spite of the rapid economic growth, income distribution seems to be relatively equitable compared to that of other developing countries. In view of the past experiences and development potential of the country, it can be expected that the Korean society and economy will undergo rapid change toward the year 2000.

This century has coincided with the Pax Americana, the period during which the United States has played the pivotal role in the world system, succeeding the nineteenth-century hegemon, Great Britain. In view of the emerging role of Japan and the development dynamics of the Asian Pacific countries, however, it is expected that the year 2000 will be a turning point in the history of the global system: it will mark the opening of the Pax Pacificana. It is, therefore, historically imperative that Korea demonstrates its full strength as a mature nation-state by the year 2000. In other words, on the basis of its consistently increasing national wealth accumulated through sustained economic and social development, Korea will be able to takes its own position in the international arena and to avoid "peripheral" dependence on the world powers.

Taken from In Joung Whang, "Korean Economy Toward the Year 2000: Historical Mandate and Policy Issues," paper presented at the Beijing Conference on the Asian Pacific Economy Toward the Year 2000, Beijing, People's Republic of China, November 1986.

Futurables: An Optimistic Scenario

The future of Korea will depend largely on how the Korean people can use potential accumulated in the past to cope with challenges and opportunities presented by their environment. Hence, the future-shaping factors include: (1) demographic changes; (2) international environment, political as well as economic; and (3) growth potential of the economy.

Changes in Population

In Korea, rapid population growth is viewed as being a burden on the national economy. To slow rapid population growth, the Korean government in 1962 introduced the national family planning program, which successfully reduced the annual population growth rate from 3.0 percent in the 1950s to 1.6 percent in the 1970s. This rate will decline further, nearing the 1 percent level by the year 2000. Despite such an effort, the population of Korea is projected to reach 50 million by the year 2000. This growth will significantly increase a population density that is already the world's third highest, following Bangladesh and Taiwan: it will reach some 500 persons per square kilometer by the year 2000. Korea's high population density combined with its relative lack of natural resource endowments causes a severe imbalance between population and natural resources, creating problems in energy, food, housing, education, and environment.

Changes in age distribution of the population anticipated in the next fifteen years will also have significant implications. The school-age population is expected to decrease from 38 percent of the population in 1980 to 28 percent in 2000, reversing the growth trend of the past two decades. Along with the population growth, the share of the economically active population will increase from 62 percent of the population in 1980 to 69 percent in 2000. This trend will increase the number of taxpayers and thus raise demand for political participation; it also implies an increase in the potential for economic growth, in view of supply-side projections. Finally, the aged population is estimated to grow at an annual rate of about 3.7 percent, with those over 65 reaching 6.2 percent of the population by 2000. This rapid growth will require that additional resources be allocated to a nonproductive sector of the population, as older citizens require more social services.

These demographic changes will impose a considerable burden on the Korean economy; they will increase the challenge of maintaining a certain level of welfare with the limited resource endowment within the given spatial boundary. Hence, the Korean economy must demonstrate an adaptive vitality spurred by industrialization and technological development if it is to ensure continued economic growth and efficiency in resource utilization in order to cope with demographic changes.

International Political Environment

Several current trends and anticipated changes in world international relations will affect Korea's external political outlook in the 1990s and beyond. The shifting mood of East-West détente initiated in the 1970s will continue to evolve and will reduce polarization. The West European countries and Japan, because of their conflicting economic interests, will move closer to neutrality and independence. At the same time, the People's Republic of China (hereafter China) and Eastern Europe may reinforce their trends toward economic and social revisionism. The growth of the nonaligned movement will also contribute to the reduction of polarization in international relations.

The United States will probably press Japan more strongly to increase its defense spending. China, with its vigorous pursuit of modernization and its open-door policies, is expected to strengthen itself militarily. As the four superpowers (the Soviet Union, the United States, Japan, and China) involved near the Korean peninsula seeks a new balance of power in the region, they are likely to pursue a peaceful coexistence that furthers their national interests. These changes obviously have ramifications for Korean development.

A most important factor directly affecting the future development is the relationship between South and North Korea. Because it is very unlikely that national unification will be realized in the near future, the balance of military power between the two seems to be of critical importance. Despite South Korea's continued efforts to achieve a self-reliant defense capability, North Korea still maintains its numerical superiority over South in military forces. Furthermore, North Korea has the ability to conduct limited guerilla warfare, mobilize the entire population rapidly in an emergency, and wage an all-out war effort with little notice. The tension in the Korean peninsula will, therefore, not ease for the time being. Nevertheless, as China pursues its modernization drive into the 1990s and as the Soviet Union begins to feel the imbalance between its economic and military capabilities, neither country is likely to favor instability in the Korean peninsula.

Prospects of the Global Economy

A major feature of renewed global economic growth will be the rapid technological transformation leading the recovery. Technological innovation will shift economies from traditional capital- and resource-intensive, pollution-inducing production methods to new energy-saving production methods that will increasingly meet personal and social welfare needs. Technological breakthrough and the ensuing transitions in the developed countries will be accompanied by rapid changes in comparative advantage. Comparative advantages in heavy and chemical industries will shift from developed countries to newly industrializing countries (NICs), while other developing countries will pursue labor-intensive light manufacturing and low-technology heavy industries.

There should be no serious global shortages in raw materials for the remainder of this century. Pressure on the global economy will diminish as world population growth rates continue to fall, as they have since 1965, in response to population control efforts. The net increase in the world population in the two decades from 1980 to 2000 is projected to be about 1.7 billion, of which over 90 percent will take place in the developing countries. Despite world dependency on OPEC oil, petroleum and natural gas may not create serious problems in terms of quantity of supply and prices. The importance of atomic power and new energy sources increases gradually and the production of coal climbs more rapidly. Finally, no serious shortages in food supply are likely in the near future, as the world's food demand continues to increase at a manageable rate of 2.0 to 2.5 percent per year.

The outlook for international trade is moderately encouraging. High levels of protectionism in the developed countries are expected to persist for several years, because of low rates of growth and slow structural adjustment. When developed countries do lower their barriers on labor-intensive goods in the 1990s, in response to their own labor shortages, it is primarily the latecomers in development who will benefit from increased trade. Overall, trade is expected to increase at a 6 percent annual rate for the remainder of this century, much slower than it did in the 1960s.

The economic situation in the Pacific Basin provides a relatively promising outlook. Because of the high growth rates of the newly industrializing countries, such as Taiwan and Hong Kong, and of the ASEAN countries, the Asian-Pacific region including China is expected to growth much faster than the rest of the world. The relative economic status of the Pacific Basin will, therefore, improve, and over the long term, the vortex of the world economy will shift from the North Atlantic to the Pacific region.

Growth Potential of the Economy

Studies indicate that increased labor inputs have been a dominant factor in Korea's rapid economic growth during the past twenty years. For the 1972–1983 period, for example, approximately 40 percent of Korean growth can be attributed to additional labor inputs among production factors. Of the rise in labor inputs, the increase in the number of workers accounted for about 60 percent, while the increase in working hours and the improved level of education contributed 17 percent and 13 percent, respectively. The second important source of growth during that period was improvement in productivity, which accounted for 37 percent. However, improved productivity was primarily attributable to economies of scale rather than to technological innovation.

Based on present supply-side projections, the Korean economy is estimated to have a growth potential of 7 to 8 percent annually until the year 2000. With economies of scale and labor inputs diminishing in importance, primary sources of growth in the future are expected to be technological innovation and capital inputs. Korea's current efforts to restructure industry, diminish industrial concentration, and secure a stable supply of raw materials should spur growth by eliminating the bottlenecks that hindered productivity in the 1970s. Despite this shift in emphasis, of course, abundant, hard-working, and well-educated human resources will continue to be one of the important sources of Korea's development in the future.

Korean Economy and Society in the Year 2000

General Features of the Future Korea

Korean society by the 2000 will have changed fundamentally in several ways. First, it will have almost completed its transition into an industrialized society, with all the characteristics of a society that has entered the high-technology information age. Second, further development will have made the society more universalistic in some ways and more diverse in others. Finally, Korea will have become an internationalized society, a full member of the global community.

Korea is expected to sustain its long-term economic growth until 2000 and, as a result, to arrive at a higher level of industrialization. Simultaneously, Korea will enter the information age as its electronic industry grows and computer facilities are widely disseminated. The industrial structure in Korea will become highly complex and will come to resemble that of the advanced countries as high value-added industries, high-tech industries, and "soft" industries grow relatively rapidly. The expanded supply of computers and the improved means of information collection, processing, and utilization will be applied to almost all activities of society, causing revolutionary changes in every facet of Korean life.

Continuing industrialization and expanding urbanization will lend urgency to the social need to address residential, traffic, and environmental problems in urban areas. Anticipated increases in income level and the reduced average working hours will accelerate the growth of leisure and sports industries. The advancement of the nation's industrial structure and the evolution of the information age will also affect the employment structure in terms of human resources and job requirements. Specifically, demand will increase for new professional and technical manpower in such industries as information and environmental protection.

As Korean society moves further toward industrialization, it will display a considerable degree of universalism and standardization characteristic of a developed society. The most notable factor contributing to this universalism is the standardization of living conditions and consumption patterns, which will eliminate the major differences between the urban and rural areas and among the different social classes. On the other hand, Korea will also experience a strong countertrend toward diversification. This trend will be intensified by the pursuit of unique ways of life that reflect individual specialization in occupation as well as diverse personal interests and hobbies. Social differentiation will be further accelerated by the increase in income level and leisure time, the extension of life expectancy, and the higher levels of cultural life.

Korean society will become more internationalized as the economy becomes functionally integrated with the rest of the world and as means of cross-country transportation and communication continue to develop. Internationalization will prevail in such areas as trade, finance, and business management as a result of Korea's move toward market liberalization. Frequent international exchanges in the fields of culture and sports as well as overseas travel will also accelerate the process of internationalization. As a result, the lifestyle and behavior of Korean people will become more cosmopolitan and the concept of a "global village" will become widely accepted, even while the cultural identity of Korea is preserved.

Sectoral Profiles of Development

Once the general profile of Korea in the future is in place, it is possible to project the effects of development on specific sectors of national life. The major sectors considered below are: increased income and its effect on the Korean lifestyle; industrial structure; social and regional development; education and culture; political development; and Korea's status in the world.

Increased Income and Its Effect on Lifestyle. As noted earlier, the Korean economy is expected to sustain its growth at an average annual rate of about 7 percent until 2000. As a consequence, Korea's real per capita GNP will increase from about US$2,000 in 1984 to about US$5,000 in 2000. Although even the latter per capita income level will be far below the average of the developed countries, it will enable the majority of Korean people to lead comfortable lives that meet their basic needs. At the same time, they will allocate growing proportions of their personal expenditure for cultural and recreational activities. Consumer durables, indicative of high living standards, will be widely supplied among even the rural population and the urban low-income classes. Increased saving capabilities will enable most households to make long-term plans to purchase a home, finance children's education, and prepare for their retirement. The demand for houses is expected to increased continuously because of population increases, urbanization, and the transition toward the nuclear family.

Change in the Industrial Structure.   Korea's industrial structure is also expected to undergo considerable change. The percentage of employment in the primary sectors is projected to decrease from 27 percent in 1984 to 15 percent in 2000. At the same time, the employment percentages of the secondary and tertiary sectors will respectively increase from 24 percent and 49 percent in 1984, to 29 percent and 56 percent in 2000.

Owing to the adjustment of the industrial structure within the manufacturing sector, the automobile, electronics, and machinery industries will continue to growth faster until 2000, while the relative importance of the textile, food processing, steel, and shipbuilding industries will decrease. As income levels and living standards improve, specialization and diversification will occur in such service industries as banking, insurance, and retailing, and demand for the "soft industries" will grow rapidly. In short, the industrial structure of Korea by 2000 is expected to become similar to that of industrialized countries.

Social and Regional Balance in Development.   With development will also come an increased emphasis on the need for balance in material progress. In part, this will be reflected in broadened attempts to provide for all members of society. In order to protect the working population from social risk, the social security system, which includes health insurance, industrial accident compensation insurance, and unemployment insurance, will be comprehensively expanded.

Despite the gradual introduction and expansion of the national welfare pension system, increasing welfare demands from senior citizens will be met partly by inducing the public to observe the responsibilities of an extended family based on traditional values and partly by providing tax incentives for families that support elderly parents. In formulating these programs, policymakers should take advantage of the merits of a traditional extended family system, in spite of the trend toward nuclear families that has accompanied industrialization and urbanization. On the other hand, the livelihood of the helpless, such as the mentally and physically handicapped and the elderly without family support, will be protected by expanding the national public assistance programs, in spite of the limited financial resources of the government.

To reduce regional differences, large segments of the population as well as political, economic, and sociocultural functions will be dispersed to appropriate regional centers. Small and medium-sized cities can serve as centers for conurbation and help adjacent towns attract new residents. In addition to providing greater opportunities to earn supplemental off-farm income in rural areas, relocation and establishment of education, health, and cultural facilities will make local cities and towns attractive enough to discourage rural-urban migration.

Improvement in Education and Cultural Identity.   Education has played an important role in Korea's post-war modernization, primarily because of the almost blind faith in the value of educational attainment among Korean people and thus their exceptionally strong motivation and desire for education. By 2000, as free education is expected to be extended to the middle school level, 95 percent of middle school graduates and 71 percent of high school graduates will seek opportunities for further education, thus creating a society with higher academic credentials.

Education in science and technology is particularly crucial if Korea is to achieve its objective of restructuring its industry to compete directly with the advanced economies. In addition, nonformal, social education will be extended in a form of lifetime education to accommodate increased educational needs stemming from rapid social change, such as the increase in leisure time, the advances in science and technology, and the onset of the information age.

In spite of an outward-looking modernization strategy, the Korean society, rooted in Confucian doctrines, will preserve its cultural identity to the greatest extent. Indigenous Korean culture and traditions will be harmonized with new values imposed by industrialization within the context of internationalization to the extent that efficiency in pursuing national development is secured.

Development of Political Institutions. As the population's income and education levels increase and as the society becomes more liberalized, it will be necessary to accommodate the rising demand for political participation. As a result, there will also be a growing need to transform those political demands systematically into one of the driving forces of national development. In order to fully represent the interests and demands of the people, the role of the political institutions in encouraging popular participation and in aggregating and articulating public interests should be strengthened. A significant step will be revitalization of the local autonomy system. The increased emphasis on local government will heighten the self-governing ability of the citizens and expedite self-reliant regional development driven by local initiative.

Furthermore, to accelerate economic development in the coming decades, it seems necessary to promulgate a series of institutional reforms, including democratization, privatization, decentralization, liberalization, and internationalization, in major political and administrative processes.

Korea's Economic Status in the World. By 2000, it is hoped that Korea will emerge as one of the world's industrialized countries. The GNP of Korea in the year 2000 is estimated to reach $250 billion in 1984 constant prices, which will place Korea among the top fifteen economies of the world. By that year, Korea is also expected to be one of the ten largest trading countries in the world. By gradually improving the current account of its balance of payments, Korea became a net capital exporter beginning in the late 1980s.

As Korea continues to industrialize, considerable changes are also expected in its level of international cooperation with both developed and developing countries. To ward off possible conflicts in trade and industrial development between Korea and other developed countries, Korea will pursue complementarity in horizontal specialization and cooperation with those countries.

At the same time, Korea will extend its mutual cooperation with the developing countries, sharing its development experience and intermediate technologies and gradually expanding its level of aid assistance. As the Pacific Basin emerges to be the new dynamic economic center of the world trade system, Korea will be prepared to play an important role in its development.

Policy Implications

What policy implications can be drawn from this image of the Korean economy in the year 2000? The primary values that the Korean people traditionally pursue include *welfare* at the individual level, *identity* at the national level, and security and *peace* at the international level. It is still uncertain whether the rosy picture of the Korean economy in the future will lead the country to become a solid nation-state that will be able to pursue the above values. To achieve that goal, Korea must address some critical issues. We can identify the issues by examining the experiences of Western advanced countries.

The Western model of development for improving in human well-being is based on three major factors: (1) industrialization, which increases income through the higher productivity of modern technology; (2) urbanization, which provides physical convenience for economic and social lives of the people through agglomerated facilities and mass culture; and (3) the institutionalization of social security measures, which protects unfortunate individuals who are excluded from the benefits of industrialization and urbanization by old age, handicaps, disease, or unemployment. The Western approach to a social welfare system is characterized by individualistic prescription, extensive government intervention, and a materialistic concept of welfare instruments. Nevertheless, fragmented human relations, social disorder, mental and emotional instability, and internal disruption of the traditional social fabric, all of which are primarily fostered by the mass culture, must be regarded as undesirable byproducts of the Western development model.

It is in this context that, as a late starter in modernization, Korea should carefully consider a number of possible issues it will face in transforming its society into a matured country.

The first issue is how to achieve modernization while minimizing the extent of Westernization. In other words, how should Korea accommodate Western values inherent in modern technology, which may come into conflict with the traditional Korean culture and indigenous value system in such a way as to maintain the stability of the social system?

The second issue is how to preserve Korea's national and cultural identity during the process of internationalization of the economy. The integration of the Korean economy into the rest of the world that has accompanied its trade expansion will likely cause an identity crisis for Korea, unless its unique national spirit is reflected consistently in both its internal societal management and its external relations. The need to serve the world through internationalization without losing its own identity will be Korea's second constraint in choosing a desirable path for development toward the year 2000.

The third issue is how to transform the traditional rural sector to make it compatible with a growing urban-industrial sector. The functional integration and harmonious development of the rural and urban sectors are of critical importance for the total development of society in terms of people's welfare. The more rapid the industrialization process, the bigger the gap between the two sectors becomes. Special attention should be paid to this issue, because the rural sector has significant implications in the context of modernity—particularly in terms of social structure, human relations, mental and emotional stability, traditional norms and standards of behavior, and mode of world outlook.

The fourth issue is how to protect individual interests in the process of holistic development. Because the maximum efficiency of the national development in aggregate terms may require some sacrifice of individual welfare, the ideal path of Korea's development toward the twenty-first century will be one protecting individuals from the hardships of industrial life that accompany rapid urbanization and materialistic development.

The Role of the Korean Economy in Asia and the Pacific Region

Another important issue to be considered is what role Korea should play in the Asian-Pacific region. We should approach this question in the context of regional prospects and the agenda for regional cooperation.

The Development Prospects of the Region

Korea is one of the "newly industrializing countries" (or NICs), which include Brazil, Mexico, Taiwan, Hong Kong, and Singapore. In part because of the success of four Asian NICs and in part because of the Japanese miracle, the Asian Pacific has been the most dynamic center of world economic growth over the last two decades. To at least some degree, these four NICs have replicated both the methods and the success of Japan, which achieved developed-country status in the 1960s after a long process of industrial development. One hopes that this parallelism will continue into the future: Japan today boasts the second largest economy and one of the highest per capita incomes in the world. One hopes that other developing countries will be able to emulate the success of the present

NICs. This hypothesis is supported by the recent emergence of the so-called near-NICs, which include India, Malaysia, Thailand, the Philippines, and Indonesia. These countries are thus well on their way toward industrialization.

The most important addition to the Asian-Pacific regional economy in recent years is the People's Republic of China. Only since beginning to open its economy to the world a few years ago has China started to fulfill the development potential so long proclaimed by international observers. China has had to undergo somewhat difficult reforms to promote her modernization. Nonetheless, no one can deny the long-term geopolitical importance of China: Rich in natural resources, with an enormous land area and a quality population of over one billion, China has tremendous development potential. China will certainly share her dynamism with other Asian countries.

All these Asian-Pacific countries have at least two basic characteristics in common: large, well-disciplined, and relatively skilled labor forces, and pragmatic and outward-oriented economic policies. All indications suggest that these will remain as common features of the Asian-Pacific countries and that any change will improve their labor forces and increase their outward orientation.

Issues in Regional Cooperation and Korea

Admittedly, this prediction may be too optimistic. Much will depend, of course, not only on the potential of the Asian-Pacific economies but also on their international environments. At least four key external conditions will have to be reasonably well satisfied: (1) stability in prices of primary products and natural resources, (2) availability of foreign capital at favorable and stable interest rates, (3) smooth transfer of more advanced technology, and (4) reasonably secure market access. These four problems have been discussed repeatedly in many international forums—most notably in the North-South arena at the UNCTAD—all to little avail. There is probably not much room for further progress at this level.

Nonetheless, the international trading environment has worsened steadily since the early 1970s. For this reason, the problems of technology transfer and market access will remain critical in the years up to 2000, and will become even more so as development competition intensifies among the countries of the region.

An alternative approach to help solve the problems, however, is regional cooperation on a collective basis. To a degree, such efforts have already begun. They have been spearheaded by the Pacific Economic Cooperation Conference (PECC), which has met regularly since 1980 to identify opportunities for economic cooperation among the nations of the entire Pacific region. On a somewhat narrower scale, member countries of the Association of Southeast Asian Nations (ASEAN) have for the last several years made some serious attempts to agree on areas for economic cooperation. Nevertheless, it is expected that Asian-Pacific countries should organize collective endeavors at a level more multilateral than that of ASEAN. Thus, for example, these outward-oriented states might get together to discuss possible arrangements to stabilize supplies of primary products and to promote technological cooperation within the region. They might also seek joint action to work toward shared goals at global forums on issues such as capital-market and trade liberalization.

To enhance its role in these efforts, Korea looks forward to entering into substantive cooperative arrangements on a bilateral or subregional basis with any of the outward-oriented countries in the Asian-Pacific region. Korea, which stands to gain in several ways from increased cooperation, can also offer various benefits. First, Korea boasts domestic markets for manufacturers and primary goods that are quite large now and will continue to grow in the foreseeable future as it continues to liberalize imports.

Second, intermediate technologies that Korea has been developing from more advanced imports should also be of tremendous value to other developing countries, to whom Korea could transfer technologies through proper channels. Of special value in this category would be Korea's experience in development planning and manpower training. One such program now in existence is the International Development Exchange Program (IDEP) operated by the Korea Development Institute in Seoul. As a Korean version of technical cooperation among developing countries (TCDC), IDEP is organized with its own financial resources to share Korea's development experience with other developing countries, particularly in Asia and the Pacific. Furthermore, Korea is in an appropriate position for mediating between developed and developing countries in the region in transfer of intermediate technology, capital, human resources, technical know-how, wisdom, and quality human relations.

Third, Korea even expects to be a source of substantial development financing in the near future. Korea has just begun to record a surplus on its current account and expects to sustain it, which would enable it to enter into financial cooperation with other developing countries in this region.

Korea's Historical Role in the Region

As important as any other factor are Korea's willingness and commitment to cooperate with any other country in the region in the pursuit of collective global goals. Korea could initiate a positive role in the region in collaboration with Japan and with other Asian NICs. As was discussed earlier, in view of its current global strategy and its future potential, Japan will play the leading role in the era of the Pax Pacificana. In support of the Japanese role, Korea should stand on the firm base of its own development without making any claims against Japan.

To hasten the opening of the Pax Pacificana in the new century, Korea should contribute to boosting the confidence of the Asian-Pacific people in transforming this region into the center of world development. One of the means toward this end is Korea's experimentation with a unique development strategy rooted in the Asian culture and its own traditional value system. In this respect, the development path to be taken by Korea in the years to come requires creative efforts not only for its own historical mandate but also for the region as a whole—"creative" in terms of concept of development, management culture, soft technology, and new commodities not in the form of material goods but in a form of human values.

Conclusion

Korea's recent performance is cause for cautious optimism about its future. Despite the deteriorating international environment and internal disruptions of the early 1980s, Korea has managed to reorient itself along a path of stable growth. The performance of the nation proves that Korea has a deep-rooted and sufficient development resource: *its people and culture.* The main task of this nation building toward the year 2000 is to realize the development potential of the Korean people by wisely focusing their skills and efforts.

In order to meet the challenge of reaching the status of a matured developing society, Korea must partly reinforce and supplement the development strategies of the past and partly develop a unique development model. The prime mover of this achieving society has always been the human factor—its desirable characteristics and traits for which government should prepare appropriate policy responses. One of the most critical is how to make best use of indigenous culture and traditions in the course of development.

The goal of Korea's development toward the year 2000 will be to advance the nation to the level of a matured country concerned both with the welfare of its people and with its contribution to international peace. This goal must be achieved within the context of Asian, and in particular Korean, culture and traditions, and it should be attained through increased cooperation for peace and prosperity of this region.

Korea has historical motives for playing a positive role in regional cooperation. The old Korea was humiliated at the turn of this century as a nation unprepared for meeting external challenges. The new Korea, as a historically peace-loving country, should neither repeat such a painful experience nor inflict it on other countries. As a full member of the center states in the Pax Pacificana, Korea should instead offer real cooperation and mutual prosperity to the countries in Asia and the Pacific region, by demonstrating a unique development strategy fitting into its own sociocultural and historical context. The development path Korea takes as it nears the next century will be an additional test as to whether the Korean approach is feasible and desirable in the broader Asian-Pacific context.

PART V

The Role of the Public Bureaucracy

CHAPTER ELEVEN

Merits and Demerits of Public Administration in Korea's Modernization

Wan Ki Paik

IN DEVELOPING AND less developed nations, the relation between modernization and the role of public administration can be termed almost fatalistic. Because the extra-administrative powers were too weak in the process of modernization, public administration had no other choice but to emerge as the main driving force of modernization, no matter whether or not this was desired. Extra-administrative powers such as the parliament, political parties, interest groups, and private enterprise could not afford to bear an effective role for modernization. The case of Korea was no exception. Against such background, the public administrative system was the only institutional setting in formulating and achieving the goals of development in all fields of politics, economy, and society. Administrative bureaucrats came to realize that the responsibility in achieving the goals of development was on their shoulders. In the case of Korea, public administration was recognized as the primary organ in carrying out the task of modernization.

In Korea the relation between modernization and public administration came to be closely bound together on a full scale following the May 16, 1961, military revolution. In other words, the leading role of public administration in the process of modernization has become conspicuous since that date. Of course, the role of administration was not meaningless even before that time, but the pioneering and leading role for the task of modernization emerged only after May 16.

Let us briefly examine the administrative system prior to May 16, 1961.

Korea's administrative system of the Yi dynasty, the colonial period of Japanese rule, and the latter period of the Liberal party regime may be

Taken from Wan Ki Paik, "Merits and Demerits of Public Administration in Korea's Modernization," *Korea Journal* 23 (2)(1983):38–47 termed system maintenance. Public administrations of these periods were typically regulatory, mainly intended for order maintenance and tax collection, among other usual functions; that is, it was a conservative type of administration mainly for maintaining order, prevention of disorder, formalistic fulfillment of responsibility, and status quo at any price rather than a positive administration for the completion of goals. The productive elements of administration for creation, induction, encouragement, or promotion for any concrete results were meager. The administrations of the time were designed to regulate the will of the people for doing something, yet they did not offer anything in particular for the people. Administrations intended for such a static role were suddenly turned into a type of value creation since the 1960s.

Despite the about-face of the administration to value creation since the middle 1960s, traditional elements for system maintenance were not weakened. Rather, these elements were further strengthened while other elements for value creation were being added. In other words, elements for productivity, performance, creation, and the pioneering role began to be heightened while the conventional elements for order maintenance were fostered at the same time. Since this time, public administration came to bear the leading role on a full scale in the process of modernization. All projects for development were formulated and performed under the auspices of public administration. The *Saemaul* (New Village) movement was initiated for the development of the agricultural community, and export-led policies were drawn for economic growth. Developmental projects in all fields at this time relied on public administration and the administration occupied a monopolistic status for value creation. Such a trend of omnipotent administration brought about the phenomenon of a political vacuum, and all organs and entrepreneurs came to be subjugated to public administration. High-echelon bureaucrats were imbued with "elitist" consciousness, claiming themselves, elatedly, to be the solvers of any and all problems.

However, what should be pointed out clearly here is that the emergence of the value creation type was brought about not by systematic improvement or renovation of public administration itself but by compulsory instructions by a leader (namely, the president). Thought it was true that a number of brilliant elites were brought into public administration throughout the 1960s after Korea's liberation from Japan, transforming the character of public administration to more development-oriented tasks, this step cannot be seen as a dominant factor in metabolizing public administration into a mobilizing system of goal achievement. Mobilization of the public administration system and subsequently its powerful administrative performance should be seen rather as an outcome of, first of all, the awe-inspiring orders, compulsory instructions, or supervision of a powerful political leader. The political leader engaged himself in on-thespot command for the sake of goal achievement. At that time, the administrative capability was fostered not by itself but by coercing compulsion. Administration had to do something for certain goals, and those who did not take some action were selected as the target of disciplinary measures. Administration came to exert its influence in its close alliance with the political power. To summarize, public administration since the 1960s has been characterized not by its neutrality, manageability, or self-autonomy but by the mere expression of a political leader's instructions and will.

What, then, were the positive aspects of public administration in the process of modernization?

First, instead of abstract and ideological values, public administration by pursuit and emphasis of concrete and tangible values helped to fix a pragmatic notion of values deep in the minds of the people. In other words, values of modernization and development were made concrete to the extent of being visible and tactile as viewed by the people.

It has been pointed out generally that the notion of modernization began to be implanted in Korean society from the Reform of the Year of Kab-o (1894). The version of modernization at this time was to introduce new trends of the time and to copy foreign institutions while exposing the traditional domestic system to the outside world, forcing itself to experience contact with the outside world. Such a notion of modernization, perceived as a mere imitation of foreign institutions from a passive standpoint, was continued up to the period of the 1950s without the process of internal sublimation. Modernization was a vague notion without any concrete content. Being abstract and vague, the notion carried no tangible substance. The notion was perceived merely to be a departure from tradition, a pursuit of Westernization, an imitation and introduction of a democratic system. Such a vague notion of modernization was far from the reality of the people's daily life and failed to function as a centripetal force in marshaling the will and endeavors of the people. Modernization was a vague ideology far removed from the living reality of the people. The vague notion of modernization may be seen as having been transformed into a "a concrete will for better life" through the developmental administrative system of the 1960s. Right or wrong, from this period of time the value of modernization began to carry an economic value of concreteness and pragmatism to drive out poverty. Modernization began to be fixed in the minds of the people as something for "a better life." Since this time, modernization has become a milestone to show the people the direction of life, functioning as a centripetal point rallying and integrating the force of the people into focus. The *Saemaul* movement, which began to be driven forward on a full scale, can be noted as a concrete illustration of the new notion of modernization. At any rate, the value creation–oriented administrative system that started to emerge from the 1960s transformed the notion of modernization into a pragmatic and practical value and fixed its evaluation of effectiveness as the tangible economic value.

Second, public administration contributed to the fixation on "power culture." The power referred to here is not a moral or ethical power but an economic, scientific, military, physical, and visible power. Public administration bore the leading role in fostering these powers.

In the traditional society of Korea, there was a strong tendency to pursue invisible, mystic, and immaterial values. Any ethical and moral value preceded any and all other values. Rather, an ethical and moral value looked down on material and ontological values. Values pursued and stressed in such a society were honor, dignity, integrity, and virtue or righteousness—not money, affluence, or any physical conveniences.

The military class, technicians, scientists, or working classes were not the objects of reverence. What resulted from the society that despised working–producing classes were stagnation and powerlessness, not dynamism or vitality. Our traditional society did not realize the reality that even ethical and moral powers could be built on economic, military, and scientific power. It again did not realize that ethical power might be weakened if it were not supported by physical power. The seriousness of such a perception came from recognizing the relationship between the two powers as mutually exclusive.

A moral and spiritual power without the support of material and physical power can be likened to a tree without roots or a castle built on sand. An economic power, a military power, or a scientific power is a concrete expression of material and tangible power. It is also claimed that such powers can produce a moral power of sound and healthy substance when they undergo sublimation and that they constitute the origin of all cultures and values in the form of an economic, scientific, and military power. It is also stressed that even though what is ultimately pursued is a moral value, it should be based on a physical value or physical power; otherwise any moral value cannot exert its power, because such physical values are directly related to existence and survival. Because they are directly related to survival, physical values form the origin of all powers. In the case of military power, its meaning consists not only in national defense in repelling the invasion of foreign enemies but also in making a society dynamic, promoting the progress of industry, science, and technology, and fostering an aggressive spearhead. Here it is also claimed that it is not a coincidence that historically advanced nations of today value the military very highly.

Our traditional society did not recognize that ethics could not function in a society lacking the support of a physical power and that an ethical power is the weakest in solving the conflicts of the society. However, our administrative system contributed to a great extent to fostering such a physical power. Good examples in which the administration contributed to the fixation of a power culture are the administration-led economic growth, strengthening of national defense, and promotion of the introduction of technology.

At any rate, the importance of physical power has begun to be recognized and emphasized since the 1960s, and public administration has contributed greatly to the fostering of such powers.

Third, public administration has also greatly contributed to the expansion (growth) of absolute figures (numbers) and the "pie." While the distribution of values is predicated upon the production and growth of values, it is claimed that public administration has greatly contributed to the production and expansion of such values. The notion of distribution is one that by necessity, calls for production. In other words, there is no distribution without production. If a society attempts to distribute first without production, this society will never extricate itself from poverty. In this sense, the notion of production is progressive, positive, and expansive, while that of distribution is conservative, passive, and equilibrating.

Obviously a society needs a production-oriented mentality before distribution if it aspires to outgrow stagnation and the status quo of a closed system. Korea's traditional and conventional structure of consciousness has been more concerned with distribution or with sharing than with producing and expanding. In other words, Koreans have been concerned with distribution rather than with the growth of absolute figures and the pie itself.

By the 1960s, a change was brought into this passive mentality, and the change took the form of production orientation and the growth of absolute figures. Public administration has carried out a leading role in building a dynamic social system by mobilizing human and material resources to the fullest extent in the expansionary process of values and production. Investment in and fostering of social overhead capital such as science and technology, highways, electric power, atomic power, and port facilities, among others, have consolidated the basis and springboard for economic growth. The expansion of such economic values has driven out poverty consciousness. From that point on, the growth of other values was considered an omnipotent possibility.

The expansion of such values led to a mentality of "the pie can grow bigger" rather than that of "the pie is constant." It has been generally noted that peoples of emerging and underdeveloped nations cannot outgrow the mentality of "the pie is constant." There is a great difference between the mentalities of "the pie is constant," and "the pie can grow." In a society where the mentality of "the pie is constant" prevails, people tend to think that if someone else's share is bigger, their own share will be made smaller. They become concerned with distribution and with guarding their own shares. In such a society one tends to regard his neighbors as enemies. This tendency leads to mutual distrust, giving no chance to an emergence of the spirit of cooperation.

However, in a society where the mentality of "the pie can grow" prevails, people are more concerned with how to make the pie grow bigger. The pattern of such a mentality favors expansion, not the status quo. These people accordingly direct their attention to production and on opening up new fields. Because they think that the pie can grow to the extent to which people exert themselves, they tend to see their neighbors as partners and tend to stress the theme of "along with my neighbors" more than that of "I alone." In such a society, what is most emphasized is how to increase the rate of productivity, not how to safeguard one's own share or how to rob others of their shares.

Fourth, public administration gave birth to a "possibility consciousness" of "anything can be done if one wills," providing a momentum for Koreans to shift their pessimistic evaluation of themselves to a positive one. The *Saemaul* movement, which became popular and widespread around this time, instilled the sense of self-confidence and the philosophy of omnipotent possibility. In other words, it helped foster the growth of a mentality to outgrow the fatalistic and self-resigning consciousness and to bring forth a dynamic mentality to challenge for the sake of development and to achieve something for the sake of goal attainment.

One of the mental tendencies that have long dominated the Korean consciousness pattern was a fatalistic complex. By origin, a fatalistic mentality is a belief that in a human life, all good fortunes or bad luck, disasters, successes, poverty, and wealth are determined not by human capabilities but by supernational powers. In other words, its belief is that one cannot escape from an inborn fate. No matter how hard one may try, we are destined to tread the course of our own fate. To people of such destiny, life is always determined by mystic and extrahuman forces, not by open, clear, and predictable forces. To those of such mentality, all relations with human beings and nature are wrought with mystic, sacred, and fatalistic complications, not based on secular and factual premises. Such people accepted their fate as it was, never knowing how to challenge it.

The value creation–oriented administrative system that emerged in the 1960s has been playing a dominant role in transforming this type of fatalistic mentality into an aggressive one of "anything can be done." Public administration has begun to implant the philosophy of possibility in the hearts of the people by successfully carrying out a number of developmental targets. The *Saemaul* projects, led by public administration, and the attainment of export goals have played a determinant role in changing the consciousness pattern of the people. In other words, public administration played an important role in transforming the self-resigning, stagnant, and passive mentality of the people into an aggressive, positive and progressive one. Passing through the 1960s, Koreans came to have an affirmative estimate of themselves and to have a sense of pride and confidence. However, the excessive sense of confidence of "anything can be done" at the same time has given rise to unpalatable side effects.

Fifth, public administration has played a pioneering and guiding role for technological propagation by introducing and providing technology and information necessary for the increase of grain production, growth of exports, computerization, exploration of underground resources, installation of atomic power plants, and the growth of the defense industry. Originally, technological introduction and collection of information were a great expense and carried some limiting restrictions. Thus, at the level of private enterprise, individuals sometimes found it impossible to perform by themselves. This was particularly the case when private enterprises were still at the stage of immaturity. In Korea, technicological introduction was actively promoted along with the formation and implementation of the Foreign Capital Introduction Law of 1962, and imported technology from advanced nations played an important role in driving forward industrialization. The role of introduction and propagation of technology contributed not only to the improvement of productivity but also to the promotion of the rationalization of life and thought.

Let us now examine some negative and dysfunctional aspects of the role of public administration.

First, while public administration monopolized the developmental function in all fields, all extrabureaucratic organs became subjugated to the administration. Not only the legislature and political parties but the judiciary was subjected to public administration. Private enterprises came to play merely a branch function under the command of public administration. In this period, nothing could be done if a nodding response of public administration could not be obtained. Extrabureaucratic organs became powerless. Because their activities were allowed within certain bounds, pluralistic development could not be expected. As all political institutions and private enterprises were under the control of public administration, only an administration-led monolithic developmental process came about, with no plural developmental progress. Political vacuums became more common, and the activities of private enterprises grew no more than heteronomous. From here on, an elitist tendency and self-complacency in public administration were furthered.

Public administration tends to monopolize not only the input function but also the output function in the political process. Generally, because its main domain of function is that of output, public administration is restricted not to play the input function. The input function is to be carried out by people at large, by political parties, by the legislature, or by pressure groups that are all outside the realm of public administration. Public administration is called on to play a role only for the transfer and output of the demands from these extrabureaucratic organs. However, the administrative system of the time monopolized both input and output functions, giving rise to political vacuums. Elites in public administration became the center of political activities by occupying the focal position in the political process and by engaging in important decision making. All reforms, changes, and modernization measures were planned and implemented by elitists in public administration. Such an administration may be called an elitists-led mobilization system of administration. As modernization and growth were pursued with hasty fervor, administrative elites, armed with high specialization, came to establish a policy-formulating group, centered around a certain political leader.

Efficiency and speed may be expected in such a society where public administration dominates all other functions, but democracy and autonomy are hardly to be expected. To summarize, the administrative system of this period sacrificed the democratic elements, as a whole, in the name of efficiency.

Second, it is claimed that the administration-led development and economic growth robbed private enterprises of their opportunities to achieve progress on an autonomous basis. In other words, excessive interferences and protective measures made the protégés grow more dependent and rid them of chances to strengthen their competitiveness and physical structure. Such excessive protection caused both the patrons and the protégés to be driven into corners. If there was no aid from the government in the case of the protégés, they became powerless when a rough wind blew in trading conditions. And the protective development measures by the government destroyed the intraindustrial relations by preferring, as a natural consequence, particular industries and enterprises and by bringing about an imbalance in development among industries and enterprises. Furthermore, the protected enterprises developed a self-complacent mentality and tendency, and they became apathetic to technological development, managerial rationalization, and entrepreneurial development through successful management. Unbalanced protective measures to particular industries and enterprises (for instance, policy financing) blocked resource distribution based on efficiency and prevented rational and efficient distribution of resources for the benefit of all industries.

Third, even from the standpoint of the government as a patron, the policy of direct interference and support involves enormous human resources and expenses, giving rise to the phenomenon, "A navel can be bigger than a belly." While the scale of economy was small, social expenses could not pose a big problem, but since the economic scale grew big, social expenses also grew huge and expenses began to offset outcomes. Moreover, after the scale of the economy grew larger, the conventional policies of direct protection and support were impossible to implement merely in the light of the volume of resources to be mobilized.

In the past, the mainstays of governmental support measures were the tariff policy, the industrial protective policy through import restrictions, and the support policy through taxation and financing. However, as has been described earlier, excessive support policies blocked the autonomous growth of enterprises, weakened international competitiveness through managerial rationalization and free competition, and prevented enterprises from strengthening their own physical constitution. Furthermore, privilege consciousness of enterprises was fostered. An imbalance among industries was a natural consequence, blocking the efficient distribution of resources. As a result, the administration-led economic growth policies helped develop a government-dependent industrial system.

Fourth, the administration-led economic growth policy, by necessity, brought about a connivance between public administration and enterprises. Such a connivance caused, without fail, structural corruption and irregularities. It was almost impossible for enterprises outside the protection and concern of public administration to aspire to growth. Thus, it was said that any development or expansion growing out of such a climate was necessarily based on injustice, and that such a patron-client relationship blocked the establishment of a market economy system based on free competition.

Zaibatsu closely connived with the political power, and they grew under the protection of the political power. They participated almost monopolistically and took part in the important policy decision-making process of public administration. The *zaibatsu* group also monopolized the process of public administration by manipulating and steering the public administration from the standpoint of the pursuit of their own interests. Because the interest group of *zaibatsu* and particular business groups aimed at pursuit of their own private and business interests, their approaches were always secretive and unofficial, and they dominantly employed acquiescence, bribery, or kickbacks instead of persuasion, mediation, or transactions. Their approaches did not take official or institutional channels but relied on deep-rooted human relations such as geography, blood, or acquaintanceship.

Accordingly, it has been generally believed that anyone could become a parvenu overnight if he or she happened to find a tie with the authorities. Such a tendency gave rise to the growth of a climate where one could make a big fortune without exerting effort. This was absorbed by every corner of society, bringing forth a social atmosphere of "betting once and for all," speculation on real estate, speculation on securities, and housing speculation by leisured and wealthy housewives. It was generally perceived that it was almost impossible to make big money through normal and legitimate means.

Fifth, public administration has been for the benefit of "those who have." This was an inevitable outcome as all-out efforts were exerted to make the "pie" grow big and to expand its value. There was no time to divert concern to the socially weak, and no attempt was made to do so. The self-complacent thought was that the question of distribution and balancing would be automatically solved in due course after growth was made. In other words, the fear was that imbalance had been intentionally fostered by public administration.

Public administration for the sake of "those who have" and for the socially strong naturally disrupted the society and promoted the growth of imbalance. In the past twenty years or so, the unbalanced growth became serious between big and middle and small industries, cities and farming regions, export and domestic-demand industries, industry and agriculture, and among regions. Though national accord and union were proclaimed as a goal, such an unbalanced developmental policy in fact disrupted the society and broke the national accord. The unbalanced policy for big enterprises sacrificed middle and small industries, blocked the birth of the middle class, and gave rise to a number of social policy issues by bringing about the unbalanced distribution of wealth.

The well-balanced development between industry and agriculture, between the central and local regions, and between A and B regions was by any means necessary for the national accord, for social stabilization, for population dispersion, and for cultural propagation. However, such a balanced development stopped short with merely slogans, and it was not the real policy for actual implementation. Of politics and culture, the economic power was concentrated only on the central region and on particular regions. Such an imbalance broke the harmony of the people and resulted in unbalanced distribution of population and irrational deployment of industries, causing a number of social and economic problems. A balanced growth among classes, regions, and industries is a necessary basis of social coexistence. However, the government instead fostered unbalanced growth by dint of its official powers in the past twenty years or so.

It can nevertheless be conceded that to some extent the preoccupation with growth and an expansion of absolute figures made the unbalanced growth inevitable. But it could be an enormous and serious mistake for the government to have regarded the question too easily. The government did not realize that an imbalance could be justified only when it was needed for the attainment of a better balance. The government also did not take heed that the malcontent of the people comes more from a comparison with others than from poverty or deficiency itself. It was one of the great miscalculations on the part of the government to have surmised that growth could automatically solve the question of distribution.

Sixth, in a headlong haste for growth and goal achievement, there arose many occasions where uncontrolled growth was made by ignoring due processes or formalities. In an excessive haste for goal attainment, the export goal was sometimes achieved even by the red figure on balance sheets.

The hastily implemented subway projects gave rise to a number of serious accidents. Heavy and chemical industries, pushed forward without definite planning or feasibility studies, brought about the waste of resources in proportion to the lack of prior planning. It was not known that the hasty growth would lead to the production of defective goods. Growth under such conditions was a defensive growth for the sake of demonstration. Not recognized was that a desirable outcome and the birth of works of good quality needed due time, processes, and formalities.

Growth-oriented policies for the sake of effect and growth merely in terms of volume led to a number of defective and faulty projects, contamination of the environment, and destruction of bioecological cycles. There were many instances where the policy was made without an honest and realistic estimate of disposable resources, thus leading to irregular outcomes. The self-confidence of "anything can be done" had many positive aspects, but it also brought forth many ill side effects, as the merit of self-confidence was overemphasized. A prevailing social tendency at this time was that any means could be justified as long as an end could be achieved. Such an outcome-oriented mentality weakened a life attitude of "we should live by legitimate means" and fostered social uneasiness. What was questioned at this time was not whether the approach was legitimate, but whether or not a goal could be and was achieved. Such concerns with the demonstration effect and goal-attainment tendency encouraged the undemocratic and self-righteous mentality that was concerned vaguely only with the materialistic volume rather than with the content. Government thinking stopped short of weighing the relationship between any particular goal attainment on one hand and the increment of happiness and the quality of life of the people on the other hand. The goal attainment was evaluated per se and no attention was paid to what effect it would contribute socially. In the production of food and grains, the important concern was what amount of the goal was achieved, not whether the increase of production would lead to the deterioration of the quality of grains, excessive use of farming chemicals, and the consequent contamination of rice paddies.

In summary, it is true that the administration's headlong concern with goal achievement has caused a number of unpalatable incidents and a trial-and-error procedure in the process of development.

So far we have examined the merits and demerits of public administration in the course of the modernization task for the past twenty years or so. The extent of demand and interference by public administration can vary from time to time and from place to place. Though a great deal would be expected of the role of public administration if there were nothing to start with, the demand would decrease where extrabureaucratic organs achieved a certain degree of plural development. It is expected, then, that the extent of demand and interference by administration will have shifted by the early 1980s.

In the past twenty years or so, public administration has greatly contributed to the task of modernization. The value-creation role of the administration may be considered as inevitable. However, because a great deal of progress has been made in the development of private groups and social organs outside the jurisdiction of public administration, the monopolizing role of public administration in the process of development is something to be reconsidered for the benefit of public administration itself. In other words, as the role-bearers of development have became plural, it would be an anachronistic, negative phenomenon if public administration goes on insisting on its monopoly of the leading role. If it continues to adhere to such a role and position, the merits of the administration that it has built up so far will tend to be offset in their entirety.

In fact, the administration will find its own limit to its capability when it attempts to undertake the demand of development alone.

Now, for its own healthy development, public administration should consider a shift of the role of development from the public to the private sector. In other words, public administration can delegate to other organs what it cannot afford to engage in itself, and it should seek to improve the quality of administration by concentrating its endeavors in its own genuine domain. It should also concern itself solely with supporting functions by not directly involving itself with value creation and value production, as far as it is possible to do so. Public administration should undertake value creation and production only when or where private enterprises and other organs cannot afford to do so by themselves.

The role and contribution of public administration would not be lessened even if its role were shifted from that of production and creation to a supporting one. Rather, public administration would increase its own merits by concentrating its endeavors in its own domain.

CHAPTER TWELVE

An Assessment of Government Intervention in Korean Economic Development

Bun Woong Kim

THE DECADE OF the 1980s has been a critical period for assessing the Korean governmental role in economic development. During the period of the 1960s and 1970s, government economic intervention was praised as a success model by many scholars and practitioners. Over the last several years the efficiency of government intervention in the Korean economy has been intensively questioned and criticized because of the latent inefficiency of public intervention and the trend toward economic liberalization. This chapter argues that government economic control should transform direct intervention to a free-market mechanism—that is, shrinking the governmental role through deregulatory reform, privatizing the public sector, and thus ensuring a greater reliance on private initiative and economic democracy.

Efficiency and Inefficiency of Government Intervention

For a quarter century Korea has achieved remarkable economic growth. From 1962 to 1985, the Korean economy grew at an average annual rate of 8.3 percent. The nation's GNP per capital increased from $82 in 1961 to $2,032 in 1985. It is generally agreed that the sustained high growth in the Korean economy over this period was largely due to a significant shift in industrialization strategy from import substitution to export promotion in the early 1960s and the successful implementation of the outward-looking strategy thereafter. Among the diverse factors contributing to accelerated growth, government intervention was mostly attributed to the export-oriented policy.

From Bun Woong Kim, "An Assessment of Government Intervention in Korean Economic Development," *Korean Observer* 17 (2)(1986):149–160.

Presidential political leadership and a significant portion of the bureaucratic elites have given their top priority to economic development. Governmental economic intervention was too strongly supported to argue against its continuation. The intervention mechanism was solidified by an exceptional commitment of the late President Park Chung-Hee to economic development. Park's strong drive motivated the bureaucracy to formulate "administratively planned" economic growth, pushed the administrative elites to put all their efforts into the effective implementation of a planned economy, and established the Economic Planning Board (EPB) in 1961 as a leading ministry in the Korean government.

However, other noneconomic factors such as political ecology, cultural heritage, and social discipline also contributed to Korea's rapid economic growth. Nevertheless, the outward-looking strategy would not have succeeded without public intervention and private entrepreneurial forces. In the last quarter century in Korea there has been a host of price controls, distribution controls, and other government interventions through direct and indirect taxes, tariffs, quotas, export subsidies, and the protection of import-substituting industries. These controlling factors could affect the actual patterns of production, trade and employment growth. Factor market interventions, including the overvaluation of foreign exchange and implicit subsidization of capital good imports, could affect the choice of techniques within industries and the relative profitability of various activity. Through government intervention the Korean economy was directed more to export promotion than to a neoclassically efficient allocation mechanism.

A reconsideration of the effectiveness of government intervention was brought about, however, by major policy shifts: the development of heavy and chemical industries and economic liberalization suggested a more open economy.

First, the Korean government pushed the heavy and chemical industry development plan, a major priority in the Third Five-Year Economic Development Plan (1972–1976), to develop technologically sophisticated industries to meet defense needs and also to upgrade the composition of exports. Unfortunately the plan was drawn up on the overly optimistic assumption that international trade would continue to expand very rapidly. To accelerate industrial growth the government intervened and founded the National Investment Fund, which allowed the government access to public employee pension funds and a substantial portion of private savings at regular banking institutions. But the funds were insufficient to finance all projects, and banks were urged to make special loans at very low nominal interest rates on a preferential basis.

Because of the projects' long gestation periods and the unexpected world trade recession, government intervention led to unwise excessive investment, particularly in such fields as power generation, electrical equipment, and diesel engines. Intervention caused a chronic excess of demand for special loans at low interest rates, which stimulated the expansion of the domestic money supply and limited the ability of banks to offer interest rates high enough to attract savings. In the long run, government intervention in the development of heavy and chemical industries proved to be inefficient and ineffective and impeded the normal growth of the Korean economy.

The share of heavy and chemical industrial products in total exports rose from 21.3 percent in 1972 to 34.7 percent in 1978. But it was achieved at the cost of a high rate of inflation, 18 percent per year between 1972 and 1979. The overinvestment in heavy industries resulted in serious imbalances in the economy, which led to the weakening of export competitiveness and brought about a slowdown in the overall growth of the economy.

Second, in the 1980s Korea has taken the free market approach toward an open economy system through deregulation of direct government control. Over the last five years Korea's economic liberalization program has achieved dramatic results. As late as 1979, Korea's import liberalization ratio was less than 68 percent. The ratio reached 84.8 percent in 1984 and in 1986 it increased to 87.7 percent. When the ratio topped 95 percent in 1988, virtually all industrial products were free of import barriers other than tariffs. The policy to remove nontariff barriers has been accompanied by measures to reduce the average tariff level and to narrow the tariff differentials among different products. By adopting a negative list system in 1984, foreign investment policy was further liberalized. This new approach may imply the government's direction toward deregulation of direct administrative intervention in the economy.

In 1981 the Korean government enacted the Anti-Monopoly Act in order to reduce monopolistic practices and to promote competition in all industries. To revitalize the market mechanisms in the mobilization of savings and the allocation of investment, the government had relinquished its holdings in all of the five major commercial banks by 1983. In order to achieve greater efficiency in investment allocation, the government has been restructuring the industrial incentive system. Government intervention in extending preferential access to credit and favored treatment in taxation for so-called strategic industries has been a major public issue. Henceforth, the pattern of Korean economic administration should be changed from direct control to an indirect guiding role, that is, providing information and incentives to industry for upgrading technology and manpower.

Administrative Elitism in Economic Development

Administrative intervention had become popular among Korean bureaucrats, as had President Park's social philosophy, for example that of the

Saint-Simonian elitist strain. President Park and government elites feared the "waste" of competition and thus deepened their drive for favored government intervention in economic development. They were certainly strongly interventionist but envisaged administrative intervention as a means for encouragement of the outward-looking strategy and particularly for the central planning of the Korean economy. The components of the Korean adminstrators' interventionist role are traceable to their authoritarian bureaucratic elitism-specific patterns of socialization and administrative culture.

Until the advent of the Park administration in 1961, Korea suffered from a stagnant economy and political chaos. The administrative elites in the Park regime recognized the material benefits of unidimensional planned economic development in an atmosphere of circumscribed political liberties and were blessed by a hard-working literate population tired of poverty and political chaos. Thus, they engineered the drastic reshaping of the nation under the guise of single-minded national and presidential devotion to economic development. The bureaucratic elites produced an extreme degree of administrative centralization and collectivism, taking their direction from the Blue House and EPB. Furthermore, government intervention in the 1960s fostered a unity of purpose for economic growth that severely restricted free-market mechanisms.

The centralized bureaucratic elites were viewed as an impediment to pluralistic participatory democracy. A complex fusion of traditional cultural-political patterns and foreign administrative practices produced a centralized system of bureaucratic thought and behavior. The authoritarian political tradition stressed popular compliance with the established leadership without question, and this nurtured bureaucratic elitism and impeded democratic pluralism. In this setting, public policy making was the exclusive domain of the bureaucratic elite and although this facilitated effective bureaucratic direction of economic and social development, it deterred the creation of autonomous centers of authority in the political arena. The overwhelming moral and political predominance of the bureaucratic elite culture over the masses was not conducive to the evolution and development of free-market mechanisms and economic democracy.

Korean bureaucrats have depended on strong central regimes in which they dominated the policy-making process as well as policy execution. The policy-planning subculture of the bureaucratic elites was characterized by (1) the "speed and flexibility" of policy response; (2) the "pragmatism" of choosing among all available instruments and tools without any ideological bias; and (3) the "particularism" of applying certain policy to a limited number of clients in a specific situation. However, it appears that the development of interventionist administrative elites was desired in Korea because (1) resource utilization control required central planning and supervision; and (2) rationally directed economic activity may produce enormous growth with stable or even reduced inputs of scarce raw materials. In sum, the ascendancy of bureaucratic elitism strengthened the administrative interventionist role in the Korean economy.

Public Intervention vs. Private Initiative

The "invisible hand" of Adam Smith has never quite been acceptable to Korean bureaucratic elites. As far as public enterprise is concerned, governments exist to intervene in the production and distribution of goods and services. Government intervention constrains enterprise behavior by the nature of bureaucratic impediments imposed on business decision making. The control may impact differently on each of the institutional forms under the public enterprise rubric. Most Korean public enterprises operate in a highly imperfect output market because of monopolies or regulations.

Public intervention identifies the "publicness" of enterprises by ownership of the means of production and control of the decision-making process. The basic question of public control is whether decisions are made by the government or the managers, owners, market, or workers.

Economic growth through government intervention played a key role in President Park's social philosophy. Park's motive for government economic intervention was to control private power and improve the welfare of the masses. He viewed intervention as a regrettable necessity to be applied not to restrict private initiative; rather "The economic planning or long-range development program must not be allowed to stifle creativity or spontaneity of private enterprise. The overall national development program may necessitate, for rational operation of the economy, reluctantly imposed administrative control over the regional allocation of various industries and planning for investment." The Park administration advocated a broad range of intervening tools, including planning, regulation, public information systems, cooperatives, and public ownership, in order to counterbalance the control of markets by private business. The private sector also would not undertake these independently because of the magnitude of capital requirements, risk, uncertainty, technological complexity, and lack of market knowledge. Thus, the government undertook entrepreneurial substitution either by providing technical assistance and subsidized credits through entrepreneurial support organizations, such as development banks or by initiating the public activity. The autonomy-entrepreneurial function of public enterprise is in question because business decisions cannot possibly be made by bureaucrats who are trained in irrelevant disciplines. Most top managers of Korean public enterprises, such as presidents, vice presidents, directors, and auditors, came from government and the military. An analysis of the social background of 357 top managers of 56 nondepartmental public enterprises shows that the primary former occupation of 43 percent had been military (21 percent) or civil service (22 percent); more important, this included fully two-thirds of all presidents and auditors as well as half of all officers in the nonfinancial institutions.

In effect, many Korean government agencies and public enterprises are monopolies. But, in the name of administrative efficiency and rational management, bureaus with partially overlapping functions have generally combined, leaving the surviving agency with monopoly status. A monopoly agency, lacking competitors, is inexorably driven to exercise its power and exploit its monolithically secure position, which may be highly inefficient and dysfunctional.

The growth of government also accounts for growing administrative inefficiency. There are undeniable tendencies for government to grow in response to public demands and as a consequence of inefficiency. If unchecked, this trend may lead to an uncontrollable spiral of continued growth of the government and its intervention motives. Along with the tremendous growth of the Korean government during the last quarter-century, the public sector has predominated over the private sector.

Because of cumulative spillover effects of "big" government's administrative inefficiency, currently a substantial number of Korean citizens no longer regard government action as synonymous with the public interest. Thus, it is necessary to recognize limits to government intervention in order to attain the public good.

It is necessary to check the growth of government and to reduce "unwarranted and unwanted" dependence on government agencies. To shrink the government's role, E. S. Savas has suggested a multipronged approach:

> (1) Reduce government provision or subsidization of certain services; (2) make greater use of those service-delivery arrangements that require a lesser role for government; (3) utilize competition to the fullest possible extent to overcome the harmful consequences of unnecessary government monopolies.[1]

His approach requires both institutional means that permit greater reliance on private initiatives and a more limited government role. In recent years, the Korean government has made great efforts to decentralize its decision-making power to local government and administrative agencies and to privatize the public sector toward more private initiative and free-market mechanisms. During 1970–1984, 2,513 administrative matters (including licensing, inventions) were delegated from central government to local governmental—provincial, city and county—level, and 360 governmental authorities were also released to the private sector. In the year 1985 alone 90 central government matters were delegated to local autonomy and 16 governmental authorities were privatized to civilian institutions. For instance, the export-import permission-licensing power of the Ministry of Agriculture and Fisheries was delegated to a private sector organization, the Korean Association of Poultry, Food Grains, and Farm Products.

In Korea, it is simply not possible to find any prolonged examples of inefficient productivity that characterize many public enterprise sectors. Indeed, in some cases, Korean public enterprise production efficiency is extraordinarily high by LDC standards, and not markedly deficient when compared with similar operations in industrial nations. It is widely believed, however, that Korean public enterprises are less cost-efficient than their private counterparts, though the public-private gap is much smaller in Korea than in most LDCs. In privatizing the Korean public sector, much attention should also be focused on how to reduce the costs and ease the burden of administrative regulation to intervene in a market economy. Concern about excessive regulatory costs is surely warranted, and Korean bureaucracy must take a number of specific steps to deal with the problem. Deregulatory reform seems essential to remove government involvement and eliminate unnecessary regulation where market forces can work to support public goals.

Government economic regulations exist to control marketplace decisions when there are certain market failures. However, many of these rules have recently stifled competition, protected inefficiency, and inflated prices in Korea. The possible instruments for government intervention vary widely and include the collection and dissemination of information, the establishment of standards, the use of taxes or subsidies, and increased reliance on producer liability. Regulatory actions may effect both economic efficiency and the distribution of income. Curing a market failure by regulatory intervention generates costs as well as benefits because, owing to certain features of potential and bureaucratic institutions, regulators cannot be expected to stop just at curing the market failure.

A major problem is the inherent inefficiencies of regulation that flow from bureaucratic organizational rigidity. Government agencies and regulatory commissions often seem to behave according to an internal logic. The organizations develop stable behavioral patterns such as certain decision-making rules to process information and to perform actions along with and according to their own concepts of the environment in which they operate.

The gains from deregulation will be substantial in Korea. In the 1980s, significant progress in economic deregulation was made in the elimination of price-propping and competition-deadening regulations in a number of Korean industries, and deregulation or drastically reduced regulation in banking and other financial institutions. The present Korean government has pursued liberal economic policies that emphasize the role of private initiatives and the advantages of a truly open economy. Under major economic deregulation Korea's import liberalization ratio will reach 95 percent in 1988, and virtually all industrial products will be free of import barriers other than tariffs.

Korea has deregulated foreign investment policy as well. In 1984 the government adopted a negative list system for approving applications for foreign investment. In that year the government also removed all restrictions on the repatriation of principal and the remittance of dividends, and made approval for technology importation automatic upon notification of the government.

The Korean government has also reduced its intervention in savings and investment decisions. In 1983, the government relinquished its equity holdings in the five major commercial banks in Korea, and has further lifted various restrictions that had limited competition among different types of financial institutions. In addition, Korea has already liberalized and opened the domestic capital market to foreign investors. Nevertheless, Korea's economy is not yet a fully open economy by any standards.

The Korean economy should continue to respond to the new liberal policies through additional privatization of the public sector and deregulation of the government intervention mechanisms. It is also worth noting that, in general, a "market-oriented" approach to regulation can replace the traditional "command-and-control" form of regulation. Innovative techniques are market-oriented alternatives that lessen governmental restraints and permit greater private sector discretion in choosing how to meet regulatory objectives. Techniques to decentralize decision making are cost-effective and use incentives similar in many cases to those of the private marketplace to achieve broad regulatory goals. Under President Carter's directive in 1980, the U.S. Regulatory Council increased systematic use of innovative techniques—alternatives to traditional methods of regulation. The innovative regulatory techniques were applied in eight categories: marketable rights, economic incentives, performance standards, compliance reform, enhanced competition, information disclosure, voluntary standards, and tiering. The same market-oriented approach to regulation is desirable in Korea.

Conclusions

Most socioeconomic policies of the government are interventions into the workings of the private market in an attempt to improve economic performance, macro- and micro-efficiency, and the distribution of income and wealth. In Korea, a very efficacious substitute for governmental economic intervention can be private entrepreneurial initiatives based on free-market mechanisms.

First, government intervention in the Korean economy was a most efficient way to achieve remarkable economic growth. In the 1980s, however, governmental economic control approached the limits of administrative intervention because of excessive growth of bureaucracy and economic policy reforms toward an open economic system. Korean economic administration has to be transformed from direct intervention to a free market approach that permits greater reliance on private initiatives and requires a more modest role for government than is usually deemed necessary.

Second, in this context, the administrative elites' development of an interventionist role in the Korean economy should be transformed into an indirect inducement role, seeking—one hopes—"economic democracy," that is, the transfer of economic decision making from the few to the many. Thus, a strategy of reform must transfer economic power from bureaucratic elites to private industries. The administrative domination of the Korean economy appears to contradict the economic liberalization policy toward an open economy system in recent years. Saint-Simonian administrative elitism in economic development was very efficient during the 1960s and 1970s, but it is no longer valid or efficient for Korea's economic liberalization in the 1980s and 1990s.

Third, privatization seems necessary to revitalize the entrepreneurial initiative of the public sector. The growth of the government should be checked to reduce unwarranted and unwanted dependence on government agencies. Like contracting, the privatization of public service delivery may foster more economic efficiency.

Fourth, excessive regulatory costs of government economic intervention should be saved through deregulatory reform based on a free market mechanism. The innovative techniques of a market-oriented approach to regulation are necessary to replace the traditional command-and-control form of regulation.

Finally, the Korean government so far has overregulated the economy. Administrative reforms toward an open economy may bring about a more autonomous, sensible, and efficient government without sacrificing Korea's economic development in the last three decades. Liberalizing the Korean economy by deregulatory reform may provide a base for administrative autonomy and a greater hope for economic democracy.

Note

1.   E. S. Savas, *Privatizing the Public Sector: How to Shrink Government* (Chatham, N.J.: Chatham House, 1982), p. 5.

PART
VI

Uneven Development

The Territorial Dimension of the Developing Capitalist State: Measuring and Explaining Centralization in Korea

Yong Duck Jung

THE SYMBOLIC USES of politics are more prevalent in the developing than in the developed capitalist states. Various developmental policies are announced by government leaders, but most of them are no more than just rhetorical manipulations of language. Even the economic growth and industrialization that some have achieved have not been accompanied by equitable redistribution of income and democratic decentralization of power. A typical case of the invalidity of the modernization thesis is found in the Republic of Korea. While economic growth has been substantial since the early 1960s, sharing of the proceeds has not been widespread, and inequalities have worsened as development has accelerated. Directed economic development has entailed political and social tradeoffs such as political restrictions involving the denial of basic human rights, the suppression of representative institutions, severe limitations on political expression, and the strong centralization of power within the public bureaucracy and in center-periphery relations.

One of the reforms that the Chun government promised since its start in the early 1980s was a change in central-local relationships toward more local autonomy and decentralization. Since then, there have been many debates in Korea on ideal types of local government systems, mainly on normative and prescriptive bases. Most of the normative discussions have tended to be partisan arguments without descriptive information, while many prescriptive presentations are unreliable advocacies without

Taken from Yong Duck Jung, "The Territorial Dimension of the Developing Capitalist State: Measuring and Explaining Centralization in Korea," *International Review of Administrative Sciences* 53 (4)(1987):517–544.

causal analyses of the problems. In the meantime, however, the government has not shown any sign of initiating the promised reform of local government, as it did with other symbolic slogans—including "realization of social justice and welfare states"[1]—that it used in order to summarize its political goals and to justify its political identity. Assuming that more effective reforms of Korean local government require more descriptive and explanatory analyses of center-periphery relations in addition to the normative and prescriptive debates, this chapter seeks to measure the degree of centralization and to explore the causes of the centralizing tendency in Korea.

The Degree of Centralization

There are many suggested approaches to measuring and explaining the (de)centralization of a country's central–local relationships. Brian Smith has presented a systematic list of hypothetical concepts and propositions to be tested for measuring and explaining (de)centralization in a country. Among the list of measurement variables, the following four, which can be defined operationally with ease, seem to be useful especially for international comparison: the functions of subordinate governments, their financial dependency, and the size and structure of area governments.

Functions of Subordinate Governments

The functions of subordinate governments are a first variable: any shifts in the territorial balance of power on the base of the functions are supposed to change the level of decentralization. Thus, "centralization can be reduced by expanding the jurisdiction of subordinate government."[2] Indicators of functional shifts between the levels of governments can be obtained from data on public spending and personnel. First, increased decentralization will be reflected in a growing proportion of public spending incurred by area governments. Korean local expenditure as a proportion of total public spending has been about 23.9 percent on the average per annum during the 1972–1984 period. Thus, Korean local governments have spent less than one quarter of the total public spending. Compared with other countries, the Korean local expenditure as a proportion of total spending is smaller than that of most West European and North American countries and Australia and Japan, but larger than that of Italy, France, and Spain, and almost similar to that of the United Kingdom.

Second, the number of public servants working in local governments as a proportion of total public servants has also been used to measure decentralization. Only one fifth (20.8 percent) of total public human resources have worked in local governments on the average per annum during the 1965–1981 period in Korea. Considering the fact that local services tend to be highly labor-intensive, the proportion of Korean local public servants can be said to be very small. Compared with other countries the proportion of Korean local public servants (28.3 percent in 1981) is smaller than that of most West European and North American countries and Australia and Japan, but again larger than that of Italy, France, and Spain.

Financial Dependency

The second variable for measuring decentralization is financial dependency: If central funding increases, *ceteris paribus* so will central control. To measure financial dependency, it is necessary to see the proportion of local revenue raised from local services compared with central grants. The local service income as a proportion of total local revenue in Korea was 63.46 percent on the average per annum during the 1976–1984 period. Compared with other countries, the Korean local tax income as a proportion of total local revenues (about 40 percent in 1983 and 1984) is smaller than that of Norway, Sweden, and Australia, but similar to that of Denmark, the United Kingdom, France, Spain, the United States, Japan, and Canada, and even larger than that of Italy and West Germany. Therefore, it can be said that the Korean local governments are not very dependent on the central government in revenue sources, though there are big differences between urban and rural areas.

Size of Area Governments

Though still very much open to debate, the size of area government has been regarded as an indicator to measure the degree of decentralization: larger local authorities could be in a better place to resist central domination than could smaller ones. Therefore, legislation creating government fewer in number but larger in population and territory might be a decentralizing measure. The average sizes of the first- and second-level local governments of Korea are not as small as those of Italy, Japan, and the United Kingdom.

Structure of Area Governments

A fourth indicator of decentralization is the structure of area governments: "A simple (or single-tier) system of unitary all-purpose authorities will be less decentralized than a complex (or multi-tiered) system of authorities."[3] A conventional belief is that the more levels in the territorial hierarchy of the state, the more opportunity for discretionary gaps and leakages of authority to occur, which should increase the discretionary power available to lower levels in the system. Korea, like most industrialized countries including Japan, the United Kingdom, and the United States, has a two-tier system of local government. As Italy and France, which have been considered as more centralized countries among the industrialized countries, have three-tier systems, it can be argued that the number of tiers is not a valid indicator of decentralization of central–local relationships.

Considering the result of application of the four conventional variables to the Korean case, we come to a conclusion that Korean local government is less decentralized than that of most industrialized countries in West Europe, North America, and the Pacific. However, skepticism will arise from the comparison of Korea with France, Italy, and Spain. The comparative data to test the four variables suggest that the Korean local government system is more decentralized than that of any of these three countries. This conclusion might be too hasty, simply because the four variables are not valid enough to show the real dimensions of center–periphery relations in Korea: The Korean local government system can be explored more realistically by specifying the concept of decentralization.

Decentralization vs. Deconcentration

The general term of decentralization can be classified into two different concepts: decentralization and deconcentration. Decentralization in French usage is "a term reserved for the transfer of powers from a central government to an areally or functionally specialized authority of distinct legal personality." Deconcentration, on the other hand, is "the French equivalent for administrative decentralization within a single government's hierarchy."[4] In other words, decentralization (or political decentralization) involves the delegation of "political" authority, through which political institutions can be created with the right to make policies for local areas. Deconcentration (or administrative decentralization), on the other hand, involves the delegation of "bureaucratic" authority, that is, the delegation of responsibility from the headquarters of an organization to its field office. If the local government is operated through political authority and lay institutions within an area defined by community characteristics, a system of devolution (or federalism) can be said to exist. On the other hand, service-defined areas, bureaucratic authority, and field personnel produce only field administration or deconcentration.

In Korea, local governments have not had substantial political decision-making power for more than twenty-five years since General Park seized power through a military coup in 1961. During the earlier period of the Republic, under the so-called Local Autonomy Law of 1949, Korean area governments had locally formed policy-making assemblies whose members were locally elected by the inhabitants. For some time in that period even the chief executives of the local governments had been elected by the area residents. In 1961, however, the military government adopted the so-called Law Concerning Temporary Measures for Local Autonomy that suspended the functions of all local assemblies, and the administrative heads of local units became appointive. Since then, local governing functions have been performed by the Minister of Home Affairs and the respective provincial governors who are appointed by the president. There has, therefore been, by definition, no political decentralization at all in Korea since 1961. Other industrialized countries, including France, Italy, Spain, and even the Communist countries like the Soviet Union and China have some kind of local political bodies, through they may not be considered democratic in a Western liberal pluralistic point of view. Thus, it is submitted that it is not yet meaningful to discuss the degree of decentralization in its general sense in Korea. It seems to be more relevant to focus our attention on the degree of deconcentration within the hierarchy of field administration in Korea.

Even in the case of no political decentralization, it is still necessary to look into the degree of deconcentration within the field hierarchy. For political centralization may coexist with administrative decentralization: administrative decentralization in which subsidiary units, governed by officials appointed by the center, have no self-government is a logical and practical possibility. Even in a case where area governments appear very centralized, with no power residing in locally based institutions, the central-local relationship within a field hierarchy can be highly decentralized, with extensive powers delegated to the field officials. This is not the case with Korea, however, for the Korean system of field administration is also highly concentrated.

Forms of Field Administration

To measure the degree of (de)concentration, first, it is necessary to assess the formal type of field administration. As usual, Korea has two kinds of field administration: the functional system (in charge of functionally specific government services such as education, health, agriculture, etc.) and the prefectoral system (involving the appointment of a general representative of the central executive to a subnational territory, like the province in Italy and the department in France). As for the relationship between the prefect and local government and between the prefect and the functional field offices, Korean field administration can be regarded as an integrated, rather than an unintegrated, prefectoral system. In relation to local governments, the prefects are the chief executives of the first and second levels of local authorities and exercise control over the smallest local units (i.e., wards and townships). In relation to other field offices, the prefect is the superior field officer to whom the field officials of other ministries are subordinate. The prefect embodies the authority of all central ministries. Therefore, Korean field administration, an integrated prefectoral system, can be regarded as a more centralized system than unintegrated prefectoral systems in which, although the prefect exercises administrative supervision and control, local authorities can appoint their own chief executives. Moreover, the integrated form of the Korean prefectoral system tends to reduce deconcentration, as it adds to the degree of central control over the field agents of functional departments.

Policies of Personnel Transferring

Deconcentration may be affected by policies of transferring personnel between headquarters and field organizations. For example, the vertical
movements of personnel counter the tendency for field service(s) to be
assigned low status within the organization. In Korea, all local officials
are appointed from above and hold offices with no fixed term. The mayor
of the Special City of Seoul is appointed directly by the president upon
the recommendation of the prime minister. The provincial governors and
the mayors of the larger cities are appointed by the president through
the prime minister upon the recommendation of the minister of home
affairs. Finally, even city mayors and county chiefs are appointed by the
president upon the recommendation of provincial governors. Thus, the
president has virtually overall control over the appointment of local government chiefs. In addition to the chief executives, all the high levels of executive positions within local government are recruited together with state
public servants (i.e., civil servants employed by the central government).
Local public servants (i.e., civil servants employed by local government) are
working only as low-level rank and file, i.e., manual and clerical workers.

Revenue-raising Power

The legal restrictions imposed on the level of local rates of tax may affect
the level of administrative or political decentralization in a system of government. The degree of decentralization may also be dependent on
"whether the delegated tax powers permit area governments to expand
their revenues in line with increases in the rate of inflation and the growth
of the economy."[5] There are two groups of local taxes in Korea: the provincial taxes for province governments and the city and country taxes for city
and county governments. The rate level of none of those taxes is decided
by the local authorities. They have only tax-collecting powers, to implement the local taxation policies made by the central government. It is unthinkable for local governments to have any power to expand their taxes
in line with increases in the rate of inflation or the growth of the economy.

Communication and Supervising Methods

The degree of (de)concentration will be affected by the ways of communication between headquarters and the field for planning and control. It
will be dependent also on the methods used for supervising the work
of field offices, some of which are more remote than others. In Korea, all
communications, whether advisory or mandatory, take the top-down
rather than bottom-up forms. Field officers gather information to feed to
headquarters, but without participating in policy-making processes. Various supervisory methods, including advance review, reporting, and inspection, are used by the central ministries and the Board of Audit and

Inspection. In addition to these rather formal channels of communication and supervision, there are other informal, but more important, channels between the center and the periphery. They include the nationwide networks of the police and of the civil and military intelligence agencies. Korean political parties have not mattered much in the policy-making process. Moreover, they have been highly centralized. The central party leaders of the ruling party control party members in local branches, while the opposition parties do not have effective local organizations.

Under these circumstances, it is hard to think that the area governments have "a general competence to do whatever is considered necessary to meet the needs of the area as perceived" by field administrators, or "need to find some statutory confirmation that they can act on a particular matter or provide a particular service."[6] The central headquarters usually employ the form of "control," backed by all kinds of sanctions, rather than "influence," which area governments are free to resist. Area governments operate not as partners but only as the agents of the center.

Korean local governments are extremely centralized not only because they are *politically centralized*, with no local self-governments, but also because they are highly *concentrated*, with little power delegated to field offices.

Causes of the Centralization

Why has such a centralization occurred in Korea? What has caused such an extremely centralized center-periphery relationship, especially during the last twenty-five years? Most discussions in Korea about the causes of centralization have been concerned with the historical and sociocultural legacy and the needs of economy efficiency and administrative rationality. However, choices of (de-)centralized institutions are also a matter of power. Any change of central-local relationships can be seen as the consequence of conflicts of interest between power groups in society, which have "something significant to gain or lose in the restructuring of local institutions, in the delegation of power to them, or in the redefinition of areas."[7] After briefly reviewing the conventional ways of explanation, this section will focus primarily on the issues of political and economic interests that may have caused the centralization in Korea.

Historical and Sociocultural Legacy

One of the conventional explanations of centralization in Korea has been made by emphasizing the historical and sociocultural aspects of the society. Traditionally, the country had been ruled by a strong central government through central government officials. Throughout the 500-year history of the Chosun dynasty, there were no such historical factors as "the existence of regions with political status predating the nation of which they form constituent parts,"[8] which may strengthen decentralization. In a predominantly Confucian society such as that of Korea, many analysts are skeptical about the possibility of the existence of a pluralist ideology or political culture. They believe that the Korean people accept the Confucian dictum that the people should follow established leadership without question, and should not be concerned about the knowledge necessary for the exercise of leadership. In their eyes, local initiative tends to be a concept alien to most Koreans. Western pluralist ideas of local government were imposed from outside in the late 1940s without having enough internal support. Without an opportunity to develop indigenous ways that suit the entities involved, the local government system could be eliminated without difficulty when strong centralizers came to power. Such historical and cultural factors of centralization have been strengthened by the homogenous characteristics of the Korean population. Decentralization tends to be stimulated in general as a response to the centrifugal tendencies of ethnic or religious cleavages. But both ethnically and linguistically, Korea is one of the most homogenous societies in the world.

Such historical and sociocultural causes of centralization in Korea must not be overemphasized. Admittedly, the rural population, kin-oriented and Confucianist, has been most conservative and resistant to social change, but rural migration has eroded traditional culture. In 1960, over 60 percent of Korea was rural, but in 1970 the figure was about 50 percent, and in 1980 less than 35 percent. Furthermore, higher literacy has improved the prospect for political participation, and if local initiative has been alien, it may have been because of lack of opportunity and government discouragement rather than lack of talent. The continuing strength of the democratic norm in the city and countryside demonstrates the persistent desire of the people to participate in the management of their own affairs. It is also noticeable that since the early 1960s Korean society, though still homogeneous, has experienced growing conflicts between the southeast and southwest regions, and between the haves and the have-nots.

Economic and Administrative Rationality

Another conventional explanation of centralization in Korea is the needs of economic efficiency and administrative rationality. First, the small size of Korea's territory has often been regarded as a causal factor for its centralization. The principle of scale economics suggest that the larger the country, the greater the decentralization. Since 1945, more than half of the peninsula has been occupied by Communist North Korea, and the South has remained a small country of only ninety-nine thousand square kilometers, less than half the size of the United Kingdom and less than one-third that of Japan or Italy. Another "rational" explanation comes from the lack of resources, both human and capital, in the local areas. The lack of financial self-sufficiency of Korean local government has been empha-sized as the most critical constraint on reforms toward local autonomy by the ruling political party and the government authorities. The county ad-ministrations, which cover rural areas, depended upon the central govern-ment for more than two-thirds of their revenues on average during the 1980s. The Korean economy has been based heavily on a small number of revenue-earning export commodities, and there have been few alter-native tax bases for the rural areas to develop. An administrative ration-ale comes from the lack of human resources in local government. The competence of the locally employed officials has been relatively low com-pared with those employed by the central government. Such problems arising from the lack of human and financial resources are not unique to Korean local government, but are common even in industrialized coun-tries. However, the need for centralization, based on the economic and administrative rationales, has been emphasized more often in Korea than in other countries, because the Korean government has stressed national security and economic growth as ultimate national goals. To achieve na-tional security and economic growth effectively, it has been argued that it is necessary to centralize the direction of the economy and coordinate nationally the development of extremely scare resources, especially capi-tal technology, and skilled personnel. Thus, the greater the involvement of the national government in the economy and in security, the less the decentralization in Korea.

Such "rational" explanations of centralization should not be emphasized too much, because it is possible to find many other interpretations of the efficiency or rationality criteria. It is true that territorial delegation of power is often a response to the size of the country and that smaller states tend to be more centralized. Although Korea is a small country in territory, its demographic size is not that small according to European standards. The current fiscal weakness of the rural areas must be an obstacle to decen-tralization in Korea.

The financial self-sufficiency of Korean local government as a whole has been as high as that of most industrialized countries. Much research also suggests that, depending on the types of grant and subsidy policies, fis-cal weakness may not undermine local autonomy or decentralization at all. Therefore, the issue of fiscal weakness or dependency must be regarded as a matter of coordination of the financial differences among the area governments in Korea.

The relatively less competent personnel in local administrations is a prob-lem common to all countries, but Korean local governments are supposed to have advantages in finding competent human resources from the pri-vate sector. In Korea, the civil service has been regarded as an honorable profession, and government officials still have great prestige compared with those in the business sector. Provided that the current closed recruitment system is opened up and local civil servants are given opportunities for promotion to higher level positions, the competence of local personnel can be improved more than that of the business sector. Therefore, the lack of financial self-sufficiency and of competent personnel should not be counted as the explanatory variables (or the causes) but as the descriptive variables (or the effects) of centralization in Korea. Finally, no one will object to the fact that national security and economic growth are important in Korea, which is still poor and menaced by militarily formidable neighbors including North Korea and the Soviet Union. It is still open to theoretical debate, however, whether centralization is more efficient for national security and economic growth than decentralization. It must be remembered, also, that the first elections for local councils were held in 1952 in the midst of the Korean War. Furthermore, in addition to national security and economic growth, the country has needed to pursue other national goals, including political democratization and the promotion of individual freedom. Among the principles of the rational explanation, such a need might have been a causal factor leading to more decentralization or local autonomy, which is often seen as the training ground for democratic leadership and citizenship.

Such explanations of centralization in terms of the historical and sociocultural legacy and of administrative and economic necessity will almost inevitably overlook important features of the Korean political economy which impinge upon its intergovernmental relations. The need for (de)centralization in developing capitalist states such as Korea reflects no less the power of different groups to promote and defend their political and economic interests. That is why we need to turn our attention to analyses of the economic, bureaucratic, and political interests to explain more realistically the centralizing tendency during the last twenty-five years in Korea.

Economic Interests

First, (de)centralization may occur as new modes of production develop with the support of state intervention. For example, federations are usually brought into being by groups seeking to benefit from wider economic association and territorial mobility. In developing capitalist states, however, emerging economic interests tend to be hostile to the fragmentation and decentralization of state power, because they are often dependent for their growth on national, not local, political power. Central governments are involved in placing many contracts with companies supplying goods and services to large developmental projects. Political office at the national level provides various kinds of rewards.

The significance of state-level government for industrial development must have had serious implications for the centralizing tendency in Korea. The Korean economic system has been a regulated capitalism in that the government will either directly participate in or indirectly render guidance to basic industries and other important sectors. Especially since the early 1960s, the government's role in the economy has become more influential through measures such as long-term economic planning (which has been more than indicative), public enterprise, fiscal and monetary policies, and economic regulations favoring certain industries.

Most government activities have been conducted in the name of economic development, and many agree that Korea's rapid economic growth during the last twenty years was engineered by the public sector employed on behalf of guided capitalism. In doing so, the Korean government has permitted large firms to conduct monopolistic pricing in order to encourage economies of scale and to enhance competitive power in international markets, but has restrained prices for labor and agricultural products in order to prevent inflation and again improve large firms' international competitive positions. Additionally, overall tax policies have disadvantaged wage earners and individual consumers more than manufacturers and the export companies. Monetary policies, including loans, have been more beneficial for firms than for households, for profit earners than for wage earners, for export-oriented than for domestic-consumption-oriented industries, and for larger than for small- or medium-sized enterprises. In the meantime, corruption and favoritism have emerged, and many Koreans have believed that a political linkage exists between the government and the *chaebol* (defined as groups of large enterprises). Such a political linkage must have caused not only the centralization of income and wealth in the hands of the *chaebol*, but also the centralization of political and administrative power in central government.

Centralization in Korea, therefore, may be seen as a product of the coalition between the state and the emerging economic forces that benefit from expansion of the central state machine. It would be exaggeration, however, to say that the state level of government has become just the instrument through which the growing business group gains access to capital for private investment. Instead, it is more correct to note that the state in Korea has not been controlled by any particular economic class or group, but has played an independent and dominant role in its relationship with the forces of capital and labor. Therefore, it is necessary to look into the policy-making process within the public sector.

Bureaucratic Interests

Instead of assuming a dispersal of power, it is more plausible to focus on the independent, self-interested role played by political and bureaucratic elites in Korea. First, a policy initiative may be the product of a government agency's effort to justify its continued existence or expand its base of support within the society. Program developments may simply flow from the standard operating procedures that an agency has developed, or from the value preference of the bureaucrats themselves. Public officials of the Korean Ministry of Home Affairs (MHA) have been known to be reluctant to decentralize. They may be afraid that their chances to be promoted to high-level positions, including local chief executive, will be overtaken by those to be elected locally, and that even if they can be appointed to be chief executives or other high-level officials, they will be controlled by the local councils to be formed.

Since the Chun government promised reforms for local autonomy in the early 1980s, most civil servant candidates who just passed the Higher Civil Service Recruitment Examination tended to regard MHA as a minor agency for choice of work. Traditionally it was one of the most important ministries, including the Ministry of Foreign Affairs, the Economic Planning Board, and the Ministry of Finance. It is clear, anyway, that if reforms for local autonomy and decentralization are conducted, MHA and other central ministries will have to face reductions of their power over field administration. The MHA has been hostile to decentralization. The central government has tried to suppress debates on the issue of decentralization, to prevent them from entering the political process, and further to shape people's preferences so that neither overt or covert disputes exist.

Such a bureaucratic–politics approach, however, does not offer many insights into the move toward centralization during the last two and a half decades in Korea. Although the Korean public bureaucracy has been more influential in the policy-making process than have legislative and judiciary branches, the political parties, or the social sector, it has played within the limited domain within the state sector. Korean public bureaucrats respond to directives issued from above and have limited autonomous inputs. They have had little power in policy planning and initiation, but rather simply implemented programs that are decided by the Blue House (the presidential residence and office compound). Most public policies have been developed with the approval of the core power elite, i.e., the presidential group. Some bureaucratic distortions or changes of policy that the policymakers intend may be inevitable in Korea, like other countries, because of organizational necessity (e.g., the organizational division of labor), but they are extremely limited in Korea. The concept of the "president as king" is much more applicable to Korea than other countries. Because the president chooses most of the important players, sets the rules, and selects those who head the large bureaucracies, these individuals must share his values and remain "the president's men." It seems to be more reasonable in Korea than elsewhere to see power as the province of a small and cohesive political elite.

Interests of the Core Power Elite

Public policy may be seen as the product of a small, closed group of the key power elite who play a relatively autonomous and architectural role.

This power group may sponsor policies as a means by which to under-mine and/or co-opt opposition forces and to strengthen the loyalty of beneficiary groups to the state. They also operate in an entrepreneurial fashion to anticipate or even to consciously mold the demands of various sectors of society. This interpretation of the policy-making process seems to be most useful in explaining the centralization tendency in Korea. Except for a short period of the populist Chang government (1960–1961), the Republic has been under authoritarian regimes. Authoritarian governments, by their nature, are inimical to decentralization. They tend to seek "ways to mobilize and incorporate the lower classes in support of [their] policies without permitting the operation of national political organizations which might threaten the current political leadership." Local self-governing institutions will not be permitted unless there is strong control over local authorities.

Moreover, the continuing political instability, caused mainly by the legitimacy problem of the regimes, has been prevalent throughout the Republic, and its intensity has been more severe since the early 1960s. During the period of 1963–1975, about 7000 people (more than 500 on the average per annum) were arrested for alleged political reasons. To maintain political stability, seven regulatory measures or laws, including the National Security Law, have been made, and the above measures or laws have been put into practice eleven times, including four proclamations of martial law, during the same period.

The threat of such political instability led to centralizing measures to weaken local centers of primordial political identity. The authoritarian power elites concerned with maintaining political stability eliminated the locally formed policy-making institutions and adopted for political purposes the highly centralized integrated prefectoral system in 1961. Since then, those highly centralized field administrations have been employed for the political objective of containing sources of instability. Field offices have been used to locate sources of internal conflict and to settle disputes that might threaten the stability of the regimes. In addition, they have been used to obstruct oppositions to the government as well as threats to the regime, which have also been removed by "manipulating the machinery for the peaceful transfer of power, notably elections."[9]

In Conclusion

The Korean central-local relationships have been extremely centralized in regard to the political aspects of both (de)centralization and (de)concentration, especially over the last twenty-five years. The centralizing tendency has been caused by the historical and sociocultural legacy and by economic and technocratic necessity. However, it is more realistically explained by reference to the interest configuration of economic, bureaucratic, and political forces that have been dominant during this period in Korea. Such extremely centralized control of the territorial dimension of the state has been an indispensable condition especially for the power maintenance of the authoritarian political elites. Normative discussion on the desirable level of decentralization or local autonomy, or any prescriptive advocacy on the methods to achieve it, has been beyond the scope of this chapter. However, the result of this study suggests that if Koreans believe it desirable to increase the decentralization or local autonomy of the local government, as many of them argue these days, they should also know that it cannot be achieved without weakening or partially reversing the causal factors of the centralization of the state. It is indicated further that the most important factor in Korea among the elements that have been observed as "leading to the successful adaptation of federal principles and arrangements is the substitution of government by [a properly structured democratic elite] in place of government by a single strong man."[10]

Notes

1. Y. Jung, "Distributive Justice and Redistributive Policy in Korea," *Korean Social Science Journal*, 11 (1984), pp. 143–162.
2. B. Smith, "Measuring Decentralization," in G. Jones (ed.), *New Approaches to the Study of Central-Local Government Relationships* (Aldershot, Hants., England: Gower & SSRC, 1980) p. 139.
3. B. Smith, *Decentralization* (London: George Allen & Unwin, 1985), p. 90.
4. *International Encyclopedia of Social Sciences,* 1968, p. 370.
5. Quoted in B. Smith, *Decentralization,* p. 87.
6. B. Smith, *Decentralization,* p. 87.
7. B. Smith, *Decentralization,* p. ix.
8. B. Smith, "Measuring Decentralization," p. 144.
9. B. Smith, *Decentralization,* p. 148.
10. D. Elazar, "Federalism, Governance, and Development in the Third World," in W. Thompson (ed.), *The Third World* (San Francisco: Institute for Contemporary Studies, 1978), p. 156.

CHAPTER FOURTEEN

Financial Structure and Management: The Case of the Seoul Metropolitan Region

Dong Hyun Kim

THE REPUBLIC OF Korea has experienced profound socioeconomic changes, particularly during the past three decades. It has observed unprecedented rates of high economic growth concomitant with rapid industrialization. A massive rural-to-urban migration, in response to high population pressure on the land as well as to expansion of the urban industrial sector, has resulted in rapid urbanization.

These societal transformations, which came to pass in a relatively short period of time, consequently produced changes in the settlement system characterized by overconcentration in large urban centers and an absolute decline in the rural population. However, the shift of population distribution to one of large urban agglomerations has frequently been thought of as inevitable to achieve fast economic growth under the unfavorable conditions that existed in Korea in the early 1960s, i.e., low levels of technology and capital accumulation and poor natural resource endowment.

The problems associated with an excessive population concentration have long been recognized by scholars and government officials, and various efforts have been made to alleviate these problems. However, it is the general consensus that the policy efforts have not been effective enough. As a result, more and more people believe that reassessment of past development goals and policy directions is imperative. In formulating relevant policies it is important to understand the past trends and the possible courses of future development.

Taken from Dong Hyun Kim, "Financial Structure and Management: The Case of Seoul Metropolitan Region," *Regional Development Dialogue* (United Nations Center for Regional Development) 10 (1)(1989):145–170.

Urban Development Issues and Strategies

Urban Sector Profile

The Republic of Korea had an area of 98,992 square kilometers and a population of about 41.2 million as of 1986. The population density was 408 persons per square kilometers. The population of Seoul was calculated to be 9,798,542; thus, 23.8 percent of the total population lived in an area that accounted for no more than 0.63 percent of the whole national territory. Of the Seoul population, males represent 50.1 percent while females represent 49.9 percent. The number of households was 2,428,173, with average family members per household being 4.0. About two-thirds of the national land area is forest, whereas the eastern section is rugged, mountainous, and sparsely populated. A large proportion of the nation's population and economic activities is concentrated along the Seoul-Pusan axis, whereas the western half of the country is mostly agricultural.

The country is administratively subdivided into nine provinces, one special city (Seoul) that is the national capital, and three cities under the direct supervision of the government, Daegu, Incheon, and Kwangju. Each province has a number of cities (*shis*) and counties (*guns*), and each county consists of several towns (*eups*) and townships (*myons*). There are a total of 61 cities, 139 counties, 201 towns, and 1,241 townships.

Urbanization

Simultaneous with the remarkable economic growth, the Republic of Korea has experienced rapid urbanization over the past two decades. The urbanization rate has increased from 28 percent in 1960 to 65.4 percent in 1985, if "urban" is defined as an area of an administratively designated city that normally has a population above 50,000. The urbanization rate is expected to reach around 75 percent by the year 2000.

In the 1960s, urban population growth was largely attributable to rural in-migration. For instance, net urban migration accounted for 77 percent of the total urban population increase during the 1966–1970 period. However, since the 1970s, the importance of net migration has been declining, whereas natural increase has become more and more significant.

The most dominant feature of urbanization during the 1960s was a rapid population concentration in Seoul from all over the country. The population of Seoul more than doubled during the decade from 2.6 million in 1960 to 5.5 million in 1970. The dominance of Seoul in the urbanization process is mainly attributable to the fact that Seoul has been the major beneficiary of the nation's economic boom. However, since 1970, the growth of Seoul has considerably slowed, from the highest rate of 9.4 percent for 1966–1970 to 2.9 percent for 1980–1985. Instead, planned industrial cities, regional centers, and satellite cities around Seoul have been growing rapidly.

The remarkable economic growth in the country has relied heavily on a strategy of maximizing export-oriented industrialization, and has thus favored large cities in the expectation that the self-reinforcing agglomeration economies will move the national economy at an accelerated rate. This policy option seems to have been inevitable at the time the country began to industrialize in the early 1960s. However, the rapid polarized urbanization and its concomitant cityward migration widened the disparities between the urban and rural sectors as well as among different regions and social groups.

Recognizing the serious imbalance between urban and rural areas and among regions, the Korean government has been attempting to mitigate the problems. Over the last ten years, manufacturing industries in the rural areas have been growing much faster than the national average, both in terms of value added and labor force, and rural-to-urban migration has been reduced in proportion over the last five years. The reverse movement has increased proportionately for the same period. Also, there have been structural improvements in agricultural production. Income generated from noncrop agricultural products and other off-farm income sources has also been increasing.

Those problems resulting from the population concentration which are most often cited by policy analysts and urban experts include: the issue of regional balance in national development; environmental quality; amenities, public services, and diseconomies of scale; and social problems.

National Objectives and Strategy for Urban Development

The main objective of urban policy in the Republic of Korea can be summarized as: control and management of growth of the large metropolitan centers, especially for Seoul; fostering development of growth poles; and strengthening various functions of small- and medium-sized cities as local service centers.

It is commonly believed that imbalances among the different regions are inevitable at the earlier stages of national development. In the Republic of Korea, like many other Third World countries, the process of rapid economic growth during the past two decades has largely ignored the spatial dimension of development. The industrialization policies of the early 1960s emphasized aggregate national growth and thus strongly favored large urban centers. Industries were concentrated in and around the Seoul and Pusan metropolitan regions where various locational advantages were readily available. The nation's economic activities have been rapidly polarized through the process of circular and cumulative causation that resulted in overconcentration of population and economic activities, especially in the Seoul metropolitan region.

It was in 1964 that the government took its first step to control the growth of large metropolitan centers, particularly Seoul, recognizing the dual problems of overcrowding in large cities and interregional imbalances. At that time, the cabinet decided to adopt the following policy measures: relocation of secondary government agencies to local areas; development of satellite cities and industrial centers; restriction of new industrial locations in large cities; and expansion of educational and medical facilities in the local areas. Since then, balanced regional development has been an objective of regional policy in the country, and numerous planning efforts have been made.

Among those various policy measures, growth pole strategy and control of growth of the capital region are worth mentioning. The Second National Comprehensive Physical Development Plan designated three relatively large cities, Daegu, Daejeon, and Kwangju, as primary growth centers. These primary growth centers were to be developed with the priority role as countermagnets to control the growth of Seoul and Pusan, and at the same time to serve as regional centers to achieve balanced regional development.

The Capital Region Growth Management Law was enacted in 1982 with the aim of controlling the population and industrial concentration on an integrated basis. The capital region is divided into five major subareas according to the degree of development and individual characteristics of each area of the region. These five areas are: development-restricted area, development-limited area, development-induced area, resource conservation area, and an area reserved for development. Various strategies for each area have been adopted and are being implemented.

Industrial Policy

It was recognized within the circle of government policymakers, even at the early stage of economic development, that industrial location was an important policy tool to achieve balanced regional development. In order to curb the rapid concentration of industries and population in Seoul, the government had first tried to restrict the establishment of new industries and the expansion of existing ones in Seoul, beginning around 1964. However, it soon realized that it would be difficult to halt the industrial growth in Seoul without creating massive attraction points elsewhere, as Seoul, because of its enormous agglomeration economies, has been the ideal industrial location relative to other regions.

This realization prompted the government into legislating the Local Industrial Development Law. The law provided legal grounds for governmental assistance to promote local industrial development such as tax exemption, infrastructure development in government-designated local industrial estates, and other financial and technical assistance. Under these government policies, thirteen heavy industrial estates, twenty-four local industrial estates, and seven special zones were created. Some were existing ones with further improvement in infrastructure and estate expansion, whereas many were newly created ones. The total area of these industrial estates is about 590 square kilometers. They accommodate more than 2,000 firms with 550,000 employees.

The other important legislative action with regard to industrial decentralization policies was the enactment of the Industrial Redistribution Law of 1977. The law authorizes the minister of industry and commerce to classify areas for the purpose of industrial location into three zones: relocation encouragement zone; limitation and coordination zone; and location encouragement zone. In the first two zones, activities such as new industrial establishments, expansion of existing industries and land development for industrial establishments, expansion of existing industries, and land development for industrial uses are either disallowed or only selectively allowed with special permission. On the other hand, relocation into other parts of the country, particularly into the industrial areas in backward regions, is strongly encouraged through incentives of various types.

The new town development policy could roughly be grouped into the following four areas: decentralizing excessive concentrations of population and industrial activities in large urban centers, particularly Seoul; building new industrial towns or bedtowns for large industrial complexes in order to foster economic growth; developing large-scale residential subdivisions to relieve the acute housing shortages in and around Seoul; and establishing induced-growth centers to stimulate the development in lagging regions.

Although somewhat conflicting to a certain extent, the first and third objectives have been put into effect through the development of satellite towns around Seoul (Seongnam and Gwacheon) as well as of massive residential subdivisions in the periphery of the built-up areas within Seoul (Yeondong, Jamsil, and Youido). The first residential new town project was Seongnam New Town (formerly Gwangju County, Gyonggi Province), the development of which began basically as a refugee camp for the relocated population from cleared urban squatter areas in central Seoul. The city grew rather rapidly during the 1970s, and currently stands as the ninth largest city in the nation with a population of 448,000.

As the country enters a second stage in industrial development, the pattern and structure of manufacturing industries have gradually changed, with increased emphasis on heavy industries. The southeastern seaboard was considered a desirable location for newly forming heavy industries. For instance, Changwon New Town, developed in 1977 next to the Changwon Heavy Industrial Complex, was basically designed to provide housing as well as other urban services to the residents, the majority of whom are employees. The city, which is now the seat of the provincial government of Gyongnam Province, has been developed to cope with an expanded population.

In the earlier new town development, the major agents or developers have been predominantly governments, both central and local, and public corporations. The typical arrangement usually starts when the Ministry of Construction (MOC) designates the site for prospective new town development. Then one of the relevant public corporations, entrusted with central government authority, comes in and takes charge of the entire process of construction. In the development of Changwon, Yeochon, and Banweol, it was the Industrial Estate Development Corporation (IEDC). In the case of Gwacheon Residential New Town, the Korea National Housing Corporation (KNHC) has played a major role in the whole development process.

Urban Development Finance

Rapid urbanization has brought about a soaring demand for urban development. Financial expansion of municipal governments mainly resulted from (1) continuous urbanization (urbanization rates of 28 percent in 1960 and 65.4 percent in 1985); (2) expansion of administrative areas of cities (2,709 square kilometers of urban area in 1960 and 6.083 square kilometers in 1985); (3) rising incomes (U.S. $83 in 1960 and U.S. $2,032 in 1985); and (4) more people using urban facilities from surrounding areas as a result of improved accessibility.

It is almost impossible to supply urban development investments from only the public sector with limited funds and manpower of city governments. There have been many attempts to induce more funds from the private sector, which have been quite successful in such urban development projects as urban renewal in residential land development and housing construction.

The maximization of investment effects on urban facilities becomes more essential to accommodate a rapidly increasing demand for urban development with limited financial resources. There are several forms of providing urban services to enhance effectiveness of urban investments such as inviting private investments, service by private company, payment through user charges, and establishment of public enterprises.

One of the most popular devices to improve urban public services is the establishment of public enterprises. In the Republic of Korea, according to the Law of Local Public Enterprises, three types of public enterprises can be established: (1) public enterprise; (2) public corporation; and (3) nonprofit private corporation on a contractual basis.

In Seoul, there are many kinds of public enterprises such as the Water Supply Construction Office and Mokdong Development Office; public corporations with both public and private corporations, e.g., Urban Facilities Management Corporation of Seoul, which manages parking lots and toll tunnels with an independent profit system.

The advantages of the public enterprise system can be recognized in the case of the garbage and human waste disposal services in Seoul. These services are individual and selective ones because the demands originate not from all urban residents but only from those people requiring the service. In this case, the principle of user charges is appropriate because the residents who enjoy public services pay for the benefit of those services. In Seoul, according to the Ordinance of Garbage and Human Waste Disposal Services, these services can be operated by private companies based on a contract with the city government. Sixty-nine companies participate in garbage disposal works and 3,043 persons are employed. Sixteen private companies with 1,078 employees are working in the human waste disposal service.

Urban Finance

Types of urban finance can be classified as either a general account or a special account, and the latter can be divided into three components: a special account of a public corporation, a special account of education, and others. There are two sources of urban finance revenue: independent source and a dependent source. The local tax and nontax revenues are the main sources of independent revenue, and national and provincial grants and subsidies and the local share tax are the sources of dependent revenue. Special subsidies are available from the central government when the local governments are faced with difficult problems such as expansion or reconstruction of urban infrastructure. However, the portion of special subsidies has become smaller since 1971.

Expenditure of Urban Governments

General administration is a major item of expenditure in general accounting, while industrial development and urban infrastructure construction are major items of expenditure in special accounting. In the 1960s, general administration and industrial development had the largest share in urban government expenditures; however, urban governments spent more money on the construction of urban infrastructure in the 1980s. Almost 60 percent of the total budget of urban governments was invested in urban public infrastructure construction when the share of other expenditures, general administration, and industrial development, became smaller.

More than 80 percent of urban investments was spent on construction, expansion, and repair of urban social overhead facilities. The largest investment in 1985 was put into road construction and improvement (16.6 percent), water supply (16.5 percent), and urban construction (17.4 percent) in that order. From 1985 to 1988, the share of urban construction increased significantly (13 percent to 17.4 percent), representing a large investment in subway and urban park construction. With the rising incomes and living standards of urban residents, the expenditures on water supply facilities and sewerage facilities construction increased from 15.8 percent and 2.3 percent to 16.5 percent and 7.2 percent, respectively. On the other hand, the share of road construction and improvement decreased from 30.9 percent to 16.6 percent.

Over 68 percent of urban investments were carried out through the metropolitan government's own financial resources, while provincial and national subsidies amounted to only 6.4 percent in 1985. Urban investment comprised 21.8 percent of the loan, and the share of local tax was only 0.9 percent. Examining the financial resources by projects, the major portion of investments on bridge construction, urban construction, and sewerage system construction came from the metropolitan government's own resources (more than 80 percent), while 65.7 percent of water supply facility construction and 49.1 percent of road improvement were financed by their own resources. The larger part of national government subsidies to urban governments went to sewerage system construction (5.9 percent) and road improvement (6.2 percent). The loans from other financial institutions were actively utilized to expand water supply (29.7 percent) and to improve road conditions (30.5 percent).

Generally the share of urban government resources to total investment increased from 60.2 percent in 1982 to 72.9 percent in 1985, while the share of urban construction by their own resources increased from 55 percent to 68.7 percent. The share of investment by their own resources on water control increased from 67.8 percent to 84.3 percent; on road improvement it grew from 20.6 percent to 49.1 percent; and on bridge construction it increased from 93.9 percent to 98.1 percent. However, the share devoted to water supply facility expansion decreased from 69.6 percent to 65.7 percent. The share of national government subsidies increased in the water control projects (3.1 percent to 7.3 percent), water supply facility expansion (23.1 percent to 29.7 percent), and sewerage construction (0.8 percent to 6.9 percent). On the other hand, the loan share decreased in the water control projects (21.8 percent to 0) and road improvement (46.1 percent to 30.5 percent).

For the profitable urban development projects such as urban renewal, parking lots, and toll tunnels, private investments have actively participated. For example, most of the financial resources for urban renewal projects in Seoul come from the private sector while the city government supports only the basic infrastructure such as access roads, water supply, and sewerage systems. As private investments in urban development seem desirable to improve urban services, institutional supports for more active private participation are therefore necessary.

Korean cities have not yet actively utilized bonds for their urban development projects. The major reasons are the lack of long-term perspectives in financing, the strong ceiling control by the central government, and the small scale of urban financial budgets. However, the recent institutionalization of the user charges system encourages the issuing of bonds for urban development. The Urban Planning Law explicitly indicates that the charges can be levied on users who receive the benefit of development of roads, water supply, and sewerage facilities. Recently, urban governments have tried to utilize bonds for initial investment in large projects. Principal and interest can be paid by user charges for long periods.

Financing Structures and Management of Metropolitan Seoul

Municipal finance in the Republic of Korea consists of the general account and several special accounts. This is also true of all government programs. The sources of financing the general account mainly depend on tax and nontax revenues from the residents. Unlike the general account, the special account is created either on an *ad hoc* basis or for specific purposes and projects.

From the early 1960s through the mid-1970s, the financial revenue of Seoul increased sharply owing to rapid economic growth, and the financial scale quickly swelled because of the expansion of various investments and social development programs. From the late 1970s to the early 1980s, however, the rate of increase in financial revenue has slowed substantially as a result of economic recession. Because a very slow rise is expected in financial receipts in the years ahead due to the consolidation of a base for stable economic growth, sound financial operations have become an important management task.

A mid-term financial plan has thus been in force since the beginning of 1982, and investment review and zero-base budgetary systems have also been introduced. This new financial operating system, along with the existing analytical system, has given the city a rational system to more reasonably operate its finances.

The new system ensures rational financial operations through the interlinking of three factors: time-horizon linkage between mid- and long-term projects and short-term ones, the linkage between projects and finance, and the linkage among the processes of operation such as planning, management, and evaluation. Under this system, financial demand and supply for mid- and long-term periods are projected in accordance with mid-term financial plans, and sector-by-sector investment amounts are determined on the investment priority order determined for the attainment of planning goals. Then, projects are selected and budgets allotted through investment studies and zero-base budgeting made from a short-term time-horizon approach. Lastly, the evaluations obtained through analysis are fed back to the planning stages.

Size of Finance

The objective of the city's financial programs is to promote the citizens' well-being to the utmost possible extent by using limited financial resources effectively. The budget amount of the 1985 fiscal year stood at 2,069.9 billion won, down 4.90 percent over 2,171.9 billion won of the 1984 fiscal year (U.S. $1.00 = 700 won at that time). Because tax sources remain limited, tax revenues are unable to meet the accelerating spending needs, causing many difficulties in financial operations.

Investment demands are ever increasing for the expansion of such urban infrastructure as transportation, housing, environmental controls, parks, piped water, and sewers. Besides, Seoul, like other large cities, is faced with various urban problems: the need to improve marketing facilities and environmental problems such as garbage disposal and pollution, to expand social welfare programs with an emphasis on subsistence care for low-income citizens, to bolster the administrative apparatus to cope with expanding administrative needs, and to raise funds to meet the increasing maintenance costs of expanded urban facilities.

Structure of Revenues and Expenditures

The major sources of revenues of the general account are municipal taxes and nontax revenues; most of the municipal tax revenues are from fixed properties acquisition tax, residents tax, registration tax, property tax, automobile tax, and city planning tax, while nontax revenues mostly comprise the proceeds from the sale of properties, workshop earnings, fees, contributions, and local bonds. In the 1985 municipal budget, municipal tax revenues were fixed at 656–688 billion won or 73.9 percent of the total revenues of the general account, while nontax revenues were set at 217.36 billion won or 24.5 percent of the total; the remaining 14.812 billion won or a mere 1.6 percent were due to be met with subsidies. Thus, the financial self-sufficiency of Seoul is as high as 98.4 percent.

Among the general account expenditures in 1985, general administration represented 21.3 percent, public utility projects encompassing various urban development and construction schemes 36.2 percent, and social welfare including health, environmental, and social care programs 16 percent.

Because special accounts mainly consist of special-purpose programs usually generating their own financing needs, which generally do not become a direct burden to the general public, it is sufficient to examine only the sources of revenue for general accounts of the city budget.

Seoul's municipal tax system is comprised primarily of property-related taxes; as in most countries, these are not dependable as ever-growing revenue sources. The largest group of taxes (acquisition plus registration) are those assessed on real estate transactions, which amounted to 43.9 percent in 1985. However, because this tax group relies on business transactions, it shows wide fluctuations depending on the general business trend of the nation. The next largest tax group (license, automobile, and property) represents 25.2 percent of the total revenue but has little elasticity.

Special Accounts

Under municipal decrees, special accounts have been established separate from the general account to execute special projects or manage special funds. They serve to better carry out urban development, environmental improvements, and welfare programs. The 1985 special accounts totaled 1,165.9 billion won, a decrease of 2.4 percent over the 1984 total.

As many interested and concerned professionals and students of finance and government have been advocating restructuring national budget systems to integrate all government financing into one total budget system and, at the same time, to separate the operating budget and the capital budget, I will not argue here the merits of special accounts. However, in spite of total size and obvious role, these special accounts are not fully understood; in fact, when we speak of the municipal budget they are usually not included. This is generally misleading to the public.

The nine special accounts are: national housing, housing improvement, land readjustment, sewage disposal plants, turnpikes, medical care, disaster relief, waterworks, and subways.

Need for Expanding Revenue Sources

Expanding the revenue sources of Seoul is one of the most challenging tasks facing the city's administration in the future. Of course, effective and efficient delivery of all public services has to be an important dimension of the urban administration's effort.

As administration and financing of the city are closely related with administration of the nation in structure and human resources, the problems that are encountered should be reviewed within the context of both national and local capacities.

First, a readjustment of the state and local tax structures is needed in order that they be compatible with the expanding role of local autonomy. Some of the state taxes have to be shifted over to local tax groups, as most of the current local taxes are usually weak or inelastic and do not produce revenue sufficient to meet the ever-increasing demands for more programs and services.

Second, expansion of the state subsidy is necessary. This guideline may seem contradictory as local administration becomes more self-sufficient, but in regard to Seoul it may well become a comforting source of revenue. As other local administrative units become stronger, relying less on the state and thus becoming more stable, there is a better chance of increased subsidy for Seoul. The city has no doubt been a very resourceful municipality while most of the other cities and localities have remained heavily dependent on the state. Therefore, Seoul's needs and the state projects in Seoul have not been proportionately rewarded by the state. This unnatural situation will change and the state's position may become easier as a result of a fairer allocation of financial resources.

Third, in addition to new tax resources a general strengthening of the existing revenue bases is necessary. The city can continuously help its residents to increase their wealth so that it can extract more from a more prosperous citizenry. At some later date, after the completion of a careful study, the city may have to impose on wage earners a fractional increase in the income tax that is already paid to the state. Also, nonresidents doing business in the city are levied a nonresident tax for benefits actually drawn and enjoyed in the city.

Furthermore, existing tax structures themselves have to be thoroughly overhauled, efficiency needs to be increased, and better scientific management of the revenue administration must be achieved. Even before the city talks about new taxes or a tax rate increase, the city administration should be able to identify all possible revenue sources within the current tax system. Once the sources are found and identified, appropriate taxes must be levied without exception and all need to be efficiently collected. In fact, trusted and professional management of the current city administration is the first task that must be accomplished.

Fourth, nontax revenue sources should be carefully studied and expanded. As urban development and renewal programs would bring many benefits to many individuals, they can be asked to return some of their gains through a kind of fee-and-charge system. The future of the city revenue sources has to depend more proportionately on nontax revenue. It may be desirable, for example, to maintain a 6:4 ratio between tax and nontax revenues.

Metropolitan Seoul Administration and Urban Development

Organization, Staffing, and Maintenance

The administration of Seoul is complex. Even though metropolitan Seoul spreads beyond the administrative boundary, the city administration remains focused on the municipality. Seoul is the capital of the Republic of Korea as well as the largest city in the country, with about one-fourth of the nation's total population in 1990, in spite of a determined and continuing government policy to restrain further growth and to disperse population to other regions. Therefore, in order to prepare for this, the administration of metropolitan Seoul should stop acting as a branch of the national government. On the contrary, because of its operational importance and access to the people, the city must inevitably assume an obligation to provide governmental leadership in dealing with local problems and in representing local interests before the national government.

Seoul is currently divided into seventeen administrative districts (*ku*) and these are again subdivided into over 426 blocks (*dong*), administrative units closest to the people. The administration of City Hall, as of December 1985, consisted of twenty-two bureaus and bureau-level offices, and seventy-four divisions under the overall direction of the mayor and vice mayor.

In addition, the city's board of education is separate and virtually independent from City Hall, except that the mayor is chairman of the board.

The human resource total in the city administration is around 55,000, a figure that includes police and public schoolteachers as well as all other municipal workers.

From the point of view of its organizational structure and number of administrative districts, the city administration has almost doubled in size during the last ten years. In 1970, there were only fourteen bureaus and bureau-level offices compared with twenty-two at present, and in that year there were only nine administrative districts compared with seventeen currently.

As far as the form of organization of the municipal administration is concerned, the city of Seoul is maintained with a strong tradition of line organization and modified with functional departmentalization. This line and functional organizational structure is rapidly becoming outmoded and has increasingly demonstrated its inadequacies under the contemporary conditions of dynamic urban environmental change. Functional organizations tend to emphasize the separate functional elements at the expense of the total organization and its goal. To meet contemporary requirements, the municipal organizations need to replace their old bureaucratic directive management orientation and structure with a philosophy, an organizational form, and managerial behavior that can meet the urban demands of modern society. Ideally speaking, the program management form may be one of the most suitable government structures. This is described as an approach to the management process that places emphasis on the organizational totality.

As far as the organization of City Hall is concerned, it may need a drastic reorganization to meet the challenge of the coming decades. The organization of the city administration is almost ineffectively large and no functional coordinative mechanism is installed. The result is that the city administration is not only unproductive and uncoordinated, but is also becoming too difficult for ordinary citizens to deal with.

As urban problems become more complex and demand experts' knowledge rather than that of traditional administrative generalists, the urban governments require various urban specialists. Recruitment of these necessitates improved and more appropriate selection procedures. At present, there are three different channels of recruitment for municipal workers: (1) a selection examination conducted by the local autonomous agency (special city or province) for positions below fourth-grade; (2) special recruitment by the local autonomous agency when it is deemed necessary; and (3) recruitment examinations conducted by the minister of general affairs, i.e., for third grade positions.

Although urban specialists are supposedly recruited through the first and second methods, planners and pollution specialists, for instance, are selected not by classification but merely through general recruitment procedures. There is certainly a need to improve this simple procedure. To recruit better qualified professionals and to promote a better professional personnel system, personnel should be divided into several groups, such as management, planning, environment, and health and welfare.

Strengthening of Institutional Capabilities

Four levels of governmental organizations may be distinguished in terms of their roles in urban planning and management processes. The first level is the central government and its constituent ministries through which urban legislation is instituted, development goals and policies are set, and project priorities are arbitrated. For instance, the Ministry of Construction (MOC) oversees and coordinates the urban planning activities of various provinces and municipalities through its policy-setting capacities and power of review and approval. The Urban Planning Bureau is an important link in this connection, as is the Central Urban Planning Committee attached to it. The Ministry of Home Affairs (MOHA) also plays a significant role, as it controls local administrative units. The Economic Planning Board (EPB) also has an important role by virtue of its budgeting function. Other ministries are involved within their respective areas of jurisdiction.

The second level is a group of national corporations, formally semiautonomous from the central government, which have the functions of executing and operating nationwide projects. The Korea National Housing Corporation (KNHC), the Korea Land Development Corporation (KLDC), and Industrial Site and Water Resources Development Corporation (ISWACO) are the primary corporations whose operations have direct bearings on local urban planning and development. Empowered by special legislation, such as the Housing Construction Promotion Law and the Land Development Promotion Law, their activities merge with those of municipal governments.

The third level consists of provinces and special cities under the direct supervision of the central government, i.e., the MOHA. Some of the central government's authorities are delegated to MOHA offices at this level. The provincial governors oversee and coordinate planning functions of cities and countries within their jurisdiction, while the mayors of the special cities formulate plans and implement them.

The fourth level consists of other cities and counties. The governments at this level are the actual organs through which plans and projects are formulated and implemented. Their autonomy is limited, however, for their proposals are subject to review and approval from higher echelons.

Frequently, coordination becomes a problem in both planning and implementation processes. These types of problems may be called intralevel, interlevel, and interfunctional conflicts, and lack of coordination. For example, coordination is often lacking between ministries concerned with urban development. Operating with different sectoral objectives, budget systems, and reference laws, ministries pursue disparate policy goals resulting in inconsistencies in development plans and projects. The economists at EPB tend to show little concern for locational aspects, while urban policies and programs lack sufficient coordination with the nation's macroeconomic plans. National budgeting on programming tends to be formed sectorally rather than spatially. Sectoral barriers sometimes form functional redundancies between ministries. These are particularly notable between the MOC and MOHA. The MOC has sectoral control over the municipalities' urban planning function, which the MOHA exercises a global supervisory power over the municipalities. To illustrate, it is within the jurisdiction of the MOC to supervise construction of water supply systems by the local governments. In 1983, however, the MOHA played this role for the construction of Asian Development Bank-financed water supply systems in seventeen cities. In addition, the Ministry of Health and Social Affairs (MOHSA) supervised the construction and management of water supply systems in small towns and rural villages. This type of sectoral overlap is often duplicated at the local government level as urban policies and project programming are carried out sectorally by an individual ministry, even down to organizations at the lower administrative levels.

Second, there is often a lack of coordination between vertical levels, i.e., between the central governments on the one hand and the local government on the other. Sometimes, inconsistencies are found between the urban development plans of the municipalities and the national development plans. Similarly, lack of coordination may be observed between municipal plans and projects undertaken by national corporations such as the KNHC. The special status of the promotion laws in relation to the Urban Planning Law breeds such inconsistencies.

Third, there are often functional inconsistencies in the implementation of urban projects. The fact that various functions are separately handled by various branches of government and that arbitration is not powerful enough make it difficult to integrate sectoral projects in an organized way. Lack of coordination is particularly visible in the development of new towns, large residential areas, industrial estates, and other large-scale construction projects where land acquisition and infrastructure installations are required.

The problems due to lack of coordination between the agencies are most acutely observed in such integrated development projects as the development of new towns. For example, the process of development of an industrial estate and new town nearby, Banwol (Ansan city), located 30 kilometers southwest of Seoul, involves several ministries and agencies at all levels.

Such a complicated institutional mechanism for the development of Banwol results in unbalanced progress in different development projects due to a lack of coordination between the agencies involved and, consequently, a significant delay in the whole development process. Factories moved out of Seoul, for instance, and began relocating to Banwol only to find inadequate dwellings for their employees or unaffordable prices for existing units. Because the construction of the electric railway linking Seoul and Banwol was considerably delayed, the KNHC and the ISWACO are suffering in terms of cost recovery in the Banwol development project. Under these circumstances, no private developers find it profitable to participate in the needed housing projects.

The Banwol New Town Development Promotion Committee, organized under the chairmanship of the deputy prime minister, has achieved a considerable breakthrough in resolving developmental bottlenecks. If this coordination committee is authorized not only to coordinate but also to regulate both vertical and horizontal relations among all the actors at all levels, and to intervene in the formulation of the overall development strategy, resource allocation program, and individual project evaluation, it will significantly improve the whole process of development.

The activities of the public authorities in urban development are divided into two categories: development control by planning, and direct participation in development as public developer. The prime activity of planning is development control. The authorities control urban development by regulating individual development and building activities according to predetermined urban development plans. It is a predominantly negative activity that, with the refusal of any application contradicting approved plans, ensures that urban development accords with what has already been considered appropriate.

Development control is primarily based on the zoning regulations and the building act. Zoning regulations, however, have limitations in directing urban development toward what is desired. They provide an overall guide for land use in a city at the macrolevel but do not respond to the particular needs of each area in the city. Actual building activities are controlled according to the building act, which regulates the use of each plot. Thus, there are no appropriate legal means to control the development of a whole area of land as an integrated land-use activity. Zoning regulations are basically two dimensional and thus inappropriate for controlling the three-dimensional aspects of urban development. They are also problematic for accommodating an increasingly diversified and complicated urban life, as by their nature they tend to spatially segregate different land uses.

In order to overcome the limitations of such negative legal instruments based on the zoning regulations, the government introduced various special laws including the Housing Construction Promotion Law, which enables planned unit development in an area. The present legal instruments for urban planning and development are thus characterized by a dual structure comprising general laws and special laws, which often become institutional obstacles to promoting balanced urban development.

Direct participation in urban development by the public authority includes both component projects such as construction and improvement of urban infrastructure and public services and integrated projects including land readjustment projects, housing estate development, and new town development. This direct state intervention in urban development is backed by the Land Expropriation Law, which allows the public developer to expropriate land to be developed in the public interest.

Enhancing Organizational Capacity

In order for any development project to respond more effectively to local needs and priorities, local governments must take the initiative in urban development. To do this, more power should be devolved to local governments while institutional organizations at the local level should be expanded and strengthened. Institutions need to be developed at all levels of government to maximize coordination between sectoral development agencies. Particularly, the institution should be established in such a way that a strong linkage among spatial planning, programming, and budgeting is ensured and economic, social, and physical aspects of any development projects are tied together.

Challenges for Urban Administration

Probably the biggest tasks confronting urban administration in the next decade will be to successfully deal with human problems. Seoul must satisfy ever-increasing demand for public facilities, public safety, and utility services. If it is to meet these challenges, the city needs continuous adjustment. It also needs to find more effective ways of doing the city's housekeeping functions so that limited resources can be directed to the basic task of developing human resources. In order to achieve this goal, the adjustments most frequently suggested include improved administrative planning and analysis, the use of systems development techniques, expanded and improved managerial staff activities, more and better personnel training programs, and intensified cooperation with other governmental agencies, as well as in the same unit in solving problems and providing services.

The following appropriate administrative environment can feasibly be established in the Republic of Korea. First, administrative centralism must gradually be abolished to encourage the new localism that is essential in guiding successful urban administration. Current demands for most local autonomy should not be labeled as political, but rather as administrative and technical demands that should be adopted to deal with complex urban issues. Local administration is slowly becoming urban administration. Various instruments have to be found to stimulate and effectuate increased interlocal relations.

Although urban administration goes beyond the present administrative boundary and there are needs for larger and broader coverage of areas and issues, these are still distinctively local concerns that are complex to deal with at the national level. Therefore, there is a greater need for strengthening local administration, which will naturally encourage resident participation and a responsive administrative milieu through the introduction of carefully framed local autonomy.

Conclusion

The modern city is increasingly only a part of a broader, ambiguous social framework that is not easy to manage.

Increased demands to provide human, as well as housekeeping, services, make metropolitan administration more complex. Governmental programs in urban regions must be more carefully and comprehensively designed so that they can tackle urban problems such as increasing resident tensions, traffic congestion, environmental pollution, housing shortages, juvenile delinquency, and official insensitivity to human problems. For all of these, there are obvious needs for good decision making, good planning, and thorough programming.

Unlike many Western nations where there are strong traditions of local autonomy resulting in government fragmentation, a country like the Republic of Korea has a different kind of problem in dealing with an expanding urban-life boundary. This is not a problem caused by strong local autonomy, but rather a problem of an overcentralized nation that cannot effectively solve local urban problems.

Therefore, a major problem of the metropolitan administration concerns the question of how to create and expand an effective and service-oriented administrative unit that is close enough to the residents to appreciate their problems. It is not only a problem of laws and regulations, but also of the correct perspective in effective dealings for adequate and appropriate decentralization of authority from the overly centralized national government down to the local government, particularly to the city and metropolitan government levels.

The urban policy issues can be broadly divided into two aspects. One is, with respect to national spatial development, the polarized urbanization of the Seoul and Pusan metropolitan regions. The other is the overall deterioration of the urban environment in the large cities due to overconcentration, in contrast to the other local cities which suffer from underdevelopment.

The first issue is closely related to balanced regional development, which has been a long-standing objective of national development since the early 1960s. As the result of the introduction of numerous policy measures, regional income disparities have tended to decrease, or at least become stabilized; the urban hierarchical system has become normalized; and industrial decentralization has been achieved to a certain extent.

However, it is also generally agreed that the effects of those policies were insufficient to ensure the attainment of the planned goal. In this respect, a few important issues have been raised, and new policy directions are being suggested. First, the concept of balanced regional development should be clearly defined in terms of both efficiency and equity. Second, policy measures have to be designed to go with, rather than against, natural trends and market forces. Third, in the selection of policy instruments, indirect incentives rather than direct controls or regulations should be emphasized. Fourth, regional consideration should be more explicitly integrated into the central government's planning and policies. Firth, better institutional arrangements need to be set up within the existing governmental structure. Frequently, there has been a lack of coordination among planning units and government implementing bodies. Conflicting interests exist among two or more government agencies without the possibility of resolution through established channels. The result has diminished the effectiveness of any implementing actions.

Particularly in the case of Seoul and neighboring Gyonggi Province, the establishment of a metropolitan government is deemed necessary. The spillover of industries and population, and subsequent economic and physical integration of Seoul and surrounding areas, makes the adoption of a more area-wide approach for service delivery inevitable. With this unified area-wide management, the formation of a vast unplanned, homogenous, sparsely built-up urban space could perhaps be avoided.

At the same time, the new policies should place additional emphasis on upgrading the citizens' quality of life. In the past, the aggregate economic growth of the nation as a whole was the primary concern of the national development policy. Consequently, a large proportion of investment went into the production side to an extent that improving the living conditions of the people was given low priority. However, in the future the demand for amenities is expected to increase with the continued growth of per capita gross national product. Therefore, more government resources should be allocated to the area of social development to meet the increasing needs for a better quality of life.

CHAPTER FIFTEEN

Decentralization and Implementation of Social Development at the Local Level in Korea

Dong Hyun Kim

IN RECENT YEARS we have been faced with demands for decentralization and local self-government in Korea. The pressure for decentralization may be viewed as an indication of the irresponsibility, unresponsiveness, unrepresentativeness, and lack of citizen's participation in the highly centralized government. It is also a reflection of the changing consciousness of the Korean people toward the government and administration. Thus, the Korean government is trying to make fuller use of local authorities and other forms of decentralization involving participation of the people in the administration of services required locally for social and economic development. Many scholars argue that decentralization is an effective way to strengthen local government, but in some countries initial attempts at decentralization have actually weakened local government. We see that cooperation between central and local government is certainly a key ingredient of successful development, but that it must be focused on long-range plans for improvement and on definite targets for generating revenue, managing personnel, and assigning functional responsibilities. Thus, improvement plans should be comprehensive, but their implementation should be incremental.

Decentralization and Social Development Planning at the Local Level

Government leaders in Korea have become increasingly aware of the close relationship between political and administrative organization and the pace

Taken from Dong Hyun Kim, "Decentralization and Implementation of Social Development at the Local Level in Korea," paper presented to the Joint International Seminar on Local Self-Government, Seoul, December 1987.

and direction of social and economic progress. Administrative capacity is now seen as one of the critical factors influencing the achievement of societal goals, and the government has increasingly tried to bring about social change by reforming administrative and organizational structures.

The Korean government has come to play the dominant role in economic and social development. Since the 1960s, the control of central government over national economics has substantially increased. It is no longer restricted to maintaining law and order or collecting revenues. The government imposed policies on all sectors and attempted to mobilize the resources necessary to implement them. It took the initiative in stimulating private investment, in promoting agricultural and industrial modernization, in providing a wide range of health, education, and social welfare services, and in directing the course of economic development. The expansion of the government's role in economic and social development has also created the need for new administrative structures to plan and implement long-range development policies.

Since the 1960s, Korean governments opted for a highly centralized system of economic planning because the capital-intensive industrialization strategies adopted by these governments required strong intervention by the national government in investment and production processes. During the Five-Year Development Plan, central planning was introduced in order to promote rapid growth in industrial output, mobilize capital for further investment, generate employment, and accelerate social and political change. It was believed that the benefits accruing from industrial investment would "trickle down" to reduce poverty and increase income and savings, and would then be reinvested to further expand production and employment.

Central planning failed, however, for a variety of reasons. Equity-oriented development programs sponsored by the central government could not be successfully implemented in part because of the lack of organization among beneficiaries. Mobilization of human and financial support for national plans proved to be more difficult than anticipated. Government agencies and ministries failed to coordinate their activities and interministerial rivalries led to conflicts during plan implementation. Efficiency in resource allocation and investment could not be achieved in administrative systems characterized by red tape, parochialism, and politically motivated recruitment and promotion. As a result, plans formulated by professional and technical elites in central planning agencies could not be fully implemented, and when they were carried out, they often produced adverse results.

Since the 1980s, the direction and priorities of development policy have shifted significantly. Planners and policymakers began to recognize the need to transform social, economic, and political structures in ways that would enable the poor to increase their productivity and incomes. Growth-with-equity policies were increasingly adopted to provide for the basic needs of the poor, to reduce interregional and rural-urban economic disparities, to provide greater access to government facilities and services for disadvantaged groups, and to elicit greater popular participation in economic, social, and political processes.

The emergence of growth-with-equity goals in the development strategies during the 1980s created the demand for new organizational structures to plan and implement equitable growth policies. Central planning is no longer considered to be the most effective means of promoting rural development and alleviating widespread poverty. Human and material resources have to be mobilized through administrative structures and planning procedures that are more decentralized. Greater responsibility for development management has to be devolved to the local level. Voluntary organizations have to be strengthened to elicit popular participation. The rigid controls often imposed by central planning agencies and ministries have to be made flexible and adaptive for identifying local priorities, designing and implementing local development projects, and safeguarding the interests of the local communities.

One of the common lessons is that centralized planning simply could not effectively achieve many of the objectives of growth-with-equity policies. Indeed, we need a concept of bottom-up planning and decentralized administration.

Social development planning in Korea seems to be a mix of a heavy top-down approach with a slight—almost nonexistent—bottom-up one. In other words, the central planning agency tends to draw up the objective functions of social development planning as basic guidelines. Implementing ministries and agencies then draft and submit project proposals along these guidelines. Through repetitive interaction between these two processes, a mutually acceptable agreement is reached, particularly at the national level, for the final commitment in term of resource allocation. There are no planning linkages at the central level for social development programs. Because macrolevel planning of social development programs at the Economic Planning Board (EPB) is simply a consolidation of budgetary resources for social development, the specific and effective linkages necessary for mutual reinforcement and adjustment between projects are lacking.

It is difficult to generalize the degree of effective community participation in the planning and implementation of social development projects. If the gestation period of the project is long, the propensity for participation tends to be low. If the results of a project are intangible and invisible, community participation is also low. If a project is undertaken in a rural area, however, community participation is more likely than it is in an urban area. Furthermore, community participation in general is more intensive where government inducement and intervention are strong.

Whereas the planning of social development programs and projects takes place primarily at the central level, the implementation of projects is the responsibility of the local government and regional branch offices. Because the Korean bureaucratic subculture is characterized by uniformity in administration under central direction, and also because effective local autonomy is not yet institutionalized, the development of social development projects at the local level is extremely limited. This holds true even for the budgetary process because, in practice, budgeting at the local level tends to be simply a listing of projects and consolidation of funds for accounting purposes.

Role of Local Government in Social Development

To what extent has local government contributed to the planning and implementation of social development projects at the community level in Korea? Historically, the central government has played the predominant role in the management of social development projects because the majority of material, financial, and human resources were provided by the central government. In addition, the central government has traditionally exercised strong control over local government action. However, the role of local governments is still significant, because they have contributed to defining the scope and nature of social development projects at the community level, as well as to their achievements.

In pursuit of this inquiry, let us briefly describe the involvement of local administration in the planning and implementation of social development projects.

Government Intervention

Social development issues are primarily private concerns because such basic needs as preschool education, nutrition, health improvement, fertility control, the spacing of children, and the quality of life are supposed to be met by individuals relying on their own judgment and personal resources. However, at least a certain level of government intervention in meeting the basic needs of low-income groups seems to be inevitable, particularly in a developing country like Korea, where social development in general lags behind the economic growth of the country.

In Korea, government intervention takes various forms including emergency measures, public assistance programs, routine administrative services, and social development projects. In organizing and implementing social development projects, government tends to encourage private initiatives, self-help, maximum community participation, and on occasion, enforces resource mobilization and popular participation. Because the government has authority and power on the one hand and resources including professional expertise on the other, it has played a critical role in social development. The local government serves in the following capacities:

1. the educator who makes community people aware of the importance of certain needs, the availability of ways and means, and also the desirability of popular behavior and attitudes;
2. the experimenter who takes risks to introduce new ideas for solving social development problems;
3. the innovator who demonstrates better approaches to meeting the basic needs of the underprivileged; and
4. the organizer who mobilizes popular contributions, channels, and public resources, and induces people to participate in local projects for the benefit of the community.

The extent of government intervention in social development at the community level can be measured in terms of the following three categories: (1) financial commitment of local government in budgetary terms, (2) the number of government officials appointed to manage social projects at the community level, and (3) the organizational arrangements for the planning and implementation of social development projects.

Local Agents and Innovation Adopters

Because the central government has traditionally controlled most of the public resources in Korea, most social development projects are planned by the central government, although they are implemented at the local level with the financial and technical support of the central authorities. In both the experimentation stage and the nationwide dissemination of a new project, local government undoubtedly plays a critical role. Local governments are the agents of the central government on the one hand and the innovation adopters on the other.

Beyond this role, local governments sometimes carry out new ideas on their own account that the central government is later persuaded to adopt. Under a centralized bureaucracy, it is difficult to expect local government to have a creative and innovative attitude toward new approaches to social welfare services and social development. However, local governments have recently been encouraged to undertake innovative projects, particularly in pursuit of the *Saemaul* movement. This is being demonstrated through UNICEF-supported projects that rely on close coordination with local governments.

Organization and Leadership at the Project Level

To what extent do local governments contribute to effective organization and leadership at the project level? In the case of the national projects such as the family planning program and the *Saemaul* movement, the local governments' most critical role is planning and organizing local resources and energy and fostering project leadership at the community level. Local governments have fostered the institutionalization of family planning clinic services and public information and education services through the government network, namely public health centers and sub-centers, while encouraging the organization of family planning associations in each county or city and mothers' clubs in each village.

Through the organization of these two nationwide projects, local governments have fully realized the importance of project leadership. Since then, local governments have taken greater initiative in fostering professional expertise, managerial competence, and the personal leadership traits of project managers, by arranging a series of intensive training programs and by taking advantage of the assistance of well-known research institutions. These institutions have been very successful at managing the pilot projects needed to develop broader programs.

Efficient Delivery of Social Services

The successful implementation of social development projects requires efficient delivery of needed services and material supplies to the project sites and client groups. Even with efficient organization, the leadership of the project implementing agency, and the strong support of community people, the project will succeed only if the necessary materials and services are available on time at the right place.

The managerial capacity of local government is another dimension of the effectiveness of the development support administration. The managerial competence of senior officials in planning service delivery, communicating and coordinating programs, and monitoring work performance was improved through extensive management training during the 1960s and 1970s.

Local governments in Korea play three significant roles in the delivery of services and support assistance. They are (1) a planning role, (2) a coordinating role, and (3) a monitoring role.

Most developing countries tend to fall into the so-called "assuming that" syndrome. This error is expressed by the view that projects should be implemented on schedule and in the way originally conceived in the minds of its designers: *assuming that* the implementing staff is appropriately trained; *assuming that* the beneficiaries of the project will recognize the utility of the project and be motivated to follow the project staff's suggestions; *assuming that* the national budgeting and auditing process will function expeditiously and funds will always be disbursed on a timely basis; and *assuming that* the governmental participants and agency actors involved in the development project will all have the same agenda, the same set of goals, and a willingness to cooperate. The tragedy of this "assuming that" approach to social development projects is the tendency to minimize, and often to ignore, the realities of the political, social, and cultural world in which the proposed social development project is to be carried out. The Korean experience in the implementation of social development projects suggests that project failure is often attributed to the technical incompetence of the project leadership and insensitivity to the political, social, and cultural realities of the project's environment. Hence, local government in Korea has made consistent efforts to overcome the "assuming that" syndrome by paying attention to the importance of these conditions.

Changes in Behaviors and Attitudes of People

In spite of a high level of popular motivation to improve the quality of life, the citizenry often does not receive the guidance needed for social welfare projects. Because they are different from economic growth and other development projects, social development issues are often not understood among the people in general because the benefits of social development projects are usually of longer term and less visibility than those of other modernization goals.

Hence, the level of popular awareness of critical issues tends to be low, and the attitudes toward social development projects are sometimes unfavorable, leading to a less than ideal individual willingness to allocate time and resources to these projects. Therefore, it is important to increase popular awareness of the priority issues and to encourage favorable attitudes toward social development projects. This aspect of social development project management is one of the critical prerequisites for promoting the popular self-help effort through participation in community development projects.

Encouraging Community Participation

The success of social development projects undoubtedly depends on extensive popular participation in the projects, not only because government resources tend to be limited in developing countries, but also because the eventual success of social development projects depends on the accessibility to the project's benefits. This accessibility is closely related to the level of popular motivation on the one hand and to the extent of popular participation on the other.

Local governments tend to play a significant role in mobilizing the people to participate in development activities. Indeed, the political system determines how and to what extent the government mobilizes human and material resources. In Korea, the voluntary participation of the people in social development projects has been limited because of the low levels of motivation and awareness of project benefits on the part of the people. Therefore, in the initial stages of the family planning program and the *Saemaul* movement, local governments, as agents of the central government, were forced to mobilize the people's energy and resources through a form of induced participation by providing various incentives and disincentives.

Local governments were in charge of providing material assistance in the form of cement and steel to each rural village at the inception of the *Saemaul* movement. The subsequent participation of community people was a response to this inducement. The government offer of this material assistance without any strings attached served as a challenge to previously static communities, creating crises of identity, leadership, participation, and management all at once for the village. The painful and protracted process of decision making at the village level induced wider participation among community members. Since then, the village general assembly has become a major channel of popular participation, decision making, and consensus building on major communal issues. The principle that "the better village should receive the first support" has served as an incentive to villages. The citations and special awards given through local government to outstanding villages and individual workers have also stimulated popular participation.

A series of organizational reforms to promote popular participation was introduced through local government. These included encouragement of the formation of community (or village) development councils (CDC) and support for consultative councils such as the *Saemaul* consultative committees, for each administrative level, as well as for a number of local consultative committees initiated by local government to maximize the input of community leaders and neighborhood goverment organizations (NGOs) in the major decisions involving social development issues. Local governments have also been extensively involved in IEC activities to motivate popular participation in government-initiated social development projects.

In sum, although local autonomy is limited under the centralized bureaucratic system, local governments in Korea do play extensive roles in the planning and implementation of social development projects, including the family planning program, primary health care services, the *Saemaul* community development movement, preschool education, the nutritional improvement project, and other child-oriented social development projects. As the success of these projects depends on the positive response and active participation of community people in these innovative projects, the first role of local governments has been to be the organizers and adoptors of innovative projects, to be institution builders for participatory organization at the community level, and to be promoters of community-based leadership. Local governments have also been educators engaging in extensive information, education, and communication (IEC) activities in order to motivate and stimulate people. In addition, the incentive scheme has encouraged popular participation based on private initiative and the commitment of individual resources.

Because local governments are presently suffering from a lack of autonomy, a shortage of local resources, and an insufficient commitment of quality human resources, the extent of intervention as well as the level of commitment by local government is still limited. Nevertheless, the roles played by local government in managing social development projects have tended to be effective and efficient, and have had a significant impact. In this respect, the Korean experience is a worthwhile example for other developing countries.

Implementation Strategy for Decentralization of Local Social Development

The Korean government is trying to decentralize development planning and management responsibilities, not only because political groups seeking greater regional and local autonomy continue to bring pressure on them, but also because they have discovered that the overconcentration of decision making and management responsibilities at the center can lead to inefficiencies and delays in carrying out centrally conceived development plans.

Strategies for implementing decentralization policies should attempt to maximize the impact of support factors yet, at the same time, anticipate and overcome constraints. Considering the Korean situation, four basic strategies for the implementation of local social development plans and projects can be identified.

Community-based Strategy

The community-based strategy involves active participation and involvement of villagers in the promotion of community development, primary health care, nonformal education, family planning, nutrition programs, and the status of women, among others. The three major objectives of this strategy are: (1) to foster the spiritual enlightenment of rural people in regard to development-oriented values, such as diligence, self-help, cooperation, and participation; (2) to integrate activities to serve the people in each respective area or community; and (3) to increase people's convenience and access to the services offered by the government in the villages.

The success of this strategy in implementation depends upon the maintenance of a high level of popular participation in local development activities. Unless individual participation is channeled into action for collective organization, it will have little real impact upon the community development process. Therefore, a thorough analysis of participation requires close examination of factors promoting participation at the individual as well as the organizational levels. Conceptually, there are two different approaches to the initiation of community participation: the top-down approach, in which the government acts as the initial motivator of participation in community development; and the bottom-up approach, in which people voluntarily participate in community activities. In addition, four major factors impact upon community participation in local social development: (1) individual motivation; (2) the role of leadership in responding to people's needs and in providing support for development projects; (3) the development of grass-roots organizations that can accommodate individual motivation at the community level and properly aggregate and articulate community interests; and (4) government mobilization of both human and other resources for community change and regional development.

Positive improvements in each of these four areas are highly correlated with greater levels of participation in community development. Thus, it is important to examine both how and to what extent these four factors influence popular participation in community development.

Integrated Multisectoral Strategy

The integrated multisectoral strategy refers to the concentrated, coordinated, and integrated efforts of a multitude of government and nongovernmental agencies from various sectors to develop a certain area at the local level. The area is selected on the basis of need identification and prioritization, taking into account the scarcity of resources available for development at the national level. The objective is to reduce poverty and substantial economic disparity between and within regions. Such a strategy is often considered more effective and efficient (or cost-effective), given the limited human and other resources and the urgency to correct imbalances in socioeconomic development along regional, rural-urban lines. The limitation of the scale and scope of the projects on the specific focus area is advantageous, as it facilitates management, monitoring, and goal attainment.

However, the successful implementation of such a strategy is dependent on a number of factors, including: (1) an adequate and efficient information system between and within the various government agencies of the different sectors and the client system or targeted population within the chosen area; (2) vertical as well as horizontal integration of development efforts to synchronize goals, activities, monitoring, and evaluation; (3) adequate knowledge, training, and skills among change agents as well as village elite (leaders), who act as the catalysts for achieving implementation; (4) stability of personnel within the change agent system so as to maintain continuity and to facilitate accountability, monitoring, and evaluation; and (5) the legitimization of village leaders and their cooperation in participating in and implementing specific activities and targeted goals (i.e., to ensure mutuality of interests, goals, and priorities between change agents and clients).

NGO Involvement in Local Social Development Strategy

The strategy or approach used by NGOs in implementing social development projects is to involve the people in the community to fully participate in all stages of implementation. A traditional cooperative working group, such as a neighborhood, will be mobilized for such purpose. In a situation where local government authorities have to be acknowledged before local development projects can be launched, the NGOs must get approval from the government agency concerned. The government authority, in turn, may assign the NGO to work in the project or area that has not yet been covered by the government. However, once the project or area has been approved, the NGO can usually organize and run the project with the least interference from the government.

In the implementation of local social development projects by the NGO, therefore, the people within the community, led by the traditional or informal leaders, like a senior household head within the neighborhood or a teacher, will be the prime movers in implementing the project. By getting the community people involved in identifying problems and implementing the projects, the people will be responsible for the projects that they have initiated. This will lead to the continuous maintenance and operation of the development projects by moving the community's own resources.

In implementing the development projects, however, NGOs encounter the following problems and constraints: (1) in spite of the government's efforts to bring development projects into the rural village communities, security and political stability are also major concerns of the government; (2) with limited financial resources and personnel, NGOs can deal only with certain local problems and needs, thereby involving only a sector of the community population—implementation of local development projects by the NGOs is sectoral, with short-lived, less comprehensive perspectives; (3) lack of coordination and cooperation with other NGOs and government agencies in some areas also obstructs NGO project implementation.

Despite these problems and constraints, there are attempts on the part of NGOs as well as the government itself to seek coordination and cooperation between themselves in their efforts to bringing social and economic development to rural communities. At the provincial or other lower levels, the NGO's development workers may become members of the provincial or subdistrict council so that they will be formally recognized by the government; they are therefore able to participate in the implementation of local social development projects with the full cooperation of the government and other NGOs in the area.

Charity Strategy vs. Centrally Triggered Local Resources Mobilization Strategy

The charity strategy of implementation is one whereby all resources deemed necessary for implementing development plans at the local level are provided by the central government. The centrally triggered local resource mobilization strategy of implementation is one whereby central-upper governmental levels allocate their resources to the locality in such a way as to generate resource mobilization—be it monetary, manpower, time, materials, and other contributions by the community—at the local level. The charity strategy of implementation will undoubtedly speed up the development process at the grass-roots level. However, the strategy is by no means educational. The dynamics of development at the local level will end whenever the resource allocation from the top is terminated. Besides, it tends to increase village dependency on central-upper levels of government. Centrally triggered local resource mobilization is more education oriented. It leads to community participation through the identification of their idle capacity and potentiality and the mobilization of local resources. It will stimulate the self-sustaining capacity of the people and prevent them from becoming too dependent on outside resources.

Generally, the charity strategy is suitable for a situation in which central resources are abundant and idle local resources are nonexistent. It can be applied differently in many parts of the country on the basis of the assessment of the potential local resources. In contrast, centrally triggered resource mobilization is suitable for situations in which there is idle capacity at the grass-roots level, central resources are scarce, and the goal of development is aimed at self-sustenance, self-reliance, and capacity building.

Conclusions and Implications

Decentralization is not a "quick fix" for the administrative, political, or economic problems of developing countries. Its application does not automatically overcome shortages of skilled personnel; in fact, it initially creates greater demand for them. Its application does not, of itself, guarantee that larger amounts of resources will be generated at the local level. At first decentralization may be more costly, simply because it encourages more groups, communities, and levels of administration to undertake development activities. Although decentralization has been modestly successful in a number of countries, an analysis of recent experiences does not establish definitively that reorganization was the only factor that increased production or improved administration.

In general, however, decentralization has contributed to strengthening the planning and management capacities of local and regional organizations. Through these programs, agricultural inputs and social welfare services have been provided to rural areas and infrastructure has been improved. The implementation of these programs has led to an increased awareness of the need for decentralization of authority and responsibility to local and regional levels. Yet the access of the rural poor to government facilities and services has not significantly improved. Social development programs in Korea are limited in scope and have been allocated only a small percentage of local development expenditure.

Future prospects for decentralization in Korea depend on the reorientation of the development concept. Development is largely conceived as the process of *economic* development. Other kinds of development, such as political, administrative, and social, are instrumental to economic development, and their further development will be the byproducts of economic achievement. The economists' view of development has many inherent shortcomings. Economists and rational planners generally underestimate the particular needs and implementation issues of local situations. Their developmental plans often tend to be unrealistic target-setting exercises, to be accomplished by the provincial and county officials. They also neglect the availability of regional resources and the psychological commitment of the local people. To understand the value of decentralization and its democratic process, the conception of development must be broadened; this step requires broad-based knowledge that can be contributed by students of political science, public administration, sociology, and other disciplines.

As Korea is rapidly transformed into an industrial state, heightening conflict and uncertainty cannot be managed through the centralized structure of government and administration. The central government must be decentralized. It is a colossal mistake to continue to regard local administration as an extension of the central government in a society consisting of over 40 million people. Local citizens as well as public servants must be participants in the creation of a democratic society. Furthermore, the desire for democratic governance must be the duty of responsible citizens. Through active participation they can learn to be responsible as well as to solve the problems and needs of their community. The greater task for policy makers is to create the conditions under which participation and representation can occur.

Lessons from an analysis of the recent experiences among developing countries make clear the policy implications that remain to be considered for Korea in the coming decade.

1. A high level of planning and management capacity in local and regional organizations is a prerequisite for the successful implementation of government policies and programs aimed at rural transformation. Local capacity building should therefore be the main focus of future administrative reform.

2. In order to strengthen local capacity to plan and implement projects, central government should (a) transfer adequate authority to local organizations to carry out their responsibilities; (b) give greater control over local resources to decentralized units; (c) provide qualified personnel at the local level; and (d) provide strong training and technical support.

3. A relatively long period of time is required before the positive results of decentralization can be seen. Therefore, planning for decentralization and the strengthening of local and regional capacities should be done on a long-term basis. Continuity in policies and programs is needed to build on existing foundations.

4. Decentralization policies and programs should focus on promoting small-scale rural development projects. Rural people are more likely to participate if the projects directly affect them or their communities and if they are assured of receiving the benefits of those generated by them.

5. Successful implementation of decentralization policies requires financial, administrative, and political support by the central government. The roles of central, regional, and local organizations in implementing decentralization programs will, of course, vary. But the major concern of central agencies should always be to support and assist rather than to control and direct.

6. The linkages between central government and local organizations in implementing decentralization should be facilitative rather than control oriented. There are many ways in which central government agencies can provide assistance to weak local administration: by providing training; by seconding personnel from central agencies to meet pressing staff shortages at the local level; by supervising and assessing local projects and providing technical assistance when problems or weaknesses appear; and by evaluating the performance and impact of programs and projects. The identification, design, and implementation of projects should be the responsibility of local or regional organizations.

7. Training is an important determinant of the success of decentralization. Decentralization requires new attitudes and behavior on the part of central officials and clear understanding of roles of implementing agencies at each level. These new behavior patterns can be created only through appropriate training programs aimed at reorienting government officials at various levels about their new roles and activities.

8. Attempts should be made to strengthen the role of voluntary organization in the local development process. The government can contribute by distributing some services and inputs such as subsidized fertilizers through them; encouraging the creation of new organizations and small groups of the rural poor; allowing some degree of conflict—which is usually generated by these organizations; and giving high priority to issues such as security of land tenure, landlessness, and productivity of small holdings.

9. The objectives of decentralization programs should be clearly stated. Attempts should be made to involve relevant implementing agencies in clarifying these objectives in the planning stages.

10. Decentralization policies planned on a small scale but expanded incrementally lead to more positive results. Drastic changes in powers and responsibilities are often resisted by administrators in central agencies and other groups who might lose some of their authority. Small programs, on the other hand, demand fewer resources and post little threat to established bureaucracies.

In sum, a decentralization program is more likely to succeed if it is small in scope, has a long period of time in which to prove itself, centers around specific financial functions, transfers responsibilities and authority incrementally, and includes a training component. The larger the number of these features, the better are the chances that staff activity and productivity will increase, that citizen participation in government activities will expand and be meaningful, that the planned goals of projects will be more rapidly and economically achieved, and that meaningful development will occur.

PART
VII

*Public Administration
Education in Korea*

CHAPTER SIXTEEN

Educational Policy Changes in Korea: Ideology and Praxis

Shin Bok Kim

WHEN KOREA ACHIEVED independence from Japanese colonial rule in 1945, her first task was to wipe out the remaining vestiges of Japanese totalitarianism and to recover her submerged national identity. Education policies in the latter half of the 1940s put emphasis on realizing the fundamental ideas of democracy and nationalism. The ultimate idea of education was expressed by the phrase *Hong-ik-in-gan*, which means "benefits for all mankind." This spirit of humanism was an ancient and popular notion and had been a guiding philosophy in Korea for many centuries. Education was seen as a means of communicating and furthering Korean nationalist values based on the traditional ideas of human cooperation and mutual prosperity. To achieve this, the goals and contents of educational policy were completely revised to reflect the democratic values of equality, individual autonomy, and fair access to opportunity and advancement. A single-track school system was adopted that encouraged public access to, and opportunity in, the education system, and the 1949 Constitution declared that "All people have the right to education." Primary education was made compulsory and paid for from public funds.

Most people believe that much discrepancy existed between policy statements and practice. One example is that free elementary education was not completely realized until the 1970s. The Korean government and prominent political leaders stressed the need for strengthening nationalism through education. Accordingly, Korean language and history were given heavy weight in the curriculum. In the 1950s anticommunism took top priority. The Student Defense Corps (*Hakdo Hokook Dan*) was organized throughout the country in both secondary and higher education levels. The corps engaged in indoctrination and institutionalized student activi-

Taken from Shin Bok Kim, "Educational Policy Changes in Korea: Ideology and Praxis," paper presented to the third International Conference on Planning and Development in Rapid Changing Societies, University of Maryland, College Park, June 1989.

ties under government supervision until it was transformed into new student associations in the early 1980s. Students were made to believe that national identity based on anticommunism was most important for political stability and national development. The students were indoctrinated to the notion that their private interests and aspirations were linked to national economic development and the prevention of possible invasion from North Korea.

It is in this political context that we should consider the 1968 proclamation of the Charter of National Education. The charter was prepared with the wide participation of the public as well as executive and legislative branches of the government. Its significance arises from its embodiment of Korean national ethic and spirit. The charter states, "We have been born into this land, charged with the historic mission of regenerating the nation. The love of country and fellow countrymen, together with the firm belief in democracy against communism, is the way for our survival and the basis for realizing the ideals of the free world." Here education was viewed as an instrument for national development.

In the 1950s, after the Korean War, a pragmatic education policy that emphasized industrial and technical education under the slogan of "one skill for one person" was very appealing in the face of the urgent need to reconstruct the economy. This instrumental view toward education became more conspicuous after the 1960s. The government frequently adopted "education for economic development" or "national building through education" as one of the major educational goals in annual policy statements by the president or minister of education. Thus, the ideology of "development education" was put into practice with concrete policy measures. This was reflected in the curriculum and in decisions regarding student admission quotas for colleges and vocational schools. The Ministry of Education was guided by the proposals of the Economic Planning Board (EPB) specifically on the basis of manpower development plans.

In reality, though the government promoted education as fundamentally contributing the economic development, major trends have not been toward skill acquisition and developmental values so much as toward the identification of students with the future of Korea as a corporate state. Korean education seems to have played a greater role in national political integration than in the development of skills and individual creativity.

Student Selection

The burning desire of Koreans for education resulted in overheated competition to enter the most prestigious secondary schools. Primary schools focused on drills in subject matter contained in examinations. They emphasized rote learning and memorization in classroom instruction. Extracurricular activities were given little attention. Students were emotionally distressed by the strain of intensive competition and numerous extra lessons that financially crippled many parents.

To reduce overheated competition for entering middle-level schools and to normalize primary education, the government adopted the "No Examination System for Middle School Admission" policy in 1968, under which students were allocated to schools within a school district by computer lottery. The reform restored to primary education its original function and normal operation of the curriculum, but it invited excessive competition for high school entrance. To cope with this, the government again launched a "Temporary Lottery and Allocation System for Screening High School Applicants" policy in 1973. Prior to this measure, each high school developed and administered its own entrance examination and selected students on the basis of test results. Today, in twenty large cities, all students take a qualifying examination given by the provincial Board of Education and those who pass are assigned by lottery to the district's high schools.

From an egalitarian viewpoint, the system of allocating students by lottery was highly commendable. It eliminated the gap between schools and provided equal opportunity to students. It also saved children from the "examination hell" and restored to normal educational practices at the lower levels. In fact, the number of repeaters was markedly reduced and student health improved. On the other hand, the new entrance system brought students with heterogeneous backgrounds into the same classrooms and thus lowered the effectiveness of instruction. The enforcement of equal opportunity submerged the islands of excellence in a sea of mediocrity. It limited student choice of school. It undermined the autonomy of private schools and stymied their efforts to promote their own education programs.

During the First and Second Republics (1948–1960), individual universities and colleges enjoyed the right of independent student selection, employing their own criteria and examinations. This system gave rise to injustice and corruption. In 1962 the military regime introduced a national qualifying examination for college entrance, but it was abandoned after two years because it had been implemented without adequate preparation. Autonomy was again granted to each higher education institution, which led to public criticism of the corrupt selection practices of some private universities.

In 1968 the Ministry of Education again decided to institute a preliminary college entrance examination system for the dual purposes of preventing unqualified applicants from entering colleges and of restraining unfair selection. Students who passed that examination had to then take another examination administered by the respective universities and colleges. As the government strictly controlled the student selection process and admission quotas, more severe competition for college entrance resulted. Excessive private tutoring caused social problems. The health of many students deteriorated. Regular education at school was not duly respected. Many families faced bankruptcy because of high tutoring expenses.

In 1980, the government changed the Preliminary Examination into the Scholastic Achievement Examination for College Entrance and abolished entrance examinations by individual institutions. The new system assigned 30–50 percent weight to the scholastic records of senior high school students. The students could apply for admission to individual universities after they received the results of the examination and school records. Simultaneously, the government imposed heavy penalties on private tutoring. The new system contributed to the normalization of high school education and provided applicants with decisive information. On the other hand, the system was criticized for ignoring the autonomy of individual universities in selecting students and for relying heavily on a national written test that had a leveling effect on educational aspirations.

Recently the Ministry of Education has modified the style of the Scholastic Achievement Examination and the process of application for college entrance. The modified system features the inclusion of subject test items. High school graduates must apply to the departments that they wish to enter before taking the examination. Individual universities are thereby given more autonomy in selection.

Access to and Conditions of Education

The government has maintained an open-door philosophy in education since national independence in 1945 through at least two conspicuous policies. One has been to encourage private schools. Because of the financial limits of government, public schools have been unable to meet public demand for education. Private schools have had to fill the gap. Furthermore, land reform has induced many landowners to invest in educational institutions to gratify both personal honor and economic interests. The other policy has been compulsory primary education. By 1959, 96 percent of school-age children were enrolled in elementary schools.

The rapid expansion of education was probably the most conspicuous feature of the 1960s. This rapid increase of students at all levels brought about a deterioration in school conditions marked by a shortage of accommodation facilities, unfavorable pupil/teacher ratios, and low per-pupil public expenditures. As public financial support was low in contrast with many others developing countries, it was maintained that the public education system of Korea was more cost-effective and that Korea had chosen to emphasize quantity rather than quality, especially at the lower levels of the system. Most public resources were used for improving compulsory primary education. High social demand for education at secondary and tertiary levels, coupled with the governmental inability or unwillingness to provide educational resources, resulted in a heavy parental burden to finance public education and in the development of a large private school system.

In the latter half of the 1970s, the government reduced the quotas of entrants to four-year colleges and universities in order to improve the quality of higher education and to balance the supply and demand of high-level personnel. Consequently, competition for entrance to universities became intense, and the situation again demanded a return to the previous open-door policy in higher education. One key element of education reform in 1980 was the "Graduation Quota Policy." In addition to a considerable increase in admission quotas, four-year colleges could admit 30 percent more students providing that the proportion was eliminated by graduation. This policy resulted in an unprecedented increase of college students and a great expansion of opportunities for higher education in the early 1980s. Since then, the ratio of enrollment in higher education against the school-age population in Korea has exceeded most Western developed countries except the United States.

The sudden increase in college students was naturally accompanied by difficulties in securing proper facilities. For instance, the number of faculty members did not increase in proportion to the student population; as a result, the overall student–professor ratio in higher education institutions went from 28.8:1 in 1980 to 39.7:1 in 1987. Presidential decrees have set minimum requirements for teaching staffs and faculties, but most schools have not met the requirements and the universities are no exception. In the early 1980s, the government mitigated these legal requirements intentionally to facilitate the accommodation of the enormously increased numbers of students. Thus it can be said that the 1980 reform has had an adverse effect on the quality of higher education.

In a broader sense, college education still limits equal opportunity. To address this, the government has put into force a series of policies for equalizing educational opportunities in a broader sense, especially between Seoul and the provincial areas. For example, the government has provided special subsidies to foster provincial colleges and universities. In addition, the higher education institutions in metropolitan areas have restrained from increasing their quotas of student enrollment. The Ministry of Education has also supported a professor-exchange program between Seoul and provincial areas. Despite these policies, however, interprovince gaps have existed in terms of the ratio between high school graduates and college entrants. In addition, interarea and interschool gaps in educational conditions have not narrowed; they have resulted in qualitative disparities between schools and in severe competition for entrance to the top-ranked universities in Seoul.

Contents and Methods of Education

What is included in the curriculum greatly influences the kind of person produced by the educational process, and how the learning experiences are organized determines the effectiveness of instruction. During the past several decades there has been little change in the centralized operational study of the standardized curricula at the national level. The Ministry of Education has set general standards for the curriculum. Until the 1970s it established detailed standards in terms of subjects and time allocation for primary and secondary education. For higher education, however, it suggested only general guidelines. In time, the standards have been relaxed to give more room for regional interpretation.

The contents of textbooks, on which the teachers have heavily depended in classroom instruction, have been carefully controlled by the government. Until the 1960s, the Ministry of Education compiled all textbooks for elementary schools and many texts for secondary education. Since then the Ministry has either published textbooks drafted by specialized research institutes, or approved a few alternative versions developed by private publishers. Reference books and teaching aid materials have also been subject to the Ministry's approval.

The government made thorough revisions of the curriculum in 1953, 1963, and 1973. Most reforms focused on the texts in social studies and moral education rather than on science and mathematics. There has been increasing emphasis on the nation, by increasing the lessons dealing with anticommunism, nationalism, and patriotism at the expense of individual initiative and entrepreneurship. Instruction had little relevance to real-life situations. Students were encouraged to memorize the textbooks.

Since the 1970s, various attempts had been made to improve conventional teaching methods, but the effects have been hampered by large class sizes and deep-rooted examination-oriented instruction. A noteworthy project was the establishment of the Korean Educational Development Institute (KEDI) to develop a new instructional system with emphasis on programmed audiovisual and self-learning materials. Its ambitious attempt turned out to be unrealistic and was partially discontinued. But it has improved classroom instruction as well as education policies.

As for the qualitative improvement of higher education, the government undertook first a control approach and then an incentive approach. In 1950 there were strong criticisms against the loose application of academic requirements for degrees. In response to the demand for excellence in higher education, the government attempted a series of radical reforms in 1961 known as "rearrangement plans." Although most of the plans were nullified, the mechanism of government control in higher education was institutionalized. The Ministry of Education intervened in the entrance examination process and began to authorize enrollment quotas, tuition levels, and degree conferment in universities. The Ministry also imposed guidelines on academic operations including curriculum development.

As an incentive approach, the government initiated the Pilot University Program in 1973. The program selectively supported pilot institutions that met some qualitative criteria and adopted experimental reforms by providing them with subsidies and allowing for greater autonomy. The reform proposal included the reduction of a dual-major gradation system, and the application of an accelerated graduation system. The program was initially applied to ten selected universities, but it has since then been extended to all universities and colleges. The government has also encouraged self-reform efforts and given more flexibility to university management of academic affairs, unfortunately more in theory than in practice. In sum, the ideology underlying policies on teaching might be characterized by conformity or standardization. It legitimized government control over what and how subjects would be taught and sharply curtailed individual initiative and creativity of teachers.

Administration and Finance of Education

Although the Constitution specified "independence and political neutrality of education shall be guaranteed," the Ministry of Education assumed power to standardize all education activities throughout the nation. For local autonomy, in 1952 school districts were created with corresponding boards of education at the levels of province and county. The county board's authority was limited to primary schools and the provincial board directly controlled the secondary schools. However, in actual administration the Ministry of Education exercised the dominant influence. Primary and secondary education was financed partly by the national treasury and partly through an education tax levied by provincial and municipal governments. During the 1950s, however, more than half of the funds for local schools were collected through Parent-Teacher Associations (PTA).

In the 1960s and 1970s the government centralized the administration system further and maintained only a nominal form of local autonomy. The county boards of education were abolished. The provincial boards, which had been chaired by the provincial governor (appointed by the president), were to be composed of members elected by the provincial assembly, but they were actually nominees of the Ministry of Education. The superintendent was also to be recommended formally by the board, but in fact, the central government controlled the election process. This pattern of centralization has continued to the present.

The abolition of the Education Tax in 1961 increased the dependence of local finance on the national treasury and accordingly resulted in strengthening the centralization of educational administration. However, the proportion of education finances in the central government budget was less than 10 percent in the 1950s and rose only to 15 percent during the 1960s and 1970s. The government enacted the Grant for Local Education Finance Law to secure a financial source for primary and secondary education in 1963. The law earmarked 11.8 percent of internal taxes for local education and guaranteed teachers' salaries. The law has been an institutional mechanism for ensuring the stability of educational administration while avoiding the politics of budget allocation. The proportion of educational expenditures in the government's budget kept increasing during the 1980s, amounting to 20 percent in 1987. The increase of public education finance in relative as well as absolute terms could be attributed to the revival of the Education Tax as a national tax until at least 1991.

Though the Ministry of Education has tried to expand resources for education, its efforts have seldom been successful. The Compulsory Education Accomplishment Plan (1954–1959), which was the first formal and energetic rehabilitation program after the Korean War, secured only 38 percent of the requested funds. The Five-Year Educational Reconstruction Plan (1962–1966) and successive mid-term plans in the education sector generated remarkable enrollment increases in excess of the targets, but they were not followed by corresponding increases in teachers and facilities. The long-term Comprehensive Education Plan (1972–1986) fell to the same fate as many other previous plans. In short, inadequate financial support from the budgeting authorities has been the single most serious constraint to implementing educational policies as well as plans.

A noteworthy attempt at alleviating these problems in recent years has been the establishment of the Presidential Commission for Education Reform (PCER) in 1985. It was the first advisory body in the education sector in Korean history. After three years of intensive activities including numerous surveys, conferences, and public hearings, the commission sent to the president a comprehensive set of controversial reform proposals for educational development and he referred it to a new advisory body on education policy that featured a more open process.

Recent Policy Alternatives

A variety of policy alternatives are now being examined and considered for implementation. Since 1988 the Ministry of Education has scrutinized the concrete feasibility of the policy proposals in the final report of the PCER. At the same time, the Advisory Council on Education Policy to the Minister has reviewed relatively short-term policy alternatives to tackle urgent problems.

Earlier Entrance into Primary School

The entry age for primary school is set at six years in Korea, and the rigid adherence to chronological age has ignored individual differences in mental age. The government plans to permit children whose chronological age has passed five to enter schools on a selective basis at the discretion of the principal. Officials fear classroom shortages. Teachers worry about parents' zeal for early entrance. Kindergartens oppose possible loss of pupils.

Accelerated Graduation and Grade Repetition

Korea has maintained a policy of automatic promotion within each school level. All children have passed to the next higher grade at the end of the academic year. The PCER proposed that promotion to a higher grade should be contingent upon the individual's pace of learning. The Ministry of Education intends to apply this promotion policy to students from grades 4 through 12.

Autonomous Operation of High School Entrance Examinations

The present system, which randomly allocates students by lottery, has more disadvantages than advantages. The PCER has recommended an autonomous operation of selection procedures. But the government fears that entrance examinations by each high school will reintroduce the old problems of intense competition and strong demands for private tutoring.

Greater Autonomy for Higher Education Institutions

The management of higher education has been fossilized into bureaucratic inertia and dependency. The Ministry of Education has made most major decisions. In response to persistent demands for autonomy in recent years, the government has delegated more decision-making authority or expanded the discretion of the universities. First, tuition and fees, controlled by the government until 1988, are now determined by individual institutions. Second, the Ministry of Education plans to eliminate the current requirement that university and college presidents must be approved by the Ministry. Third, the Ministry intends to grant full autonomy to individual universities in the selection of students. The Central Education Evaluation Institute will transform its present achievement test into a Scholastic Aptitude Test and its future adoption will depend on the decision of individual universities.

Abolition of Periodic Reappointment of Professors

Since 1976 the government has enforced a system of appointing all faculty members with terms ranging from two to ten years according to rank. The periodic reappointment of professors undermined the consistency of their research activities, and the sense of insecurity curtailed any sense of freedom. Furthermore, the vagueness of its criteria rendered the system vulnerable to political abuse.

Strengthening of Local Autonomy

In early 1988, the National Assembly passed several acts concerning the realization of local autonomy in the near future. The amended Education Law stipulates that the local board of education should changes its role and status from an executive body to a decision-making body, and that the local assembly should appoint board members, who would then have the power to elect the superintendent. The law also provides for the considerable delegation of functions and powers away from the central government to the local authorities, especially in the spheres of financial and personnel administration. So far, political disputes over control and finances have prevented implementation.

Reform in School Management

The organizational structure of schools makes promotion remote, and principals can retain their position until retirement. Teachers now demand set terms of office for principals and a greater say both in selection and in running the schools. The government is sympathetic to their demands.

Permission of Private Tutoring by College Students

In 1980 the government prohibited all kinds of private tutoring except in the field of arts and music. However, the ban has been considerably weakened by the democratization trend in society, and private tutoring has again come to the fore, albeit in secret. The government has decided to permit private tutoring by college students only (not schoolteachers) and to televise lectures.

Conclusion

Excessive control has hampered the initiative and creativity of both educational institutions and individuals. Centralized control prevents the educational system from responding to the diverse needs and conditions of different areas and schools. Government control should be scaled down.

The new national Constitution contains a clause for "university autonomization." The government has begun to grant more discretion to higher education institutions and to delegate many functions to local administrative authorities. The call for reform in school management is expected to result in autonomous decision making at each school level. Uniform control is neither desirable nor feasible.

Conformity in educational policy may be justified as an effective means for standardization and for quality control. In fact, this policy has contributed to the enhancing of national integration and secured education standards above the legal minimum level. On the other hand, the policies enforcing standardization have also suppressed creative and innovative efforts by individual institutions. In addition, the policies emphasizing conformity have hampered abilities to adapt to changing situations and needs.

As Korean education has had to meet rapid increases of students at all school levels, it may have achieved quantitative growth at the cost of quality. The equality of education opportunity seems to have precluded excellence of education. A few typical examples of such policies would be student selection by lottery, overly large classes, and automatic promoting between grades. Equality of education opportunity means a fair and equal chance of receiving education, without any discrimination due to social class, locality, or gender. However, the concept does not mean an absolutely equal chance, but relative fairness in accordance with capability and merits.

The time has come for Korean education to end its marriage with quantitative expansion and instead to pursue individual excellence. In this context, we may recognize positively such recent policies as accelerated graduation and grade repetition, autonomous operation of high school entrance examinations, and permission for private tutoring. Education that seeks excellence requires highly qualified teachers, well-developed education programs that can cater to diverse needs, and advanced facilities. In addition, the government should seek fair competition, objective evaluation, and proper compensation.

CHAPTER SEVENTEEN

Korean Public Administration: Education and Research

Jong S. Jung

PUBLIC ADMINISTRATION HAS a short history in Korea as a field of study, but today it is geographically far-flung, having active groups of scholars in virtually every major city in the country. There are respectable journals and an active professional association, the Korean Association for Public Administration. Teaching and research activities are rigorous, and place a strong emphasis on the scientific aspects of public adminis-tration. Today education in public administration may be more active in Korea than in any other Asian country.

Korean public administration has developed in response to the neces-sity of managing the complex problems faced by the country after the liber-ation from Japanese colonial rule in 1945. Korea was a newly emerging nation, and the lack of efficient administration was as crucial as the lack of economic resources and political capability. Political leaders had to find a means of maintaining government functions in order for Korea to sur-vive as a nation. They had to employ any bureaucrats and lower-level clerks who had learned basic technical and control skills under the Japanese. As a result, administration during the first fifteen years after World War II was characterized by archaic forms and procedures. Since then, Korean public administration has come a long way. The government has devel-oped a rather efficient form of public bureaucracy, and to a large extent, the building of a strong executive branch can be credited to the role exer-cised by students of public administration.

Progress in Public Administration Education

Interest in the promotion of public administration education first emerged in Korea with the inception of the Korean Association of Public Adminis-

Taken from Jong S. Jun, "Korean Public Administration: Education and Research," *Interna-tional Review of Administrative Sciences* 49 (4)(1983):413–420.

tration in 1956. Since then, the Association has been holding an annual conference on public administration, sponsoring occasional seminars, and facilitating information exchange. The systematic educational endeavor began in 1959 with the establishment of the Graduate School of Public Administration at Seoul National University. Shortly afterward other universities set up public administration programs to train people for public service. By 1981 there were fifty undergraduate degree programs and twenty-four graduate programs in public administration. By comparison, there were only seventeen degree programs in the much older field of political science.

Korean public administration is in fact an offshoot of political science and of another older field, administrative law. Traditionally, students interested in public service who were preparing for the higher civil service examination had to be particularly knowledgeable in public and administrative law. To a certain degree, this legalistic orientation continues at the undergraduate level. Almost all undergraduate degree programs require four major courses: an introduction to public administration, organization and management theory, personnel administration, and public finance administration. However, more than thirty universities and colleges still require at least one course in administrative law.

At the graduate level, there are also common course requirements such as organizational theory, personnel administration, financial administration, and research methodology. Some graduate programs are beginning to require a course in public policy. Administrative law is not required for all graduate students, though a student can take it as an elective. Although some graduate courses carry the same course titles as the undergraduate programs do, the graduate courses focus on advanced issues in personnel administration, organization theory, and public financing. In general, graduate programs have tended to adopt a public management orientation, gradually expanding toward analytical courses in policy sciences, quantitative decision making, planning, and statistics. Both undergraduate and graduate programs lack courses teaching qualitative methods and oriented to the social sciences. This seems to reflect the strong scientific and technical emphasis of many American public administration programs. It is also commonly known among Korean scholars that the educational curricula are geared to the higher civil service examination, which emphasizes technical ability. Innovative curriculum change is considered undesirable because a program's reputation, to a large extent, depends upon the number of successful examination candidates. As a result, public administration programs tend to concentrate on the basic required courses. Furthermore, most universities and colleges do not have internship programs for public administration majors to provide students with experience in government agencies.

Public administration education possesses a goal and at the same time provides a means to other goals. Its goal is to develop proactive and change-oriented individuals who are interested in careers in public organizations. It is also a means for facilitating the process of problem solving in government and contributing to the promotion of developmental goals of society. Thus it is in the very nature of public administration that actions of public administration must be related both to government problem solving and to the promotion of the public interest.

Public administration education in Korea has long been regarded as having important outcomes. It has made at least five major contributions to the improvement of administrative capability. First, the most prevalent view of the role of public administration education focuses on those aspects of the educative process that prepare individuals for the mainly public service occupations. Public administration education is viewed as having its greatest impact as a supplier of much needed management skills to the government as well as to the private sector. Second, it has contributed to the development of administrative leadership, which provides decision-making skills, central planning, coordination, efficient government services, and mobilization of resources. Third, it develops in its broadest sense, not only rational and efficient administration, but also students' attitudes concerning the ethical responsibility of government administration toward society and its citizens. Fourth, public administration contributes not only administrative theories and concepts, but also advice and participation in the formulation and implementation of public policies and developmental programs. Finally, it is largely responsible for the establishment of a stable government bureaucracy—not necessarily an innovative one—that sustains social order through the enforcement of government regulations and rules and the maintenance of technical and productive functions.

Intellectual Orientation

A preliminary search for public administration literature revealed an amorphous intellectual milieu. If there is any distinctive academic thrust, it is the movement toward the conception of public administration as a field for professional practice. The intellectual milieu is in part shaped by the influence of American public administration and public policy studies, an influence that is readily visible in virtually every publication and research work. There is also a hidden competition among scholars to introduce new foreign theories, concepts, or publications sooner than anyone else. As a consequence, theories and concepts presented in the articles and textbooks tend to be simplistic and less critical of their implications. Since it is difficult to delineate different theoretical perspectives, I will attempt to discuss three intellectual orientations: (1) the Western orientation, (2) the ethnocentric orientation, and (3) the reform orientation.

The Western orientation may be characterized as an uncritical acceptance of theories and methods developed mainly by American and British scholars. A number of scholars are preoccupied with translation or illustration of foreign concepts, and this tendency is very much reflected in published articles and textbooks. Scholars who are busy emulating Western ideas tend to have a positivistic inclination; that is, they believe Korean administrative problems can be solved through the adoption of management principles and systems theories that have been widely used in American settings. These scholars tend to assume that the models of management and policy analysis used successfully in the United States will yield the same successes when applied to Korean administrative and policy issues, and that scientific research methods are the means to administrative knowledge. This orientation is very common among people with academic interests in policy science, management science, quantitative decision making, and functional management techniques.

If the Western orientation seems scientific and objective, the ethnocentric approach appears historical and subjective. It is historical in the sense that ethnocentrically oriented scholars tend to analyze past administrative systems such as the Yi dynasty (1392–1910), the Japanese colonial administration (1910–1945), and the U.S. military government (1945–1948). It is subjective because its epistemological method is to understand the unique reality of Korean administrative culture. Scholars in this category assume that Korea needs a public administration firmly rooted in its own culture to enable Korean society to gain a full understanding of its own essential character. Basically, this study method establishes Korean administration philosophy (except Confucianism) and cultural norms as the core of administrative reality and people's behavior and actions. Without historical and subjective perspective, according to ethnocentric scholars, one cannot fully understand even one's own administrative culture, let alone what similarities and differences are involved cross culturally.

There are numerous historical studies, but *Historical Study of Public Administration in Yi Dynasty* by Woon Tai Kim and *A Historical Development of the Bureaucracy in Korea* by Dong Suh Bark[1] are convincingly ethocentric, and use indigenous concepts and terms to arrive at a historical understanding of Korean bureaucracy and its possible implications for today's administrative behavior. Although there are other recent studies, the number of unique case studies of Korean administration is relatively small. Despite shortcomings in scientific rigor, knowledge derived from the analysis of the unique Korean background provides an invaluable explanation of the behavioral and action patterns of bureaucrats. It explains, for example, their orientation toward loyalty, obedience, ethics, corruption, and so forth. The weakness of the ethnocentric orientation is its dependence upon knowledge that is linked with solutions to old problems. It lacks the analytical power to investigate contemporary problems, as the attempt to solve complex technical issues through cultural norms is often inappropriate to administrative systems in constant turmoil.

Finally, scholars inclined toward a reform orientation stress a prudent acceptance of external knowledge with a view to modifying the Korean system. From an epistemological point of view, people with this intellectual orientation are interested in the integration of the first two approaches in order to understand Korean administrative phenomena—that is, they try to develop a dialectical relationship between the objective nature of foreign ideas and the subjectivity of domestic norms and values. The former may provide new theoretical possibilities, while the latter focuses on idiosyncrasies of Korean public administration. Reform-minded scholars are interested in development administration—that is, in the role of public administration in the promotion of the developmental goals of the government. Thus they are committed to the development or importation of theories and concepts that may furnish various strategies for the improvement of administrative capability. But their assumption is that although the developmental strategies of Western industrialization and administrative development may be useful to Korean development, the pattern of development must inevitably reflect the values and behavioral problems of Korean administration. Implicit in their orientation is the assumption that successful developmental programs must be based on existing norms of Korean reality, more generally that all major administrative and social norms are deeply ingrained in tradition and history. Because these subjective considerations are often detrimental to modernization and development, reform scholars believe, however, that outside knowledge is equally important.

The most representative works in this endeavor are the publications of Dong Suh Bark, Suk Choon Cho, and Hahn Been Lee.[2] Even in their work, a Western positivistic epistemology tends to predominate. Again, the most important contributions made by the reform-oriented scholars is in the formulation of various developmental strategies and management possibilities for administrative reform. Their reform strategies have focused on the improvement of administrative capability for the purpose of social and economic development, leadership skills, decision-making process, personnel administration, motivational strategies, and decentralization.

In recent years, the reform orientation has been revived—as the "indigenization of public administration"—by scholars who are more critical of the blind acceptance of alien theories. Chong Bum Lee defines indigenization as "the process whereby the Western science of public administration is introduced into Korean culture and takes on a new form through interaction with the existing concepts and practices in the area of public administration, as well as with overall Korean cultural patterns, which leads to changes and assimilation."[3] Indigenous and reflexive thinking was also stressed by Suk Choon Cho, former president of the Korean Association for Public Administration. He has made three well-stated points: first, that Korean scholars must import foreign theories with the criterion of relevancy in mind; second, that a "sense of proportion" must be exercised in order to avoid overreliance on American administrative theories and that equal attention should be paid to other systems such as those of Europe and Japan; and third, that there should be a reasonable synthesis between domestic and foreign ideas and knowledge sources, rather than a continuation of the present circumstances, in which scholars are largely speaking in terms of foreign ideas and concepts.[4]

Research Activities and Its Limitations

There was not much theoretical and empirical research activity in Korea until the early 1960s. With the beginning of graduate education in the late 1950s, however, methods of behavioral science began to be imported by young scholars returning from the United States. Library research—research concentrating on the examination of new theories, concepts, and models—is still common among Korean scholars. However, there is a growing trend toward empirical behavioral research. Empirical research tends to rely heavily on the use of problem-focused survey methods. These methods are generally based on techniques of sample selection, structured questionnaire design, and data analysis; however this kind of research does not contribute much to the practice of administration and management.

Among Korean scholars, there are several limitations around conducting serious research. First, scholars tend to focus on already popular topics rather than on exploring new and complex issues. Thus selection of a research topic and problem area is affected by considerations such as how others may feel about a particular study, or the possibility of receiving recognition by the mass media or by government agencies. In these circumstances, there is an urgent need to open up new research interests utilizing both quantitative and qualitative research methods.

Second, administrative research in Korea has been dominated by a few major universities, all of them located in Seoul. Specifically, many research grants have been given to a few senior professors from the Graduate School of Public Administration at Seoul National University. Professors from other universities, particularly from small colleges, are in a disadvantageous position if they wish to engage in any type of empirical research that requires substantial resources.

Third, most grants and research activities are colored by the interests of government agencies. Outcomes of government-backed research projects tend to favor agency policy and its directions: they are largely "bureaucratized research"—research to satisfy the views of bureaucrats and policymakers. Grants are usually given on the basis of agency invitation or an individual professor's relationship with a particular agency.

Finally, researchers tend to pursue government research projects as sources of extra income rather than as opportunities to generate knowledge that will improve policies and administration or make contributions to the discipline. Research projects are performed rather expediently. Of course, there is no way to guarantee that practitioners will use research findings to improve administrative processes or to develop better alternatives to current programs, but clearly it is the responsibility of academics to study problems and produce unbiased results and recommendations.

There is an urgent need for opportunities to be opened to anyone who wishes to conduct either theoretical or empirical research. The government should encourage innovative research as well as research relevant to the solution of public problems and the improvement of administrative effectiveness. In redefining the directions of future research activities, academics representing different universities and colleges can play an important advisory role by assisting government agencies, such as the Ministry of Education and the Ministry of Government Administration which provide various research grants.

Future Agendas

The continuing education and intellectual development of Korean public administration requires a great deal of rethinking on the part of academics. The factors influencing Korean society are obviously different from those affecting other societies. Because Korean public administration cannot afford to follow the trends in American public administration, the reform orientation seems to be the most desirable alternative.

Redefining Educational Purpose

Every public administration program in Korea claims to prepare students for a public service career. A career in government is traditionally recognized as a typical bureaucratic life in a government agency, accompanied by organizational power and prestige. That is, administrators are understood to be responsible for implementing policies and directives of policymakers, and it is understood that in so doing, they must commit themselves to the maintenance of organizational order and functional services.

Though these traditional roles are important, the administrator's life should not be encompassed by them. Administrators need to create their own roles, ones that are ethically responsible and personally rewarding. They need to have mental skills to think intelligently, to see value conflicts and personal biases, to take responsible actions, and to be proactive toward their own working environment. This way of behaving and acting is an important quality of modern society. To enhance it, educational programs, particularly at the graduate level, must teach the importance of the changing image of public administrators and stress their responsibility toward themselves and society.

Korean public administration education today is largely aimed at the professional training of administrative technocrats. The content of curricula is designed to meet the requirements of the higher civil service examination. Because educators realize this limitation, it is their responsibility to overcome this and other educational obstacles and to seek innovative approaches. The process of redefining educational goals can begin with discussions within and outside the university setting—discussions involving practitioners, students, and academics—on such topics as curriculum innovation, the future role of administrators, the relationship between the administration and society, and changing work ethics and values.

Questioning Assumptions and Generating Grounded Theory

Scholars who emphasize the reform and indigenization of public administration have a strong interest in searching for "good," relevant theories, and in testing or modifying them in the context of Korean public administration. Because their aim is mainly to adopt or formulate a deductive theory, their bias is toward inquiry into administrative phenomena. That is, in order to prove a particular theory, the individual researcher must be able to say, at best, what would verify it and what would falsify it, or what experiences or knowledge it explains. If a theory were applied to a given administrative context with such a task in mind, we would experience only those elements of the context that the theory attempted to explain. Any elements that did not fit into the established theoretical framework would not be disclosed.

The reform and indigenization processes must go beyond positivistic epistemology, and experiment with an approach to generating theory that is less culturally biased. This does not imply that Korean scholars should not import theories and concepts from outside. In fact, researchers should also be concerned about the cultural bias involved in *not* adopting a foreign theory. Without some comparative perspective, Korean public administration runs the risk of misunderstanding its own institutions and losing the opportunity for learning various strategies for change that may become viable alternatives to indigenous problem-solving.

Conducting Qualitative Research

The pursuit of empirical-behavioral research in Korea will be increasing and is likely to enjoy even greater popularity, for both practitioners and academics rely on objectively derived data (factual information). But the indigenization of administration also requires a research methods that can reveal subjectively disclosed experiences (qualitative information), a method that can examine administrative problems as they are experienced by administrators (or clients) in their ongoing, everyday life.

There are various useful methods for conducting a qualitative (phenomenological) inquiry into the nature of indigenous culture. Such methods include case studies, document analysis, open-ended interviews, analysis of language and symbols, and participant observations. Whichever method is used, qualitative researchers must seek to arrive at a dynamic insight into the nature of the Korean administrative phenomenon, one that can fruitfully incorporate varied perspectives. In great contrast to behavioral research, qualitative research does not try to manipulate reality. Rather, it attempts to highlight the feelings, emotions, and ideas of people working in an administrative setting. Of course, neither qualitative or quantitative studies can be truly accurate in describing the reality, but it is nonetheless important that researchers explain their assumptions and biases clearly. The use of qualitative research, along with behavioral research, will enable Korean public administration to gain a full understanding of its own essential character.

Relating Theory to Practice

The most important question concerning public administration education and research is its relevance—relevance to students of public administration, to public organizations, and to Korean society. Education and research should deal with realistic and normative questions concerning the development of people and administrative institutions. Above all, though, it should deal with practical questions and address society's need for developmental guidance. Whether or not the values and perceptions of the academic community are relevant to our students depends ultimately upon their own perceptions and understanding. Whether or not our theories and concepts are relevant to administrative problem solving also depends upon how well we develop theoretical knowledge based on human actions (practice). Thus, the integration of theory and practice requires a series of human interactions, between educator and student, educator and practitioner, and practitioner and the public.

Theoretical knowledge only become relevant when an individual—student or practitioner—organizes, internalizes, and applies it to his or her own situation. But students and practitioners often have trouble interpreting theories, concepts, and research findings. To relate knowledge to action, we need an ongoing dialogue between actors, for example, between academics who are interested in communicating theories to practitioners and practitioners who seek to apply them to the problem-solving process. Dialogue is the basis for mutual learning, the most important means of communicating, and the best way to integrate theory and practice.

Finally, in order to increase the reliability of theories applied to practical situations, we must realize the significance of grounded theory. Grounded theory directly generated from the indigenous culture tends to bear higher applicability to practical problem solving and to facilitate more intellectual understanding of social reality than formal theory—in particular established foreign theory—possibly can.

Notes

1. Woon-tae Kim, *Historical Study of Public Administration in Yi Dynasty*, rev. ed. (Seoul: Pakyŏng-sa, 1981); Dong Suh Bark, *A Historical Development of Bureaucracy in Korea* (Seoul: Korean Research Center, 1961), in Korean.
2. Dong Suh Bark, *Korean Public Administration* (Seoul: Bup Moon Sa, 1973); Suk Choon Cho, *The Study of Korean Public Administration* (Seoul: Bark Young Sa, 1980); Hahn Been Lee, *Korea: Time, Change, and Administration* (Honolulu: East-West Center Press, 1968).
3. Chong Bum Lee, "A Prolegomenon to the Indigenization of Public Administration," in Bun Woong Kim and Wha Joon Rho (eds.), *Korean Public Bureaucracy* (Seoul: Kyobo, 1982), pp. 363–364.
4. Suk Choon Cho, "Foreword," *Korean Public Administration Review*, 15 (1981), pp. i–ii.

CHAPTER EIGHTEEN

The Study of Public Administration in Korea

Jong Hae Yoo

THE HISTORY OF the study of Korean public administration is short. The first Korean textbook on public administration, written by Chung Inhung, was published in 1955. In 1956, Fred W. Riggs delivered the first lecture on public administration at the National Officials Training Institute, now the Central Officials Training Institute (COTI). The first department of public administration at an undergraduate level was established at Yonsei University in 1958. Moreover, American public administration, which had initially influenced the study of public administration in Korea, has a short history too. The beginnings of modern inquiry into American public administration is usually identified with Woodrow Wilson's essay on "The Study of Administration" published in 1887. Wilson's theory of administration was based on the sharp line between politics and administration, with administration having its own scope of study. This essay inspired the independent and separate study of public administration in the United States.

We should immediately recognize the existence of an "identity crisis" in the study of public administration. It cannot be known what the study of public administration means exactly or how it can be distinguished from political science. There is a tendency to view the study of public administration as part of the science of law in Korean society. Even in banks and corporations, it is commonly recognized that the study of public administration is closely related to the study of law. This identity crisis stems from the fact that the department of public administration and the department of law coexisted in the law school (college) immediately after the liberation of Korea in 1945; this is still the case now in some universities. Thus, the identity crisis remains a serious problem today.

Taken from Jong Hae Yoo, "The Study of Public Administration in Korea," in Chung-Hyun Ro and Mila Reforma (eds.), *Social Change and Administrative Reform Towards the Year 2000*, Eastern Regional Organization for Public Administration, Manila, the Philippines, 1985, pp. 192–197.

A second problem relates to the lack of legitimacy in the study of public administration in Korea. In the past, public administration often served as a government tool to advocate a particular or partisan interest. This problem is similarly felt by those in the political science field.

There is also the related problem of indigenization. Since the beginning of the Korean study of public administration, the theories based upon the experience of foreign countries have been introduced without considering the unique peculiarities of the Korean situation and without testing the hypothesis in the Korean context. This has caused the problem of indigenization or Koreanization of the theories of public administration.

Another problem stems from the lack of understanding of the study of public administration in Korean society. Even those who major in the study of public administration at the undergraduate level seem to have little understanding of it.

There is also the problem caused by the gap between scholars and bureaucrats. On the one hand, scholars perceive bureaucrats as those who implement policies at random without the benefit of any theoretical framework. On the other hand, bureaucrats view scholars as too idealistic, advocating academic theories without considering efficacy and reality. Generally, therefore, bureaucrats do not want scholars to participate in the decision-making processes of government. In addition, bureaucrats have little appreciation of the necessity for scholars to give lectures in government employees' training institutions. It is believed that scholars' lectures have no relevance to the practical affairs of public administration. In the present ever-changing social environment, a reciprocal exchange between scholars and bureaucrats would be an important factor for fostering Korean public administration.

Future Tasks of Korean Public Administration

Great social changes have been developing in Korea over the past few decades. Some of these significant developments are listed here.

1. Gray areas between government and business are increasing because the terms and values prevailing in business are also penetrating into government circles.
2. The advent of management science has made it necessary to develop the ability to use computers to deal with large-scale administrative problems.
3. Scientific techniques are being introduced into public administration. A technological revolution or technotronic age is occurring in Korea. Administrations cannot as yet catch up with this revolutionary change in society. The study of public administration must play a special part in coping with this tremendous change.

4. The level of people's expectation of administration is increasing.
5. The need to think in terms of systems is becoming acute.
6. The world is getting smaller and smaller.

The question remains: how can public administration respond to these great changes? To help answer this question, first, the "three Es" of public administration should be adopted. The "three Es," derived from the 1968 Minnowbrook Conference, represent the values of efficiency, effectiveness, and equity. The value of efficiency is and will be always a part of the foundation of public administration. The value of effectiveness has a close relationship with democratic administration, whereby our society can be made responsible and productive. The value of equity emphasizes responsiveness to the needs of the common people rather than the needs of bureaucrats. It is necessary for scholars to consider alternative approaches to maintain these values, with particular regard to effectiveness and equity.

Second, cooperation between scholars and bureaucrats needs to be achieved. Without reciprocal cooperation between them, administration cannot cope with the changes and problems occurring in our society. Scholars must endeavor to suggest administrative theories that are practical and prescriptive. In this respect, one cannot overemphasize the role and responsibility of scholars. It goes without saying that the role of bureaucrats is also important.

Third, there is a need to indigenize and localize the study of public administration. There is no book that provides a case study of Korean public administration in practical terms. To make matters worse, although a few books with some case studies of American public administration have been published, these can hardly serve as good references because of differences in social settings between the two countries. As far as administrative philosophy is concerned, there is a need to indigenize values and norms that have been penetrating the society. And it is equally important to reflect the history of Korean public administration in order to systematize the continuity of it. For the purpose of accomplishing this task, a larger number of scholars has to study the history of Korean public administration and combine it with modern public administration theories, by using various viewpoints. If this can be done, such theories for Korean public administration can be established.

Fourth, there is a need to enlarge the scope of the study of public administration; that is, it is necessary to make the study of public administration rich in content. For example, many new fields such as policy science deal with quantitative theories to assist large-scale administration. In addition, there is a need to study more widely and systematically such fields as the theory of administrative responsiveness to the needs of people; research into human behavior, by which factors that motivate the populace can be understood; and welfare administration. Particular attention has to be paid to the quality of life in the field of welfare administration. What sense is there in discussing increases in GNP and per capita income statistics, if the people themselves do not believe that these are happening? Because the true quality of life is estimated by subjective values, surely it is necessary to measure and estimate the responsiveness and the service of public administration by the subjective value of its client. The measurement of the productivity of administration, which has been often ignored, is also an important problem. The quality, cost, and utility of administration has not been considered in the process of policy formulation and policy implementation. But future administration must supply the resources and capabilities necessary to guarantee quality of life for the people.

Fifth, there is a need to make public administration responsive to changes like internationalization. For example, it is often necessary to discuss the study of Korean public administration in English. As preparation, there should be more vigorous efforts to publish papers on public administration in English.

Sixth, there is a need to bridge the regional gap in public administration in Korea. Some 80 percent of Korean professors with PhD degrees live in Seoul. Thus, not only is there an imbalance among the local regions, there are also not enough qualified professors to teach the study of public administration in the local regions. To solve this problem, there should be constant exchange of information between Seoul and the local regions. Holding regional academic seminars or meetings in local regions would be an effective alternative.

Finally, public administration should initiate the creation of new values for improving public life and developing Korean society. Rather than remaining merely a science or a subsystem, public administration must play a key role in developing creativity, value orientation, future orientation, and scientific knowledge.

CHAPTER NINETEEN

A Critical Evaluation of Education for Public Administration in Korea

Chong Bum Lee

EMPIRICAL DATA OF the past thirty years have indicated a massive growth in education for public administration (EPA) in Korea—in terms of institutions, government and university training programs, and membership in professional associations related to public administration. The quantitative change, however, has not been followed by satisfactory quality in terms of its output, content of teaching materials, pedagogical methods, and research.

There are four distinctive stages of disciplinary development, including initiation, simple imitation, adaptive imitation, and creativity and maturity. In the initial stage, scholars and pioneers introduce new ideas to the discipline by borrowing from other countries or by developing them from within. At this stage, pioneers often find it difficult to create a critical mass to fully integrate all these new ideas. At the simple imitation stage, a group of colleagues or an enclave is being formed. This group might introduce parts of newly adopted or newly created ideas to their community, but they would not critically differentiate among the new ideas. Nor would they be sufficiently sensitive toward the implications of cultures. Here, ideas are flowing in or are being created without assessment of their practical application.

These disparities set the adaptive imitation stage in motion. At this stage, major activities are concentrated on self-regulation and self-criticisms with regard to the previous stages. These efforts are usually followed by the emphasis on indigenization, making a new discipline more relevant to the home environment. Scholars reexamine the relevance of borrowed theories to their own culture and society. They do this by involving them-

Taken from Chong Bum Lee, "A Critical Evaluation of Education for Public Administration in Korea," revised from a paper presented at the Eastern Regional Organization for Public Administration Conference on the state of education for public administration, Manila, the Philippines, November 1987.

selves in the following activities: (1) replicating the studies in their own sociocultural environment; (2) confirming or rejecting foreign theories; (3) finding the relevance or nonrelevance of the foreign theories; and (4) developing new theories, models, and concepts in their specific cultural context.

The final stage of disciplinary development is the creative or mature stage. In this stage, rather than searching for the particularistic theories and models in the previous stages, scholars are motivated to seek general theories and models. Hence, students would search for a general theory of public administration, taking relevant cultural variables into account. Consequently, scholars may engage in research among themselves within the country or in collaboration with scholars from overseas. During this stage, there will be a supply of necessary manpower—practitioners and scholars—so that they may not be totally dependent upon the knowledge industry of other countries. This is the most desirable stage of disciplinary development.

Overview

During the last forty years Korea experienced two events that had enormous impact on government administration: the Korean War of 1950–1953 and the military coup of 1961. The Korean War changed public administration from legal-oriented thinking to management-oriented practice. The Park Chung-Hee regime, which came with the 1961 military coup, enormously expanded the government apparatus in regard to the regulatory and supportive functions of national economic development by establishing or strengthening the Economic Planning Board, the Ministry of Trade and Industry, the Ministry of Construction, the Ministry of Home Affairs, and the Ministry of Science and Technology. Rapid economic growth continued through the period of the Doo Hwan Chun government, but both regimes produced income inequality, regional disparities, labor disputes, environmental pollution, corruption, and a credibility gap between government and the public. Since the late 1970s governmental responses to these problems have been reflected in the expansion of some functions related to regulation or control of these negative effects, for example in the Ministry of Labor, the Ministry of Health and Welfare, the Environmental Protection Administration, and the Board of Audit and Inspection.

The Beginnings of Public Administration Education in Korea

Korean public administration has branched out from two different paths— the "literati-bureaucratic" tradition and the legal-bureaucratic tradition. The literati-bureaucratic tradition used Confucian and historical literature as the main subjects for civil service examinations in the Yi dynasty. The legal tradition, which had been established during Japanese occupation, emphasized administrative law. During the thirty-six years of Japanese rule, the literati-bureaucratic tradition was replaced by the legal-bureaucratic tradition. After independence, a "government-centered" tradition of public administration, combining both literati-bureaucratic and legal-bureaucratic characteristics, continued in the new republic for the purpose of guiding, ruling over, and controlling the public.

Following the Korean War, Korean public administration was influenced by the management-oriented American tradition as it was introduced to the Korean military. At the same time, the pioneers of public administration began to introduce the new administrative knowledge to the academic community, in which practitioners and academicians in law, political science, economics, and public administration were dominant members. Consequently, the legal tradition has been gradually replaced by a management-oriented administration and a government-centered approach is being edged out by a more participatory one, although government-centered practices still predominate.

Initiation Stage: From 1945 Through the Late 1950s

From 1945 until the late 1950s, there were only a handful of newly trained scholars or practitioners, but many administrative scholars who were trained under Japanese colonial rule. Knowledge of public administration was then introduced by scholars with two different backgrounds—one American-trained and the other, Japanese-trained. Because of the dominant influence of Japanese-trained scholars, departments of public administration were initially established in law schools. Before 1960, there were only four undergraduate programs and one graduate program in Korea. Public administration was not a subject matter in the higher civil service examination.

In 1956, the Korean Association for Public Administration (KAPA) was the first organized by a group of academicians and administrative practitioners. The members of the association were composed of professors of public administration, administrative law, political science, and economics in several universities, and administrative practitioners. Most scholars were lecturers in the Central Officials Training Institute. Before KAPA was temporarily dissolved (by the military in the 1961 coup), the association published two books: a translation of L. D. White's *Introduction to the Study of Public Administration* and a lexicon entitled *Public Administration Terms and Phrases.*[1]

Simple Imitation Stage: From the 1960s Through the Early 1970s

In this period, new contents of public administration were imported from the United States without much adaptation in terms of their relevance to Korean circumstances. A major event in Korean public administration for this period was the establishment of the Graduate School of Public

Administration at Seoul National University (GSPA–SNU) in 1959. The GSPA–SNU was the product of the so-called Minnesota Plan by the U.S. International Cooperation Agency, basically a faculty training program for the establishment of the new institution in Seoul National University. Nineteen candidates were recruited, mainly from the law school at Seoul National University, and they were sent to a two-year graduate program at the University of Minnesota. Upon completion, eight of them were appointed faculty members at GSPA-SNU, and the remainder were assigned to other universities.

This new group of scholars became the chief advocates for a transfer of American public administration to Korean soil. They acted primarily as salespersons for the principles-oriented American discipline. Their roles are described below:

1. In regular classes they taught both students who wanted to be government officials and those who wanted to be academicians. In the evenings they taught students filling higher civil servant positions (fifth grade and above). They also became part-time instructors at the Central Officials Training Institute for in-service training.
2. In the early part of the Park Chung-Hee regime they actively participated in reforming government administration, as they were called upon to serve as members of advisory committees and consultants. They actively applied their knowledge of development administration, such as institution building for administrative reform. These activities were continued until the early 1970s.
3. They also contributed to introducing public administration knowledge by writing introductory textbooks.
4. They revitalized KAPA, which later became predominantly an academic circle because of changes in its membership and its ideology. The new KAPA is a representative organization of public administration rather than a composite of other disciplines.

Despite these achievements, the GSPA–SNU and other universities were limited in their capacity to educate or supply public administration teachers. They merely provided students with a preliminary level of knowledge for further studies abroad. However, they did make some effort to adopt many foreign theories and develop new theories and models that might be relevant to an understanding of Korean bureaucratic phenomena. The imitative activities of the first generation, which were criticized by practitioners and young scholars returning from abroad in the late 1970s (the second generation of public administration), led to the so-called indigenization of public administration in Korea.

Education for Public Administration in the Adaptive Imitation Stage

Newly educated scholars from abroad saw the shortcomings of the past academic activities. Critical of the first generation of public administration scholars, they began to modify foreign theories and to build new theories that might better fit the Korean context. Meantime, there had been substantial changes both in quantitative and qualitative aspects in Korean public administration.

Universities. Public administration programs in universities have greatly increased in number. In 1965, there were twenty-seven undergraduate programs, eleven master's programs, and three doctoral programs. In 1975, there were thirty-four undergraduate, twenty-nine master's, and nine doctoral programs. By 1986, there were sixty-nine undergraduate programs, seventy-one master's, and thirty doctoral programs. Student enrollment in undergraduate and graduate programs also increased. Public administration programs have been introduced as well in two-year vocational colleges—some thirty-two such colleges by 1986. At the undergraduate level, public administration is second only to business administration among the social sciences.

Between 1979 and 1985, the number of public administration faculty doubled from 177 to 363. The number of universities offering the subject increased from forty-six to sixty. Yet the increased number of faculty was still insufficient to meet the soaring student enrollment in undergraduate programs, especially after the law-oriented curricula were replaced by social science-oriented public administration during the late 1970s. This replacement resulted in changes in the affiliation of public administration programs. From 1978 to 1983 nine universities changed the affiliation of public administration departments from the college of law to the college of social sciences. The change directly or indirectly reflects the diminishing number of law courses in EPA.

Government Training Institutes. In 1985 there were forty government institutes, of which twenty-three had been established before 1970, and sixteen institutes after 1970. Government training institutes were established to train public officials; however, the quality of their course work, instructors, and their training materials and pedagogical methods had room for improvement.

Professional Orientation. Membership in KAPA increased more than threefold from 211 in 1968 to 730 in 1986. In 1968 the association had had more practitioners than academicians, but in 1986 the ratio had become seven academicians to every practitioner.

Student Enrollment. As the undergraduate programs drastically increased, student enrollment and the number of graduates also rapidly increased. In 1965 student enrollment was 2,573; in 1976, 4,725; and in 1986,

25,340. Thus, undergraduate student enrollment of 1986 was almost ten times that of 1965. Also the number of graduates in 1965 was 1,031 and in 1986, 2,654.

The output of graduate programs changed more dramatically than those of undergraduate programs. The late 1970s and early 1980s may be characterized as the epoch of quantitative transformation in graduate studies in public administration in Korea. The students enrolled in master's programs in 1965 numbered 170; in 1976, 929; and in 1986, 4,348. Only two students were enrolled in doctoral programs in 1965. In 1976 the number had increased to twenty-three, and in 1986 to 252. In 1973 universities produced fifteen MAs, 183 MPAs, and three PhDs. In 1986, the numbers increased to 136 MAs, 743 MPAs, and twenty-six PhD degrees, respectively. The statistics show that the turning point of EPA quantitatively was the late 1970s and early 1980s.

In order to analyze the characteristics of graduates, let us use the Graduate School of Public Administration of Seoul National University (GSPA-SNU) as an example. While evening programs emphasize the training of the middle and higher level civil servants, the regular (day) programs focus on full-time students who plan to pursue a public service career. Most students in the evening class are public officials at the fifth grade in the civil service hierarchy. The number of graduates from 1961 to 1984 listed in the *Alumni Yearbook of 1987* totaled 2,268 students, of whom 777 were in public service, 296 in business, 190 in teaching, and eighty-eight in other public corporations. During the period of 1961–1984, a total of 459 graduates from the regular classes went on to serve in government. About 40 percent of these graduates became high officials.

Publications.   The major academic journals of public administration include the *KPAR* (a biannual since 1984), *Korean Political Science Review, Korean Journal of Public Administration,* and monograph types of journals published by various universities. Most Korean universities with MPA programs publish their own journals. More than 100 textbooks related to public administration have been published in Korean. Most of them are written for college students and readers who prepare for the civil service examinations. Recent years, however, have witnessed a growth in original research focusing on the indigenization of public administration theory.

Evaluation of Education for Public Administration

A Theoretical and Empirical Framework

The major theories introduced to Korea to date include the following.
1. The literature introduced to Korea in the late 1950s and the early 1960s was the POSDCORB-related organization and management

(O&M) theory. Its predominant concern here was building or developing administrative practices.

2. The second wave of public administration literature introduced to Korea focused on the scientific theory of management. Examples are the behavioral approach to administration put forth by March and Simon.[2] The Weberian approach represented another area of interest, greatly supplemented in the late 1970s by open systems literature, contingency theory, and other new social and sociopsychological approaches. Little emphasis has been placed on the psychological dimensions of administrative behavior.

3. A third wave was the theory of comparative and development administration addressing national development. Because it was compatible with government-directed social change and community building, development administration received a good deal of official encouragement during the late 1960s and 1970s.

4. New public administration, policy science, and management science have been introduced since the late 1970s. They have been concerned with the improvement of decisionmaking in government and the problems of value, equity, and citizen participation.

Largely neglected in Korean public administration have been the philosophy of social sciences and social philosophy. Perhaps one reason for this has been their normative character. Positivistic behaviorists have distanced themselves from philosophical issues based on intuitive speculation. But public administration is as much a study of speculative judgment as it is a science of rigorous scientific inquiry. Thus, public administration students should pay greater attention to philosophy. On the basis of his survey using a Delphi method, Kang[3] predicts that epistemological theory will become dominant in public administration in the 1990s. The surge of interest in this area results from skepticism over the positivistic philosophy of the social sciences.

Closely related to philosophical considerations is the issue of incorporating Western and East Asian thought and values together in the study of public administration. In the past, untested Western thought became dominant over East Asian thought as underlying value issues of public administration. Since the 1960s, more attention has appropriately been given to East Asian thought.

Two prevailing assumptions in public administration should be mentioned. The first assumption is that clients or members of government organizations are merely instruments for achieving given goals or objectives rather than as dignified human beings. Another assumption is that governmental goals or objectives are givens. Thus, research efforts have been directed only at finding means to achieve these goals, but not at questioning the desirability of set goals and their priorities. These two assumptions have contributed to distorting bureaucratic realities and to reinforcing the authoritarian attitude of government officials. In turn, the government has enlarged its domain and sphere of influence, thereby shrinking the sphere of individual freedom. In short, these two assumptions support the dominance of government-centered activities.

Today, government-centered planning, specifically manifested in strong government regulations and exclusion of public input in the policy-making process, needs to be reexamined. Government now has to pay much more attention to the opinions and demands of the citizenry in regard to public planning. This will require changes in the basic assumptions of public administration. Public administration as a discipline should concentrate on studying how the public articulate and organize their opinions and claims in various policy arenas. The development of a new framework based on different assumptions is of major importance.

Curricular Content

The curricular structure of public administration can be analyzed from two different perspectives: one is education for practitioners and the other, education for professional scholars. For practitioners, the public administration curriculum is composed of process knowledge and the substantive knowledge of economics, science/technology, transportation, and other related specific policy areas. For those who are pursuing an academic career, the curriculum emphasizes knowledge of the administrative process.

One way of evaluating the curricular structure is to look at it both from the "within variety" (disciplinary) and the "between variety" (interdisciplinary) perspective in public administration programs. Because the major clientele of the undergraduate and MPA programs is those who pursue a public service career or those who are already in public service, the curriculum for them emphasizes the "between variety." In contrast, the curriculum for those who pursue advanced graduate training such as a doctorate emphasizes the "within variety."

The Between Variety and the Within Variety of the Undergraduate Program. The between variety perspective in EPA has been decreasing. From the 1950s through to the early 1960s law courses and political science had dominated the undergraduate curriculum. The trend changed in the late 1960s when more public administration courses were adopted and law courses were dropped. By the late 1980s, the ratio of public administration to law had become 72 to 17. At present the undergraduate EPA may be characterized as social science-oriented, and the within variety appears dominant.

A public administration-dominated undergraduate program is not deemed desirable for training of practitioners because it does not provide them with substantive knowledge and skills necessary for them to function effectively on the job. In this regard, the present undergraduate curriculum in Korea is too narrow in breadth and scope. This type of EPA may produce myopic or crippled practitioners. In the future, more emphasis must be placed on the between variety for the undergraduate curriculum.

How did the curricula of public administration become diversified and differentiated within the discipline? The curricular differentiation within public administration came from three sources.

1. A set of courses was added by the returnees who were trained abroad, especially with American scientific fashions (e.g., O&M in the 1950s and 1960s; comparative and development administration since the early 1970s; and policy analysis since the late 1970s.)
2. Certain courses have been developed for domestic needs, including local urban administration, Korean government (or administration), and Korean administrative history.
3. The self-interest of individual faculty in creating their own "pet" courses has also increased the within variety of curriculum. Included in this category are such courses as human relations, office management, administrative management, and public relations.

The within variety increased in time as the academicians' specialization of major fields became diversified. In the simple imitation stage, scholars were mainly trained in principle-oriented O&M; thus, the within variety was not possible. In the adaptive imitation stage, the returnees specialized in comparative and development administration, system analysis, quantitative methods, and policy analysis. In this stage, scholars trained in the domestic doctoral programs also contributed to increasing the within variety. But the within variety in the undergraduate curriculum does not necessarily reflect societal needs in Korea.

The relative importance of O&M to other courses has decreased in time, and the quantitative administration and research methods and policy courses have increased in importance since the early 1980s. Comparative and development administration introduced in the late 1960s has also decreased. Although ethical studies emerged in the 1980s, they are still not sufficiently incorporated in the undergraduate curriculum. Courses like policy analysis and administrative ethics will be emphasized more heavily in the future.

Pedagogical Methods

Incremental change has occurred in teaching methods. As graduate programs have expanded, the seminar type of teaching gradually has replaced the lecture style and/or independent reading. In the late 1970s, when graduate programs began, independent reading and lecture style prevailed as pedagogy in graduate classes. As resources for public administration education gradually improved with the influx of the second generation of returnees from abroad, together with scholars trained in the domestic doctoral programs, the courses began to be taught in a seminar style. There have been some spillover effects of the graduate program on the undergraduate and MPA programs. Several undergraduate courses linked to the graduate programs have operated as seminars, a practice that helps students get both an academic and a problem-solving orientation.

Training Materials and Research

Publications have increased during the last twenty years. For example, the number of articles published in *KPAR* during 1986 had doubled compared to the number per year in the 1970s. The number of textbooks published in the 1980s has increased about three times compared to those in the 1970s. Little original research was published before the early 1970s, but in the 1980s ten such books were published. In spite of publications in Korean, the most important teaching materials still remain American public administration literature. These original English texts have been used at the graduate level, and Korean texts, translated from the English and synthesized, have been used at the undergraduate level.

Deficiencies or shortcomings in these books abound. First, the contents of one book are not very different from others. Second, the contents lack underlying logic or systemic structures. Most are mere collections or aggregations of vastly different theories and viewpoints on public administration. Thus, invariably, new books are lengthier than the old ones! Third, a mere aggregation of all theories results in the neglect of specific theories. However, recently published books are relatively systematic in their contents, and more theoretical information is contained in them. Fourth, only a few professional books have been published in Korean. The call for original research in public administration stimulated some scholars to write new books based on either newly developed theories or revised theories. The fact is that even after the outcry for indigenization, preference for publishing textbooks as opposed to professional articles has hardly changed.

Reflections and Prospects of Education for Public Administration

1. A large number of the second wave of young scholars has returned from abroad since 1970. According to the KAPA membership list in 1986, there were seventy-four new PhDs among these returnees. Moreover, the fields of specialization among them were diverse. Some of them were well equipped with quantitative methods. Whereas the early returnees had a tendency to major in development administration and comparative administration, the later returnees came with emphasis on policy analysis and management science.

Several Korean schools also began to produce PhDs in public administration, and by 1986 the number of PhDs produced internally reached 110. The new PhDs from both inside and outside the country were appointed as new faculty members of various universities, and they helped enrich Korean public administration in rigor and in specialization. The infusion of these young scholars reduced the monopoly of GSPA–SNU in the development and steering of Korean public administration.

2. Indigenization has been accelerated by works of new returnees who recognized the irrelevance of some American administrative theories in explaining and understanding Korean bureaucratic phenomena.

3. The period witnessed a drastic shift in disciplinary orientation from administrative law to the social sciences. The government's higher civil service examination also reflected this shift. Concomitantly, additional change occurred with the movement of the administrative structure of departments out from law schools to under the social science umbrella. The curricula of public administration have gone through extensive revision.

4. Korean public administration scholars have frequently participated in international bodies and conferences, including the International Institute of Administrative Sciences, Eastern Regional Organization for Public Administration, and the American Society for Public Administration.

5. The effort to develop a specifically Korean public administration brought debate on ethics and epistemology. For the most part the newly returned scholars led the debate by introducing the logic of social inquiry and methodological frameworks based on the philosophy of science, and they have been challenged by epistemologists.

In quantitative terms, the EPA in Korea has experienced rapid changes, including institutional restructure, increases in public administration programs, growing student enrollment, and professional activities associated with the KAPA. The quantitative growth, however, has not been accompanied by qualitative strength.

1. The faculty-student ratio is much too high to adequately meet the needs of graduate and undergraduate students. Five or six faculty members in each program can provide only the minimum standard of teaching. If Korean public administration is to move beyond the present state of mass education, faculty size in each program must be increased.

2. The undergraduate curricula are concentrated disproportionately within the disciplinary core and are sparse in the interdisciplinary fields. There is an urgent need to enrich the undergraduate program by incorporating relevant academic disciplines including economics, science, and technology, and a broader liberal arts curriculum.

3. On the research side, many writers have regurgitated known principles keyed to the civil service examinations. Far less effort has been given to original research. Basic and applied research must be given higher priority.

4. Cross-fertilization among different disciplines and practitioners is essential. Administrative scholars must deal with important societal problems and practices that are interdependent in nature. This focus will reduce the disparity between theory and practice.

5. In the future, Korean scholars should participate more often in international collaboration, including research projects and publication in international journals—sharing the Korean experience with the rest of the world.

Since 1981 there has been an explosive student exodus from Korea to foreign countries, especially to the United States. Most of these students have been enrolled in graduate programs, and it is expected that they will return to Korea in the early 1990s. In the 1980s there was also a rapid expansion of domestic graduate programs, especially at the doctoral level; the expanded programs will produce many PhDs in the 1990s. In combination, these two groups will result in a new third wave of scholars able to contribute to solving the problems of public administration existing in Korea.

Notes

1. L. D. White, *Introduction to the Study of Public Administration* (New York: Macmillan, 1926), translated by Inhung Chung, Hahn Been Lee, Hyo-Won Cho, Byong-Tae Min, Se-Chang Yoon, and Tong-Won Kim (Seoul: Ulyoo-moon-hwasa, 1958); Korean Association for Public Administration, *Public Administration Terms and Phrases* (Seoul: Korean Association for Public Administration, 1959).
2. J. G. March and H. A. Simon, *Organizations* (New York: Wiley, 1958).
3. Sintaek Kang, "Scope and Modes of Analysis in Public Administration: Past and Future," *KPAR*, 22-1 (1987), pp. 3–32.

PART
VIII

*Administrative Reform
Strategy*

CHAPTER TWENTY

Two Critical Combinations for Successful Administrative Reform

Hahn Been Lee

ONE OF THE recurring questions asked by many students of administrative reform in developing countries is: Why among so many administrative reforms undertaken were so few successful? Were they wrong reforms in the first place? Or were some right reforms undertaken at wrong times?

This paper discusses two crucial combinations deemed essential for successful conduct of administrative reform. One is related to the combination of right reform ideas with right demands of social change; the other is the combination of competent reform agents with enlightened political leadership.

Combinations of Right Reform Ideas with Right Social Demands

The initial stage of socioeconomic development usually involves a rapid spread of education often accompanied by some sweeping social measures, such as land reform, designed to redress some conspicuous imbalances in antecedent social structure. Whatever shape the initial developmental thrust may take, socioeconomic development of a country unleashes an enormous amount of pent-up social energy and produces a large number of new social groups such as the educated youth, the intelligentsia, the military, the industrial managers, and the new urban citizenry.

These pose a serious challenge to the bureaucracy of a developing society, for the bureaucracy in such a society tends to be static and closed. Thus, a precondition to administrative reform in such a dynamic social

Taken from Hahn Been Lee, "Two Critical Combinations for Successful Administrative Reform," in Chung-Hyun Ro and Mila Reforma (eds.), *Social Change and Administrative Reform Towards the Year 2000*, Eastern Regional Organization for Public Administration, Manila, the Philippines, 1985, pp. 30–36.

context is the opening up of the bureaucracy itself in order to meet the new demands of the fast-changing society.

How can the bureaucracy be opened up? The most suitable instrument for this purpose is the creation of new programs and organizations. On the surface, retrenchment in programs and organizations might seem to contribute to reform, but the realities of bureaucratic life show the contrary. When a closed bureaucracy has to retrench, it tends to cut off its most flexible elements and hence becomes all the more rigid and closed. This often occurs when the bureaucracy of a developing country tries to introduce "economy and efficiency" measures under the name of administrative reform. Usually the more reformist elements are weeded out.

The right reform for a closed bureaucracy is programmatic. Thus, when a government launches major substantive programs in such fields as agriculture, education, community development, and public works, mobilizing a substantial part of its human and financial resources and bending its organizational structure and procedures to carry out such projects, the move itself is a major administrative reform. Some of its best administrators have to be employed. New blood must be brought in and many technical and professional people become involved to make the program a success. As new norms are created by the sweep of new programs, a new sense of rationality and efficiency emerges among the implementors of major development programs. Consequently a new-method consciousness emerges after the initial push. This is usually the best time to introduce method-oriented reforms.

But someone must pave the way. Who makes the necessary tools or reform ready when major programs are undertaken? There must be some one to do the preparatory work. Thus, we come to the concept of innovational enclaves.

In any bureaucracy in a rapidly changing society, there always exist some units or islands in which some relatively change-prone and reformist elements find themselves. They are usually senior career administrators with professional competence and relative external exposure. They are interested in applying new approaches to their tasks. The new ideas may have come from their earlier contacts with the outside world either through training or tours. Because of their reputed competence they are secure enough in their work setting and are sufficiently motivated to try new ideas. We might call these islands *enclaves of innovation*.

Members of these groups are usually technically minded and tend to become method-oriented reformers. Being buried in a conservative bureaucracy, still being interested in promoting new ideas, they are eager to find similar-minded elements in other organizations in and around the bureaucracy. Thus, there evolve some informal alliances among more reform-minded senior administrators across ministerial boundaries, often reaching out to some parabureaucratic organizations such as research organizations in and around the bureaucracy.

Finally, when some major political event takes place that enables the launching of major substantive programs necessitated by the changing time, it is usually from these enclaves of innovation that the task elites necessary for the implementation of major programs are drawn. This way they become the advocates of administrative reform.

Combination of Reform-Minded Administrators with Enlightened Political Leadership

Administrative reform is a deliberate effort to introduce innovative ideas into the working of government, i.e., into the structure, process, and conduct of government administration. Even a small administrative reform started in a limited sphere can eventually involve a government-wide change. But government bureaucracy is basically conservative and resistant to change. In the beginning, administrative reform may be regarded as a technical matter but it soon becomes a highly political matter. Thus, for any administrative reform to be implemented, it requires a congruence of strong innovative forces at work.

Who initiates the process? In a governmental setting, it is usually some innovative higher civil servants who play the advocating role. They form the crucial link between the rank-and-file bureaucrats and the political decisionmakers. Thus, a prerequisite is that there must exist within the higher echelons of the bureaucracy some innovative "technocrats" secure enough in their work situation but sufficiently motivated to advocate new ideas.

This is not enough, however. To secure such a contribution from the reformist elements of the higher civil service requires a parallel existence of enlightened political leaders willing to adopt such ideas for their own political reasons. Innovation takes root only when new ideas are forcefully advocated and become vigorously adopted.

In the practical world of government, it is usually some innovative higher civil servants who have to take the advocate role and some political leaders who have to take the adopter at their own risk in order that any serious administrative reform can be undertaken and carried through. It is absolutely important that this combination occur. This is the crucial combination of task elites with power elites. This is the necessary condition for administrative reform.

The Korean Experience, 1955–1965

The overall administrative experience of the Korean government during the eventful ten-year period covering the latter half of the 1950s into the first half of the 1960s illustrates the importance of these combinations.

The mid 1950s was a period that saw the country busy in rehabilitation and reconstruction of the war-torn economy while building a large peacetime army. Various detailed tasks to receive and absorb massive economic and defense assistance were being carried out. The foundations were laid for more systematic development planning.

Among many governmental agencies engaged in these activities, several "islands" stood out in terms of concentration of professional expertise and innovational activities. These initial reform-related activities included, among many others:

1. the preparation of a system of national income accounts at the Research Development unit of the Bank of Korea;
2. a series of budgetary reforms at the Budget Bureau of the Ministry of Finance, starting with a new system of budgetary reclassification into functional and economic character categories (which would assist the system of national accounts mentioned above, and would automatically feed itself into the later schemes of multiyear economic development planning), followed by the initiation of a business-type accounting system into major government enterprises such as the National Railroad, the Post and Telecommunication System, and the Tobacco Monopoly;
3. the preparation of a preliminary three-year economic development plan by the Planning Bureau and the Economic Development Council of the newly established Ministry of Reconstruction; and
4. the efforts of the Planning and Programming Unit and other related offices of the ROK Army in transplanting the "programming budget and control system" of the U.S. Army.

Young and task-oriented leaders in these organizations were extremely serious about their individual reform efforts and busy building their respective technical staff. In the process, they actively reached out for contacts and mutual reinforcement among similarly reform-minded groups elsewhere. Several new parabureaucratic or extrabureaucratic institutions served as autonomous forums of exchange of ideas and talents. Prominent among these linking institutions were newly established professional schools such as:

1. the Graduate School of Public Administration of Seoul National University;
2. new Schools of Business Administration at two prominent private universities, i.e., Yonsei and Korea; and
3. new military service schools, especially the National Defense College and the Army Logistics School.

We should note here that the civilian educational institutions mentioned above drew many military officers as students and the military training schools reached extensively into civilian sources for teaching talent.

A favorable congruence of reformist energies was obtained when the new military regime that took power in 1961 sought its primary legitimation though an all-out adoption and vigorous implementation of systematic economic development planning, and, in the process, mobilized most of the reform-minded task elites hitherto scattered in the various enclaves. The central thrust of such a confluence of reformist energies was the creation of the Economic Planning Board, a new superministry representing in essence the marriage of the former Ministry of Reconstruction and the Budget Bureau, formerly of the Ministry of Finance. Over the succeeding years, many of the members of the several enclaves of innovation were recruited extensively into various leading positions of this new superministry and through it branched out into the entire spectrum of the government as economic development proceeded.

Lessons to Be Drawn

The Korean experience outlined above offers some lessons in regard to administrative reforms in developing countries.

The first lesson might be that administrative reform must be generated from within the bureaucracy, that is, it has to be nourished in some enclaves before it is carried out on a broad scale. In a developing society the types of reform in the initial stage of development are more likely to be new methods of technical procedures because of the generally technocratic orientations of the senior civil servants who occupy strategic positions of innovational potential. It is important at this stage that the types of reform advocated be relevant to the urgent needs of the society. The task of selecting the right types of reform is patently the responsibility of the administrative elites.

Two caveats are in order in this connection. One is that technical reforms conducted mainly under the aegis of foreign experts are seldom successful. Another caveat is that a reform project by whim or by fiat has little chance of success, however eager the reform leaders may be.

In the Korean case, there were indeed massive inputs of external economic and military assistance at the time, but there was no assistance specifically geared to stage a comprehensive "administrative reform," other than building some educational and training institutions designed to increase the general administrative and managerial capabilities. Yet, there emerged in time indigenous centers of reform-minded individuals and groups within the bureaucracy who became the spearheads of innovation when the favorable time came.

A second lesson that could be drawn is that the bureaucracy must be made relatively flexible, that is, loosened and opened up at least to the extent that innovative administrators interested in reform could feel secure enough to build a core of staff to do the spade work. To enable the reform ideas of the task elites to be implemented, they must be matched by a truly enlightened political leadership. However reform-minded some leaders of innovative enclaves may be, they alone cannot carry out major administrative reforms. Minor technical reform experiments in their limited domains will be all that is possible. Major administrative reforms involving significant changes in work programs, structures, and procedures across many governmental organizations are political in nature and produce major political repercussions. Administrative reforms must therefore have political sponsorship. Accordingly, there is no substitute for an enlightened political leadership adopting reforms as instruments of political legitimation.

Many countries in the Asian-Pacific region are in the midstream of nation building and socioeconomic development. One sincerely hopes that lessons can be drawn by some countries from the Korean experience. From the point of view of practical conduct of administrative reform, one cannot put too much emphasis on the need for bureaucratic flexibility to allow for reform-oriented senior civil servants to initiate innovative ideas at their level and steadily build up staff capabilities toward their intended reforms. At the same time, lateral channels of entry into the higher positions of the bureaucracy are highly desirable to reinforce such flexibility. Tight closure of the higher echelons of bureaucracy against lateral entry is, in my view, a sure guarantee of blockage of administrative reform in the country.

As for the emergence of requisite political leadership, this is the function of the larger political system, which goes beyond the sphere of this chapter. But one has to try to convince political leaders in various countries that it is to their basic advantage to espouse and adopt genuine administrative reforms relevant to the current stage of their respective national development.

The Right Administrative Reform Toward the Year 2000

In a country like Korea, which has attained the objectives of the first stage of socioeconomic development, there arises a new administrative challenge. This stems from the very success of the earlier stage. The spectacular economic and social development of the past quarter century has generated an immense social change, the primary consequence of which is that there is now prevailing in this country a highly educated, highly urbanized, and highly citizen-conscious society.

Thus, the country now comprises a qualitatively different society from that which it had a quarter century ago. Above all, this change requires a drastically different bureaucrat-citizen relationship. The citizens are highly self-conscious and bound to be increasingly tax-and-service conscious. Bureaucrats who could claim an almost exclusive preeminence in earlier periods now confront many competing elite groups in the society. Thus, new behaviors are required by them. The future requires more people-oriented administrative reforms. It also necessitates a more decentralized administrative system. The demand for administrative services is made at the same time that people insist they are delivered with an efficiency not inferior to that of industry.

How can the bureaucracy change its attitude and behavior to meet the new citizen demands of the more mature society? It is precisely this kind of administrative reform that will be most demanded by countries like Korea between now and the year 2000.

CHAPTER TWENTY-ONE

Democratization and Administrative Reform in Korea: A New Direction

Bun Woong Kim

KOREA'S REMARKABLE TRANSFORMATION into an industrialized nation has substantially changed the very nature of its sociopolitics and administration. Although many indicators are mixed, socioeconomic and political trends are generally progressing in a positive direction resulting in increased popular political participation, free enterprise, and a more open society. Democratic government and greater individual freedom now represent the wave of Korea's future.

In his inauguration speech, Korea's president Roh Tae Woo assured that he would put forth all his best efforts toward democratic reform, proclaiming "the era of the common man."

> The day when freedoms and human rights could be slighted in the name of economic growth and national security has ended. The day when repressive force and torture in secret chambers were tolerated is over.

Nevertheless, four decades of autocratic rule have left Korea with few liberal-pluralist politics and institutions. The authoritarian government bureaucracy has consistently resisted calls for genuine administrative reforms. Korea is now in the process of creating an equally dynamic political and administrative system to match the vitality of the "newly industrializing" economy and rapidly changing society.

However, Korea faces new stresses, a wide range of challenges that require enduring political stability as well as economic prosperity. Success in meeting these will necessitate a creative, responsive politico-administrative system. Naturally, old patterns of bureaucratic politics no longer suffice in a new Korea. Clearly, Korea's move toward political maturity

Taken from Bun Woong Kim, "Democratization and Administrative Reform in Korea: A New Direction," paper presented to the 49th National Conference of the American Society for Public Administration, Portland, Oregon, March 1988.

must proceed with socioeconomic progress and administrative reform as well.

Bureaucratization of Politics vs. Politicization of Bureaucracy

Most newly industrializing nations must face the paradox of development administration that "effective administration is essential to accomplish development, and yet its very effectiveness can also stifle and inhibit political development."[1] The trouble is that strengthening administration may inhibit the course of political development in both political power and political institutions. Since the early 1960s government intervention in Korean economic development has been justified as a success by ruling party politicians and bureaucrats. Economic growth has taken precedence over political development, reflecting a "bureaucratization of politics."

In the governmental setting of the 1960s and 1970s, the policy role of bureaucrats was exceptionally dominant over the interest aggregation of organized political forces. Bureaucratic policy making was too strongly advocated to argue against its prevalent role images. Some innovative higher civil servants usually initiated a leading role in administrative reform, although the government bureaucracy was basically conservative and resistant to change. However, to secure such a reformist innovation required a parallel policy advocation of enlightened political leaders. In fact, an effective combination of rank-and-file task elites with power elites nurtured and encouraged a bureaucratic politics as well as administrative reforms.

There is tacit agreement among Korean intellectuals that the components of the Korean government interventionist role are traceable to its authoritarian bureaucratic elitism, culturally pervasive in sociopolitics and administration. A consistent reliance on the centralized administrative elites nurtured a bureaucratization of politics, impeding the democratic pluralist setting that was on trial.

Second, an alliance of the senior bureaucrats and the military turned-politicians has resulted in a "politicization" of bureaucracy since the military intervention of General Park's regime in politics. Various groups of ex-generals and colonels from the Second Republic (1961) to the Sixth Republic have occupied the key governmental positions at ministerial and agency head levels, provincial governorships, and heads of public enterprises, and also have held the essential positions of viable ruling political parties.

A hybrid praxis toward democratization must be pursued to reconcile the setting of both the bureaucratization of politics and the politicization of bureaucracy. A possible synthesis—an integration of politics with administration—should be reexamined toward the "hypothetical" convergences of the roles of Korean bureaucrats and politicians, with the backgrounds, structures, functions, group behaviors, and system dynamics.

In this reciprocally synthesizing context, possible images and strategies of administrative reform should be reviewed and modeled in the process of political democratization.

Political Maturity and Administrative Reform

Korea's ongoing move toward political democratization is expected to mature with its continued industrialization, a new popular consciousness, greater national self-confidence, proliferation of technocratic elites, and a new generation of democratic leadership. Koreans also face the challenge of permanently "civilizing" their politics and government, calling upon all their talent to lead an increasingly complex economy and society. Korea's industry and business compete aggressively and impressively on the world stage. Today its international trade ranks twelfth in the world. Koreans' GNP per capita is now U.S. $3,450 and expected to reach U.S. $5,800 in the year 1992 (when the Sixth Five-Year Socioeconomic Plan ends). Korea has already made an historic commitment toward greater democratization. Accordingly, there appears to be a general consensus among Koreans of various political persuasions that government institutions and administrative practices up to now are inadequate to meet Korea's complex present and future demands. A drastic administrative reform will be a critical part of the political democratization.

Korea now has the opportunity to match its socioeconomic progress with great politico-administrative reforms. If it succeeds in reestablishing a better administrative apparatus, it will have laid the groundwork not only for enduring democratic progress but also for enduring economic prosperity.

Some broad generalizations about current Korean politics and administration are widely assumed: First, the simultaneous pursuit of political development and stability will invigorate the democratic liberalization and inspire a greater public participation gradually shifting from "crisis politics" to "interest politics."

Second, administrative reforms should be directed toward deregulation, decentralization, popular participation, and more openness in the government, shifting from bureaucratic authoritarianism to democratic autonomy. Anticipating the structural–functional changes of the government, a more adequate institutional framework should be based on establishing a new tradition of peaceful political leadership succession, enlarging citizen participation, revitalizing local autonomy, realigning the governmental roles, and strengthening law and order.

Third, current economic order and institutions should be reframed to enhance the quality of life, and to draw social equity and justice that promote economic efficiency, provide equal opportunity, and enforce fair remuneration. To meet this objective, a free-market mechanism is required to keep a competitive spirit and to encourage private initiative through setting innovative entrepreneurship and liberalized principles.

Specifically, government policy should be directed to the prevention of economic power concentration; promotion of fair competition, autonomy, and liberalization in the financial sector; privatization of the public enterprises; modifications in land use and transactions; institutionalized consumer protection; and encouragement of private sector initiative.

The Korean experience in recent decades may prove the reality that "democracy is unlikely to last without economic progress, but economic progress does not necessarily guarantee democracy." Here the public bureaucracy must play an intermediate role to parallel balanced economic growth with democracy. The crucial questions of administrative reform concerning this task are indeed: what and how?

New Constitution and Governmental Reorganization

In the context of these guidelines for reform, the new constitution of the Sixth Republic of Korea intensifies legislative/judicial control over the executive and revives local self-government autonomy, liberalization of the economy, promotion of social equity, the guaranty of freedom of expression, association, organization, and so forth. A recent national policy seminar report recommends the reorganization of Korea's national government ensuring the principles of simplification, democratization, and economic self-regulation.

The functions of the Ministry of Home Affairs should be reexamined under the context of the new political environment. The police function should be neutralized from politics by bringing it under an independent regulatory commission. The Bureau of Budget should be removed from the EPB and be placed directly under the prime minister. The Ministry of Education should be relieved from university administration, and this function should also belong to an independent commission. The Ministry of Culture and Public Information also has to be relieved of its propaganda function.

The legislative control over the reorganization process should be enhanced. Bureaus of the central government agencies and the field offices should be stipulated in the laws rather than in presidential decrees.

The establishment of committees and councils including those of advisory capacities should be encouraged rather than restricted.

The establishment of endowment institutes belonging to individual ministries should also be restricted because these institutes perform functions that were originally supposed to be the main duties of civil servants.

Finally, the delegation of functions to the private sector and to the field should be closely accompanied by a corresponding reduction of workforces of the delegating agencies.

The reforms suggested above should be feasible but may be somewhat "revolutionary" in the administrative dynamics of structural-functional change of the Korean governmental apparatus.

Regulatory Reform and Economic Democracy

For the last quarter century the efficiency of government intervention in the Korean economy has been praised as a success, and no one could argue against the very necessity of this intervention. The regulatory mechanism was solidified by the presidential leadership drive and the interventionist roles of the bureaucratic elites. In recent years, however, its effectiveness has been intensively questioned and argued because of the latent inefficiency of the government control mechanism and the economic liberalization trend. Especially in the 1980s, governmental intervention was challenged by Korea's economic management for structural adjustment, i.e., the Comprehensive Measures for Economic Stabilization (CMES) initiated on April 17, 1979. In the words of In Joung Whang:

> CMES signified a drastic policy change in the sense that proposals for a gradual reduction of fiscal and monetary incentives for export promotion and agricultural subsidies, decreases in rural housing loans, and a realignment of investment schema for heavy and chemical industries could be hardly discussed in the 1970s. They were treated as "taboos" before these policy issues were raised in the process of decision making with regard to CMES. The adoption of CMES indeed implies a fundamental deviation from the philosophy and the way of thinking underlying management of the national economy applied by the government in the 1960s and early 1970s. Because policy change imposes both benefits and costs, CMES faced resistance from various groups of society. The resistance to policy changes envisaged by CMES stemmed primarily from bureaucratic inertia, vested interest groups, and sometimes from institutional constraints.[2]

A very efficacious substitute for governmental economic intervention can be private entrepreneurial initiative based on the free-market mechanism.

First, Korean economic administration should be transformed from direct intervention to a free-market approach that permits greater reliance on private initiative and requires a more modest role for government than is usually deemed necessary. The administrative elites' development of an interventionist role in the Korean economy should be diverted to an indirect inducement role seeking, one would hope, economic democracy— the transfer of economic decision making from the few to the many. A strategy of reform must transfer economic power from bureaucratic elites to private industries.

Second, excessive regulatory costs of government economic intervention should be saved through deregulatory reform based on a free-market mechanism. The innovative techniques of a market-oriented approach to regulation are very necessary to replace the traditional command-and-control form of regulation.

Third, the Korean government has so far overregulated its economy. Administrative reforms toward an open economy may bring about a more autonomous, sensible, and efficient government without sacrificing Korea's economic development in the last quarter century. Liberalizing the Korean economy by deregulatory reform may promise a base of administrative autonomy and a greater trust in economic democracy.

A New Direction

In Korea today, administrative change is propelled by socioeconomic development and democratic necessity, by international trends and internal popular pressures. The progress of democracy and administrative reform in Korea is now at a crossroads. A democratization of far-reaching breadth and meaning is presently sweeping Korea. Hence, what role for government? Korea has the very opportunity to match its economic development with a great political democratization. However, it is evident that Korea now faces a troubling paradox: a strong administration can retard the course of political development, whereas the generation of political power—both of leaders and of the public—can weaken the growth of administrative capacity.

In this context, we argue and emphasize some administrative reform strategies for a lasting democracy in Korea.

First, the extreme policy role disequilibrium between politicians and bureaucrats—a bureaucratization of politics vs. a politicization of politics—should be readjusted toward a possible hybrid in praxis.

Second, given the limits and inefficiency of government intervention in economic development, the effectiveness of bureaucratic elitism and the civil–military rule of the guardian model of the Paraetorian military should be questioned in the current Korean socioeconomic and political setting. A shift from bureaucratic authoritarianism to democratic autonomy is anticipated through the process of deregulation, decentralization, citizen participation, and more openness in the government. Third, past Korean experience also proves that economic progress does not necessarily guarantee democracy. The administrative interventionist role should be transformed to an "indirect inducement role" heading positively for an economic democracy and enhancing the private entrepreneurial initiative posited on a free-market mechanism.

Finally, we should address the belief that Korea's administrative reform in the process of political democratization is expected to seek its own possibilities for development *sui generis,* on the basis of indigenous archetypes and circumstances.

Notes

1. C. Bryant and L. D. White, *Managing Development in the Third World* (Boulder, Colo.: Westview Press, 1982), p. 25.
2. In Joung Whang, "Korea's Economic Management for Structural Adjustment in the 1980s," paper presented at the World Bank and Korea Development Institute, Washington, D.C., June 1986.

Selected English-Language Bibliography

Ahn, Byung-joon. "Progress of Democracy in Korea: A Comparative Perspective," in *Progress in Democracy: The Pacific Basin Experience* (Seoul: Ilhae Institute, 1987), pp. 19–33.

Ahn, Chung Si. "Korean Politics in a Period of Transition," in John W. Longford and K. Lorne Brownsey (eds.), *The Changing Shape of Government in the Asia-Pacific Region* (Halifax, Nova Scotia: The Institute for Research on Public Policy, 1988).

Bark, Dong-Suh, and Lee, Chae-Jin. "Bureaucratic Elite and Development Orientation," in Dae-Sook Suh and Chae-Jin Lee (eds.), *Political Leadership in Korea* (Seattle: University of Washington Press, 1976), pp. 91–133.

Bayard, Thomas, and Young, Soo-Gil (eds.). *Economic Relations between the United States and Korea: Conflict or Cooperation?* (Washington: Institute for International Economics, 1989).

Bridges, Brian. *Korea and the West.* Chatham House Papers: 39 (London: The Royal Institute of International Affairs, 1986).

Chang, Dal-Joong. *Economic Control and Political Authoritarianism: The Role of Japanese Corporations in Korean Politics 1965–79* (Seoul: Sogang University Press, 1985).

Cho, Chang-hyun. "The Ideals and Practices of Local Self-Government in Korea," in Chang-hyun Cho and Roswitha Rothlack (eds.), *Local Self-Government* (Seoul: Center for Local Autonomy, Hanyang University, 1987), pp. 19–36.

————, and Weckbecker, Arno (eds.). *Political Parties, Local Autonomy and Democracy* (Seoul: Center for Local Autonomy, Hanyang University, 1989).

Choi, Byung Sun. "Political and Economic Liberalization and Its Impact on the Government-Business Relationship in Korea," *The Korea Journal of Policy Studies* 3 (1988):31–60.

Chung, Chung-Kil. "Policy-Making within the Executive Branch—Application of an American Model to Three Korean Cases," in Bun Woong Kim, David S. Bell, and Chong Bum Lee (eds.), *Administrative Dynamics and Development: The Korean Experience* (Seoul: Kyobo Publishing, 1985), pp. 116–137.

Clough, Ralph N. *Balancing Act: The Republic of Korea Approaches 1988.* FPI Policy Briefs (Washington, D.C.: Foreign Policy Institute of the Johns Hopkins University School of Advanced International Studies, 1987).

_____ . *Embattled Korea: The Rivalry for International Support* (Boulder, Colo.: Westview Press, 1987).

Cole, David C., and Lyman, Princeton, N. *Korean Development: The Interplay of Politics and Economics* (Cambridge, Mass.: Harvard University Press, 1971).

Cole, David C., and Park, Yung Chul. *Financial Developments in Korea, 1945–1978* (Cambridge, Mass.: Harvard University Press, 1983).

Economic Planning Board. *Social Indicators in Korea 1989.* (Seoul: National Bureau of Statistics, EPB, Korea, 1989).

Haggard, Stephan, and Moon, Chung-In, "The Korean State in the International Economy: Liberal, Dependent, or Mercantile?" in Ruggie, John Gerald (ed.), *The Antinomies of Interdependence: National Welfare and the International Division of Labor* (New York: Columbia University Press, 1983).

Hahm, Pyoung Choon. *Korean Jurisprudence Politics and Culture* (Seoul: Yonsei University Press, 1986).

_____ . *The Korean Political Tradition and Law* (Seoul: Royal Asiatic Society-Hollym Corporation, 1967).

Hamilton, Clive. *Capitalist Industrialization in Korea* (Boulder, Colo.: Westview Press, 1986).

Han, Sung-joo. "Political Institutionalization in South Korea, 1961–1984," in Scalapino, Robert A., Sato, Seisaburo, and Wanadi, Jusuf (eds.), *Asian Political Institutionalization* (Berkeley: University of California Press, 1985).

Hasan, Parvez, and Rao, D. C. *Korea: Policy Issues for Long-Term Development,* The Report of a Mission sent to the Republic of Korea by the World Bank (Baltimore: Johns Hopkins University Press, 1979).

_____ . *Korea: Problems and Issues in a Rapidly Growing Economy.* A World Bank Country Economic Report (Baltimore: Johns Hopkins University Press, 1976).

Henderson, Gregory. *Korea: The Politics of the Vortex* (Cambridge, Mass.: Harvard University Press, 1968).

Hong, Wontack. *Trade, Distortions, and Employment Growth in Korea* (Seoul: Korea Development Institute, 1979).

Jacobs, Norman. *The Korean Road to Modernization and Development* (Urbana and Chicago: University of Illinois Press, 1985).

Johnson, Chalmers. "Political Institutions and Economic Performance: The Government-Business Relationship in Japan, South Korea, and Taiwan," in Robert A. Scalapino, Seisaburo Sato, and Jusuf Wanadi (eds.), *Asian Economic Development—Present and Future* (Berkeley: University of California Press, 1985).

Jones, Leroy P., and Sakong, Il. *Government, Business, and Entrepreneurship in Economic Development: The Korean Case* (Cambridge, Mass: Harvard University Press, 1980).

Jun, Jong Sup. "Decentralization and Local Administration: A Step Toward Democratic Government in Korea," *Political Studies Review* 1 (1985):53–73.

Jung, Yong Duck, and Siegel, G. "Testing Perceptions of Distributive Justice in Korea," *Journal of Northeast Asian Studies* 2(2) (1983):45–66.

————. "Distributive Justice and Redistributive Policy in Korea," *Korean Social Science Journal* 11 (1984):43–62.

Kim, Bun Woong, Bell, David, S., and Lee, Chong-Bum (eds.). *Administrative Dynamics and Development: The Korean Experience* (Seoul: Kyobo Publishing Co., 1985).

Kim, Bun Woong, and Rho, Wha-Joon (eds.). *Korean Public Bureaucracy* (Seoul: Kyobo Publishing Company, 1982).

Kim, Chong Lim (ed.). *Political Participation in Korea: Democracy, Mobilization, and Stability* (Santa Barbara, Calif.: Clio Books, 1980).

Kim, Dong Ki, and Kim, Linsu (eds.). *Management Behind Industrialization: Readings in Korean Business* (Seoul: Korea University Press, 1989).

Kim, Hyung Kook, and Geisse, Guillermo. "The Political Economy of Outward Liberalization: Chile and South Korea in Comparative Perspective," *Asian Perspective* 12(2) (1988):35–68.

Kim, Ilpyong J., and Kihl, Young Whan. *Political Change in South Korea* (New York: Paragon House Publishers, 1988).

Kim, Kihwan. *The Korean Economy: Past Performance, Current Reforms, and Future Prospects* (Seoul: Korea Development Institute, 1985).

Kim, Kwang Suk, and Roemer, Michael. *Growth and Structural Transformation* (Cambridge, Mass.: Harvard University Press, 1980).

_____. "The Korean Patterns of Economic Management: Lessons from Experience in the 1960s and 1970s," in Yoon Hyung Kim, Chung Hoon Lee, and Daniel B. Suits (eds.), *Anatomy of Korean Economic Policies in the 1960s and 1970s: The Interaction of Government and Business in Economic Development* (Honolulu: The East-West Population Institute, 1987).

Kim, Kyong-Dong (eds.). *Dependence Issues in Korean Development: Comparative Perspectives* (Seoul: Seoul National University Press, 1987).

Kim, Se-Jin, and Cho, Chang-hyun (eds.). *Korea: A Divided Nation* (Silver Spring, Md.: The Research Institute on Korean Affairs, 1976).

Kim, Young Jong. *Bureaucratic Corruption: The Case of Korea* (Seoul: Choon Choo Gak Publishing, 1986).

Kwak, Tae Hwan, Kim, Chonghan, and Kim, Hong Nack (eds.). *Korean Reunification: New Perspectives and Approaches* (Seoul: Kyung University Press; Boulder, Colo.: Westview Press, 1984).

Koo, Hagen. "The Interplay of State, Social Class, and World System in East Asian Development: The Cases of South Korea and Taiwan," in Frederic C. Deyo (ed.), *The Political Economy of the New Asian Industrialism* (Ithaca, N.Y.: Cornell University Press, 1987), pp. 172–179.

Koo, Youngnok, and Han, Sung-jee (eds.). *The Foreign Policy of the Republic of Korea* (New York: Columbia University Press, 1985).

Korea Development Institute. *Korea Year 2000: Prospects and Issues for Long-Term Development* (Seoul: KDI Press, 1986).

Korean Political Science Association. *The Korean National Community and State Development* (Seoul: Korean Political Science Association, 1989).

Kuznetz, Paul W. *Economic Growth and Structure in the Republic of Korea* (New Haven: Yale University Press, 1977).

Lee, Changsoo. *Modernization of Korea and the Impact of the West* (Los Angeles: East Asian Studies Center, University of Southern California, 1981).

Lee, Chong Bum. "A Prolegomenon to the Indigenization of Public Administration," in Bun Woong Kim and Wha Joon Rho (eds.), *Korean Public Bureaucracy* (Seoul: Kyobo Publishing, 1982), pp. 362–387.

Lee, Chung H., and Yamazawa, Ippei. *The Economic Development of Japan and Korea* (New York: Praeger, 1989).

Lee, Hahn Been. *Korea: Time, Change, and Administration* (Honolulu: East-West Center Press, 1968).

————, and Kang, Sintaek. "Development of the Study of Public Administration of Korea," in Bun Woong Kim and Wha-Joon Rho (eds.), *Korean Public Bureaucracy* (Seoul: Kyobo Publishing, 1982), pp. 18–45.

Lee, Seong Hyong, and Kwak, Tae-Hwan (eds.). *Koreans in North America* (Seoul: Kyungnam University Press, 1988).

Lim, Gill Chin. *Korean Development into the 21st Century: Economic, Political and Spatial Transformation* (Seoul: Myung-Bo Publishing, 1988).

Lim, Youngil. *Government Policy and Private Enterprise: Korean Experience in Industrialization* (Berkeley: University of California Press, 1981).

Mason, Edward S., Kim, Mahn Je, Perkins, Dwight H., Kim, Kwang Suk, and Cole, David C. *The Economic and Social Modernization of the Republic of Korea* (Cambridge, Mass: Harvard University Press, 1980).

Michell, Tony. "South Korea: Visions of the Future for Labor Surplus Economies," in M. Bienefeld and M. Godfrey (eds.), *The Struggle for Development: National Strategies in an International Context* (New York: John Wiley & Sons, 1982).

Ministry of Government Administration. *Korea Yearbook of Government Administration*, 1989.

Olsen, Edward A. *U. S. Policy and the Two Koreas* (Boulder, Colo.: Westview Press, 1987).

Pae, Sung Moon. "Korea Leading the Third World in Democratization," in Korean Political Science Association, *The Korean National Community and State Development* (Seoul: Korean Political Science Association, 1989), pp. 167–190.

————. *Testing Democratic Theories in Korea* (Lanham, N.Y.: University Press of America, 1986).

Paik, Wan Ki. "A Psycho-Cultural Approach to the Study of Korean Bureaucracy," in Bun Woong Kim and Wha Joon Rho (eds.), *Korean Public Bureaucracy* (Seoul: Kyobo Publishing, 1982), pp. 46–63.

Park, Chong-kee. *Human Resources and Social Development in Korea* (Seoul: Korea Development Institute, 1980).

Park, Chung-Oh, Lovrich, N. P. and Soden, D. L. "Testing Herzberg's Theory in a Comparative Study of U.S. and Korean Public Employees," *Review of Public Personnel Administration* 8 (Summer 1988):40–60.

Park, Chung Hee. *Our Nation's Path* (Seoul: Hollym Corp., 1970).

Rhee, Yang Soo. "A Cross-Cultural Comparison of Korean and American Managerial Styles," in B. W. Kim, D. S. Bell, and C. B. Lee (eds.), *Administrative Dynamics and Development: The Korean Experience* (Seoul: Kyobo Publishing, 1985), pp. 78–98.

Rho, Wha Joon. "Individual, Organizational and Socio-Political Determinants of Organizational Identification," in Bun Woong Kim and Wha Joon Rho (eds.), *Korean Public Bureaucracy* (Seoul: Kyobo Publishing, 1982), pp. 262–284.

Scalapino, Robert A., and Han, Sung-joo (eds.) *United States–Korea Relations.* Research Papers and Policy Studies No. 19. (Berkeley: University of California, Institute of East Asian Studies, 1986).

Secretariat for the President. *The 1980s: Meeting A New Challenge I–III* (Selected Speeches of President Chun Doo Hwang), 1981–1984.

Suh, Dae-Sook, and Lee, Chae-Jin (eds.). *Political Leadership in Korea* (Seattle: University of Washington Press, 1976).

Wade, L. L., and Kim, Bong Sik. *The Political Economy of Success: Public Policy and Economic Development in the Republic of Korea* (Seoul: Kyung Hee University Press, 1977).

Whang, In Joung. *Social Development in Action: The Korean Experience* (Seoul: Korea Development Institute, 1986).

_____. *Management of Rural Change in Korea* (Seoul: Seoul National University Press, Korea, 1981).

Woronoff, Jon. *Korea's Economy: Man-Made Miracle* (Seoul: Sisayongosa Publishers, 1983).

Wright, Edward Reynolds (ed.). *Korean Politics in Transition* (Seattle: University of Washington Press, 1975).

Yoo, Se Hee. "The International Context of US-Korea Relations: Special Focus on the 'Critical Views of the United States' in Korea since 1980," in Robert A. Scalapino and Sung-joo Han (eds.), *United States–Korea Relations* (Berkeley: Institute of East Asian Studies, University of California, 1986).

Yoon, Woo Kon. *Korean Public Bureaucracy: A Behavioral Perspective* (Seoul: Sung Kyun Kwan University Press, 1982).

Contributors

BELL, DAVID S., Jr., Ph.D., Indiana University, is Professor of Government at Eastern Washington University. He was a Visiting Fellow at the Institute of Southeast Asian Studies (Singapore, 1975–1976), was Exchange Professor at Dongguk University (Seoul, 1981–1982) and was on sabbatical leave at Dongguk University in 1984. He has lectured in Southeast Asia and in the Republic of Korea under the auspices of the United States Information Service. He has presented numerous papers at professional meetings and his articles have appeared in *The Journal of East Asian Affairs*, *The Asian Journal of Public Administration*, *Korea Observer*, and *The Korea Journal*.

CAIDEN, GERALD E., Ph.D., University of London, has served on the faculties of the Australian National University (1961–1966), Hebrew University (1966–1968), University of California, Berkeley (1968–1971), Haifa University (1971–1975), and the University of Southern California (1975–present). He has been visiting professor to Yonsei University (1983). He has published over twenty-five books and monographs and over one hundred and fifty journal articles. He has acted as an editorial consultant to several leading journals in the field of public administration and as a reader for notable publishing houses. He has also been consultant and researcher to a wide variety of public organizations.

CHOI, BYONG SUN, Ph.D., Harvard University, is assistant professor of public administration at Seoul National University. He has published many articles on government regulation, trade policy, economic policy making, and government-business relationship in *Korean Political Science Review*, *Korean Journal of Public Administration*, *Korean Journal of Policy Studies*, and other professional journals.

JUN, JONG S., Ph.D., University of Southern California, is professor and chair in the Department of Public Administration at the California State University, Hayward. He has served on several national committees of the American Society for Public Administration and on the editorial boards of *Public Administration Review* and *Administration and Society*. He has been a consultant to government agencies at the U.S. federal, state, and local levels. He is the author of *Public Administration: Design and Problem Solving* (1986) and *Management by Objectives in Government* (1976, and coauthor of *Tomorrow's Organizations* (1973) and *Administrative Alternatives in Development Assistance* (1973).

JUNG, YONG DUCK, Ph.D., University of Southern California, is associate professor of public administration at Sung Kyun Kwan University. He is the coauthor of *Public Administration* (1988) and *Korean Public Policy* (1984), and he has translated many works into Korean including Arthur M. Okun's *Equality and Efficiency*. He has published a number of articles on public policy analysis and management, regulatory policy, and welfare policy in *the Korean Social Science Journal*, *Korean Public Administration Review*, *Journal of Northeast Asian Studies*, *Journal of International and Public Affairs*, and *International Review of Administrative Sciences*.

KIM, BUN WOONG, Ph.D., Claremont Graduate School, is professor of public administration and Dean of Planning at Dongguk University. He was a visiting professor at the University of Southern California (1984), has served as a member of the Executive Committee of the Korean Society for Public Administration and Korean Political Science Association (1980–1982), and was consultant to the Economic Planning Board and Seoul City Government (1981–1983). He is the coeditor of *Administrative Dynamics and Development: The Korean Experience* (1985) and *Korean Public Bureaucracy* (1982); and has coauthored *Seminar in Public Administration* (1982), *Public Administration* (1981), and *Handbook of Korea* (1979). He has published numerous articles on public bureaucracy and comparative politics in *Korea Journal*, *Korean Public Administration Review*, *Korean Political Science Review* and *Asian Journal of Public Administration*.

KIM, DONG HYUN, Ph.D., University of Missouri, is professor of public administration and Dean of the Graduate School of Public Administration at Sung Kyun Kwan University. He was a senior fellow at the Korean Development Institute (1978–1981) and has served as a consultant to UNICEF, Seoul, and several ministries of the Korean government. He is the author of *Development Theories and Strategies: Critical Perspectives* (1984), and coauthored *Public Policy in Korea* (1984), *Public Administration Dictionary* (1984), *Foundation of Development Theory* (1988), *Professional Ethics and Occupation* (1985), *Understanding the Social Sciences* (1982), *Child Development Policies in Korea* (1982), and *Social Security in Korea* (1980). He has also published a number of articles pertaining to public policy and development administration in the *Korean Public Administration Review*, *Technology Transfer*, *Policy Regional Development Dialogue*, *Korea Journal*, and other professional journals.

KIM, MAHN KEE, Ph.D., University of Pittsburgh, is professor of public administration at Hankook University of Foreign Studies. He was Director of the Korean Association for Public Administration (1985–1986), Director of the Institute of Korean Regional Studies at the Hankook University, and a consultant to the Ministry of Government Administration. He is the author of *Cases of Educational Innovation* (1973), coauthor of *Public Administration* (1988), and numerous papers and articles on the Korean educational administration comparative administration, and public personnel administration in *Korean Political Science Review, Journal of Korean Public Administration, Korean Social Science Journal,* and other professional journals.

KIM, SHIN BOK, Ph.D., University of Pittsburgh, is professor of public administration at Seoul National University and Director of Korean Association for Public Administration. He was a visiting professor at UCLA (1989); he served as consultant to the ministries of Education and Government Administration, Economic Planning Board, and Board of Audit and Inspection, and a member of the Five-Year National Planning Committee in Korea. He is the author of *Development Planning* (1983) and has coauthored *Policy Science* (1989) and *Education and Development* (1980). He has published a number of articles in *Korean Journal of Public Administration, Korean Public Administration Review, Korean Political Science Review,* and *The Economist.*

KIM, SUK JOON, Ph.D., University of California, Los Angeles, is associate professor of public administration at Ewha University. He is the author of *The State Public Policy and NIC Development* (1988) and has published numerous articles on comparative and development administration, and public policy and state in *Asian Perspective, Pacific Focus, Korean Journal of Public Administration,* and *Korean Political Science Review.*

LEE, CHONG BUM, Ph.D., University of Pennsylvania, is professor of public administration at Korea University. He was Research Fellow at the University of Pennsylvania (1982) and served as chairperson of the Planning Committee, Korean Association for Public Administration (1981). He has published *Korean Public Bureaucracy: A Search for Pluralistic Society* (1986) and a number of articles on organization theory, research methodology, and development administration in the *Korean Social Science Journal, Law and Administration Review,* and *Korean Public Administration Review.* He has translated many works into Korean, including Herbert A. Simon's *The Sciences of the Artificial.*

LEE, HAHN BEEN, Ph.D., Seoul National University, is professor of public administration at Kyung Hee University. He has served as Vice Minister of Finance, Ambassador to Switzerland, Deputy Prime Minister, and Minister of the Economic Planning Board in the Korean government; Dean at the Graduate School of Public Administration, Seoul National University; Director of Technology and Development Institute, East-West Center; chairman at Korea Advanced Institute of Science & Technology; and President, Soong Jun University and Ajou University. Among his major books are *Korea: Time, Change & Administration* (1968), *Theory & Strategy of National Development* (1970), and *The Road to the Future* (1980). Dr. Lee has published numerous articles on development administration in the *International Review of Administrative Sciences, Philippine Journal of Public Administration,* and *Policy Sciences.*

PAIK, WAN KI, Ph.D., Florida State University, is professor of public administration at Korea University. He was president of Korean Association for Public Administration (1984) and was an editor of *Korean Social Science Journal* (1983–1985). He is the author of *Korean Public Administration* (1988) and *Korean Administrative Culture* (1982) and coauthor of *Korean Politics* (1976) and *Korean Political Process* (1982). Professor Paik has written a number of articles pertaining to development administration, comparative politics, and the Koreanization of American public administration.

WHANG, IN JOUNG, Ph.D., University of Pittsburgh, is Vice President of the Korea Development Institute. He was professor of public administration at Seoul National University (1968–1976) and served as a senior expert with the United Nations' Asian and Pacific Development Administration Center, Kuala Lumpur, Malaysia (1973–1978). His publications include *Public Administration and Economic Development* (1970), *Management of Family Planning Programs in Asia* (1976), and *Management of Rural Change in Korea* (1981), and a number of articles on the policy sciences and social development administration in *Asian Survey, Korea Journal, Journal of Korean Public Administration,* and other professional journals.

YOO, JONG HAE, Ph.D., University of Michigan, is professor of public administration and Director of Research Institute for Community Development at Yonsei University. He has served as President of the Korean Association for Public Administration (1983), assistant professor at Eastern Michigan University (1969–1971), a member of Special Committee on Local Government Autonomy of Prime Minister, and consultant to the Ministry of Government Administration. Professor Yoo has published over twenty books including *Modern Public Administration* (1988), *Development Administration* (1988), *Korean Dictionary of Public Administration* (1987), *Modern Organization Theory* (1986), and *Seminar in Public Administration* (1982); and journal articles in *Korean Public Administration Review, Korean Political Science Review, Korea Journal,* and *EROPA journal.*

YOUN, JUNG SUK, Ph.D., University of Michigan, is professor of political science at Choongang University, where he was Dean, College of Social Science (1983–1985), and Director, Institute of Area Studies (1986–1988). Dr. Youn has served as a consultant to the ministries of Defense and Home Affairs and as a member of Special Committee on the Constitutional Reform in Korea. He was research fellow at Japan Foundation and visiting professor at Keio/Rikkyo University, Japan, and University of the Philippines (1988–1989). Professor Youn has published *Japan's Foreign Policy and Korea* (1982) and *Japanese Political Leadership* (1980) and journal articles in *Korea and World Affairs, Pacific Focus,* and the *Korean Journal of International Relations.*

Index

Administrative reform
 conditions for success
 of, 239–241
 in development
 administration, 6, 243
 proposals for, xxvi–xxvii
 role of foreign experts,
 243
amae, meaning of, 29
American military
 government (AMG),
 reforms under, 65
Anticommunism,
 education and, 199–200
Anti-Monopoly and Fair
 Trade Act (1981), 89,
 106, 137
April Student Revolution
 (1960), 64, 65
Association of Southeast
 Asian Nations
 (ASEAN), 117–118
"Assuming that"
 syndrome, 186
Authoritarianism
 decentralization and,
 159
 democracy and, in
 Korea, 10
 East Asian societies
 compared, 33–34
 increase in unlikely,
 76–77
 in Korean political
 tradition, 246, 247

Banking, liberalization of
 government policies,
 142
Bank of Korea, Research
 Development Unit, 242
Banwol New Town, 176
Bark, Dong Suh, 213
Bell, David S., Jr., xvi
Bonds, in urban finance,
 168–169

Buddhism, in Korean
 culture, 27
Budgeting systems, EPB
 and, 98
Budgets, urban, 167–169
 reform of, 171
 in Seoul, 169
Bureaucracy
 Confucianism and, in
 East Asia, 27–28
 as criterion of state
 type, 62
 in developing nations,
 6–7, 19, 243
 Korean characteristics
 of, 73, 213
 in local government,
 148–149
 opening up a
 precondition to reform,
 239–240, 244
 policy-making role of,
 138–139
 prestige of, 155–156
 Rhee vs. Park on role
 of, 86
 role in modernization,
 xxi–xxii
 see also Civil service
 examinations; Elites,
 administrative;
 Recruitment; Training
Bureaucratic authoritarian
 (BA) model of
 development, 59
Bureaucratic politics
 model, for economic
 change, 103
Business administration,
 schools of, 242

Cabinet ministries
 as personal fiefdom of
 minister, 75
 role in economic
 planning, 92

Capital formation,
 government role in, 89
Capitalism. *See* "Guided
 capitalism"
Capital Region Growth
 Management Law
 (1982), 164
Centralization,
 administrative, 153–159
 development con-
 sequences of, xxii–xxiii
 in education, 205–206
 Korean tradition, 24, 138
 measurement of degree
 of, 148–149
 see also Decentralization
Chaebol (large enterprises)
 centralization and, 157
 government agencies
 and, 100
 government policies
 toward, x
Change, management of,
 5–6
Chang government
 (1960–1961), populism
 of, 159
Chang, Myon, 64
Changwon New Town, 165
Charismatic leader, Rhee
 as, 44–45
Charity strategy, for social
 development programs,
 192
Charter of National
 Education (1968), xxv,
 200
Chayu-dang (political
 party), 46
China
 basis of social actions
 in, 29
 Confucianism and
 Taoism in, 27
 development potential,
 117

familism in, 30–31, 33
legal system in, 34–35
public administration
in, xvii
"rule of courtesy" in, 37
see also Confucianism;
East Asia
Choe, Tu-sŏn, 46
Choi, Byung Sun, xx
Choi, Jae-sok, on *nunch'i*,
29
Chŏlla, influence of in
cabinet, 49
Chon, Hae-jong, on blood
lineage, 31
Cho, Suk-choon
on foreign
administrative theories
in Korea, 215
on Korean
administrative culture,
30
on Korean attitude to
law, 35–36
Chosun dynasty, 153
Chun, Doo-Hwang
CMES and, 93
economic growth under,
225
goals of regime, 64
new constitution of, 80
Chung, Inhung, 220
Civil service examinations
in China, 31
in East Asian societies,
27
educational curricula
geared toward, 211
under Yi dynasty, 50
Civil service. *See*
Bureaucracy
Clan systems, East Asian
societies compared,
32–33
Class struggle, role in
regime change, 64–65
Collectivism, East Asian
societies compared,
31–32
College entrance
examinations, 201–202
Commission of Military
Revolution and Military
Government, cabinet
members under, 52–53
Community-based strategy,
for social development
programs, 189–190

Community participation
NGOs and, 191
in social development,
183–184, 187–189
Comprehensive Measures
for Economic
Stabilization (CMES;
1979), xiii, xx
fundamental policy
changes, 250
main components of, 89
reasons for creating,
92–93
Computerization,
economic growth and,
111
Conflict resolution, in
economic policy
making, 98
Confucianism
authoritarianism and,
33
ethical view of, 28–29
hierarchical order
stressed by, 35–36
in Korean
administration, xvii
in Korean culture, 26, 28
pluralism in
government and, 154
rule of virtue vs. rule of
law, 34
Confucius, Analects, 28
Connolly, William, on
pluralism, 21
Consensus-building, in
economic planning, 92,
94
Constitution, revision of,
79–80, 95, 249
Coordination, interagency,
urban planning and,
174–177
Corporations, national. *See*
State-owned enterprises
Corruption, in public-
private development
partnership, 131
Costs
of public-administration-
driven development, 130
see also Efficiency
Council on
Democratization
Promotion, 72, 73
Crisis, types of, 60–61
Curricula
educational, 204–205

for public administration
schools, 231–232, 234

Dahl, Robert, 20, 68
Decentralization
administrative, political
centralization and, 151
defined, 150
in local social
development programs,
192–195
in urban administration,
178
see also Centralization,
administrative
Decision making
democratization of as
goal of reform, 95
effort to decentralize,
140
see also Policy making
Deconcentration, defined,
150
Democracy, 10, 69–72, 114,
248–249
bureaucratic elite and,
23–24
consociational, 77–78
economic, 143
reforms toward,
250–251
recruitment of elites
under, 50
Democratic Justice Party
(DJP), 78
dissolution of, 80
membership, 71
organization of, 70
patronage networks,
73–75
support for status quo,
79
Democratic Liberal Party,
formation of, 80
Democratic Republican
Party
dependence on military,
71–72
dissolution of, 70
Democratization,
administrative reform
and, xvii–xviii
Demographic change
future effects of, 108
in world population,
110
Demographic profile, of
ROK, 162

Dependency, financial, of
local governments, 149
Dependent development
model, 59–60
Deregulation
gains from, 141–142
see also Free-market
policies
Détente, East-West, Korea
and, 108–109
Developing societies
administrative reform
in, 243–244
military role in, 53
political pluralism and,
21–22
Development
changing concepts of,
10–11
shift from public to
private sector needed,
134
see also Bureaucratic
authoritarian (BA)
model of development;
Dependent
development model;
Economic development;
Social development
Development
administration
agendas for, 4–5
defined, 3–4
study of, 230
Development
administrators
characteristics of, xv
role of, xiv–xv
Development models,
Western, 115
application to Korea, xvi
Dictatorial leader
elites and, 47–48, 54–55
Rhee and Park as, 47
see also Charismatic
leader
Dimock, Marshall, on Jap-
anese bureaucracy, 37
DJP. *See* Democratic Justice
Party
Dong-A Ilbo (newspaper),
46
Duvergier, Maurice, 78

East Asia, development
prospects in, 116–117
Economic development
agendas for, 5

centralization of
government and, xxii–
xxiii, 156
concept of expanding
economy, 127–128
models for, 9–10
political and social
tradeoffs, 147
public administration
involvement in, 129–133
social development and,
193
urban, 166–167
Economic Management
Plans, formulation of,
91–92
Economic Planning Board
(EPB), xx–xxi, 174
autonomy of, 99,
101–102, 104
CMES implementation
and, 93–94
five-year development
plans and, 91–92
functions of, 96–97,
100–101, 105–106
influence in policy-
making, 102–103
origins of, 86–87, 243
policy and jurisdictional
conflicts, 97–98
political change and,
103–104
role in formulating
CMES, 92–93
Economic policy
after Korean War, x, xii
after Park, 103–104
changes under CMES,
93
conflict resolution in, 98
institutions involved in,
96–103
models for change in, 103
procedures for
establishing, 92
proposals for reform,
xxvii–xxviii
Economy
advanced, political
pluralism and, 67–68
internationalization of,
110, 116
see also Planning,
economic
Education
attempts at regional
balance, 203

financing of, 205–206
government role in, xiv
growth/quality tradeoff,
202, 209
local autonomy in,
205–206, 208
policy alternatives,
206–208
post-World War II
policies, xxiv–xxv, 199
rapid expansion in
1960s, 202–203
role in postwar
modernization, 113–114
role of reform in regime
change, 65
see also Curricula,
educational; Public
administration
education; Schools
Education, elementary,
199, 202
age of entry, 206–207
methods, 200–201
Education, higher
improvement of,
204–205
increased autonomy of,
207
as route to elite status,
50–52
Education Tax, 205, 206
Efficiency
democracy and, in
modernization process,
129–130
government growth
and, 140
of local government, 186
in public
administration, 222
Egalitarianism, in
education, 201
Elections, 71
in pluralistic system, 68
Electoral laws, proposals
for change, 78–79
Elites
in developing countries,
43–44
educational background,
50–51
functional, role of,
56–57
industrial, bureaucracy
and, 7
replacement process,
52–55

in society with monolithic power structure, 47–48
support for status quo, 79–80
see also "Strategic elite"

Elites, administrative
avoidance of local government agencies, 158
defined, 44
democracy and, 23–24
development and, 23
in economic development, 137–139
in Korean public administration, xvii, xviii–xix
policy concerns of, 158–159
in public policy making, 20

Elites, political
charismatic leader and, 45
defined, 44
dominance over other elites, 56–57
under Park, 46, 54
under Rhee, 45–46

Endowment institutes, 249

Equity
neglect of in Korean development planning, 182–183
in public administration, 222

Evans, Peter, "dependent development" model of, 59

Examinations. *See* Civil service examinations; College entrance examinations; Schools, entrance examinations

Expenditure, public
local as proportion of total, 148
political rationales for, 75

Exports
government policy regarding, 90
heavy and chemical industrial share, 135, 137
in Korean development strategy, 58–59

Extrabureaucratic organizations, role in reform, 242

Faculty, academic, appointment reforms for, 207

Fair trade policies
EPB and, 106
legislature's opposition to, 89

Familism
in East Asia, 30–33
in Korean society, xvii

Family planning, 108, 185–186

Fatalism, in Korean traditional thought, 128

Feudalism
in Japanese society, 30–31
prestige of military under, 53

Field administration
forms of, 151
political role of, 159
supervising and communicating methods, 152–153
see also Local government

Finance. *See* Urban finance

Five-year plans
central planning under, 182
EPB and, 91
First Five-Year Economic Development Plan (1962–1966), 107
public sector emphasis, xix–xx
Third Five-Year Economic Development Plan (1972–1976), 136

Foreign aid, Rhee vs. Park on, 86

Foreign capital, policies concerning, 60, 137, 142

Foreign Capital Introduction Law (1962), 129

Foreign exchange, government policies toward, 89

Foreign experts, role in reform, 243

Foreign study, for Korean public administration students, 235

Formalism, in East Asian societies, 37

Free-market policies
of 1980s, 137
see also Deregulation

gakubatsu, social significance of, 32

Gorbachev, Mikhail, xxix

Government
research into goals of, 230–231
see also Local government

Grant for Local Education Finance Law (1963), 206

Great Britain, influence of Oxford and Cambridge universities, 51

Gross National Product (GNP), 107, 112, 135, 248
government spending as percent of, 88
growth of, x

Guerreiro-Ramos, Alberto, 19

"Guided capitalism" theory, 87, 157

Gwacheon Residential New Town, 166

Hahm, Pyoung-choon, on Korean personality, 34

Hahn, Seung-jo, on Rhee's elite recruitment, 45

hakbŏl, social significance of, 32

Hakdo Hokook Dan. See Student Defense Corps

han system, in Japan, 31

Hermens, F. A., 78

Hierarchy, East Asian societies compared, 35–36

Historical Development of the Bureaucracy in Korea, A (Bark), 213

Historical Study of Public Administration in Yi Dynasty (Kim), 213

Hong-ik-in-gan ("benefits for all mankind"), 199

Housing Construction Promotion Law, 177

Human resources, centralization and, 155

Ideology, as criterion of
    state type, 62
Income, 112
    of local governments,
        149
    per capita rise since
        Korean War, x
Indigenization, xvi
    defined, 20
    of public administration
        education, 234
    of public administration
        research, 214–215,
        217–218, 221, 222
Industrialization
    export strategies, 135, 137
    government policies to-
        ward, 86, 163
    growth of, 111
    heavy industrial
        development, 136–137
    regional decentralization
        efforts, 163, 164–165
    in Western model of
        development, 115
Industrial Policy
    Deliberation Council
    (IPDC), 105–106
Industrial Redistribution
    Law (1977), 165
Industrial structure
    changes by year 2000,
        112–113
    see also State-owned
        enterprises
Inequality
    economic development
        and, 9–10
    see also Equity
Inflation
    EPB and, 101
    Park's policy toward,
        102–103
Information, education,
    and communication
    (IEC) programs, of EPB,
    93–94
Innovation, islands of
    in bureaucracy, 240–241
    in government, xxvii,
        242
Innovation, social, local
    government role, 185
Instability, political, 159
Integrated multisectoral
    strategy, for social
    development programs,
    190–191

Interest groups,
    government agencies
    and, 99–100
"Interest politics," shift
    toward, 248
Interest rates, government
    policies toward, 89
International Development
    Exchange Program
    (IDEP), 118
International Economic
    Policy Council (IEPC),
    105
International system, role
    in regime change, 65

Japan
    absence of bureaucratic
        culture in, 27
    basis of social actions
        in, 29
    Confucianism and
        bureaucracy in, 33
    economic development
        patterns, vs. Korean
        patterns, x–xi
    familism in, 31
    future role in Pacific
        Basin, 118
    influence of rule on
        Korean public
        administration, 225, 226
    legal system in, 35
    pragmatic mental
        culture of, 37–38
    public administration
        in, xvii
    vertical culture of, 34, 36
Jung, Suk Yoon, xix
Jung, Yong Duck, xxii–xxiii
Jun, Jong Sup, xxv
    on administrative
        centralization, 24

Kang, Shin-pyo, on East
    Asian cultures, 29
Kang, Sintaek, 230
Kariel, Henry, on
    pluralism, 21
Keller, Suzanne, on
    strategic elites, 23
Kim, Bong-shik
    on Korean
        administrative culture,
        30
    on moodism, 29
Kim, Bun Woong, xvi,
    xxii, xxvii

Kim, Dae-Jung, 80, 81
Kim, Dong Hyun, xv–xvi,
    xxiii–xxiv, xxviii
Kim, Jae-Ik, 104
Kim, Jong-phil, 81
Kim, Shin Bok, xxv
Kim, Suk Joon, xviii–xix
Kim, Woon-tae, on
    Confucianism, 28, 37
Kim, Yong-woon
    Japanese and Korean
        society compared, 36, 38
    on Korean society, 30,
        34
Kim, Young-Sam, 80, 81
Korea
    basis of social actions
        in, 29
    centralization, social
        forces and, 153–154
    familism in, 30–31
    hierarchical social
        networks, 72–73
    horizontal culture of,
        34, 36
    legal system in, 35
    power structure of
        society in, 44
    public administration
        traditions, 123, 225–226
    status at end of World
        War II, 85–86
    value systems of, 37–38,
        126
    see also Korea, Republic
        of; North Korea
Korean Association for
    Public Administration,
    xxv, 210–211, 226, 227
    membership, 228
Korea National Party, 70
Korean Democratic Party, 71
    formation of, 80–81
Korean War (1950–1953)
    consequences of, 86
    economic outlook after,
        ix–x
    impact on government
        administration, 225
Korea, Republic of
    abolition of caste
        system, 49
    administrative divisions,
        162
    development
        indices of, 58
        prospects for, xxi
        regional, 179

social vs. economic,
15, 193
Western model and,
19
dominance of political
elites in, 56–57
economic growth
potential, 111
economic growth rate, 9
economic role of central
government, 182
institutional structure, 69
local government in,
148–150
major political crises
since World War II, 61
political instability in,
159
proposals for political
change, 76–80
prospects for year 2000,
111–115
regime type analyzed,
62–66
regional economic
agreements, 117–118
social challenges facing,
246–247
social changes and
public administration
in, 221–222
social structure and
political culture, 22
state intervention in
economy, 87, 90
see also Economic policy;
Gross National Product
Kyŏngsang
elites from, 54
influence of in cabinet,
50

Labor, role of in economic
growth, 110
Land Expropriation Law,
177
Land reform, role in
regime change, 65
LaPalombara, Joseph, on
bureaucracies and
change, 22
Law
administrative, shift
away from, 234
public administration
and, 211, 226
rule of in East Asian
societies, 34–35

study of, and public
administration research,
220
Law Concerning
Temporary Measures for
Local Autonomy (1961),
150
Lee, Chong Bum, xxvi
on indigenization,
214–215
Lee, Chul, 81
Lee, Hahn Been, xxvi
career of, xiv
Legislature, government
reorganization and, 249
Liberalism, 78
Life expectancy,
improvement in, x
Literary class, under Yi
dynasty, 53
Local Autonomy Law
(1949), 150
Local government
centralization, 153–159
debate over systems,
147–148
decentralization of, 181
delegation of authority
to, 140–141
devolution of authority
to, 177
efficiency of, 186
elections suspended
(1961), 150
fiscal condition of, 155
power of, 148–149
revenue sources, 152
role of, xxiii–xiv
two-tier system, 149
see also Field
administration
Local Industrial
Development Law, 164
Local resources
mobilization strategy,
192
Lowi, Theodore, on
pluralism, 21

Management theory,
229–230
Martial law, 159
Masanori, Moritani, on
familism in Korea, 30
Migration, rural-to-urban,
154, 161
Military
accounting reforms, 242

political role, 52–54,
69–70
in public administration,
xviii–xix, 242–243, 247
Military service schools,
242
Mills, C. Wright, on
pluralism, 21
Ministry of Construction
(MOC), 166, 174, 175
Ministry of Culture and
Public Information,
propaganda function of,
249
Ministry of Education
college entrance
policies, 202, 204–205
control over higher
education, 207, 249
curriculum standards,
204
EPB and, 200
standardization of
educational activities,
205
Ministry of Finance,
Budget Bureau, reforms
at, 242, 249
Ministry of Home Affairs
(MOHA), 158, 174, 175
reforms needed, 249
Ministry of Reconstruction,
economic development
plans, 242
Minnesota Plan, 227
Minnowbrook Conference
(1968), 222
Modernization
Anglo-American model
of, 11
bureaucracy as primary
agent of, xxi–xxii
education and, 113–114
public administration
and, 123, 125–134
Westernization and, 115
Monetary policies, 157
see also Foreign capital
Municipal governments,
expansion of, 166

National Investment Fund,
136
Nationalism, Korean,
education and, 199
National security
centralization of
government and, 156

Korean political
repression and, 59
see also Security-oriented
state
Neomercantile security
state (NMSS), 63–64
Neomercantile welfare
state (NMWS), ROK as,
64
Nepotism
influence in Korea, 32
see also Patronage
system
New Korea Democratic
Party (NKDP), 71, 72,
73
Newly industrializing
countries (NICs),
116–117
ROK as, 58
New towns, development
of, 165
NGOs. *See*
Nongovernmental
organizations
NICs. *See* Newly
industrializing countries
NKDP. *See* New Korea
Democratic Party
Nongovernmental
organizations (NGOs),
in local social
development, 191–192
North Korea
economic policies after
Korean War, x
relationship with ROK,
109
nunch'i, meaning of, 29

Office of National Tax
Administration (1966),
88
Office of Planning and
Coordination (1961), 87
Oh, Se-chol, on *nunch'i*, 29
Olympic Games, Korea as
host, ix
on, meaning of, 29
Organization and
management (O and M)
theory, 229–30, 232

Pacific Basin, economic
future of, 110
Pacific Economic
Cooperation Conference
(PECC), 117

Paik, Wan Ki, xviii, xxi
on Korean administrative
culture, 30
pao, meaning of, 29
Pareto, Vilfredo, on
revolutions, 52
Park, Chung-Hee
cabinet appointments,
46, 50, 51, 53
dictatorial personality
type, 47
economic growth
policies, 62, 136, 139
expansion of
government economic
apparatus by, 225
fall of, 70
industrialization
policies, 86
Park, Jyun-kyu, 80
Paternalism, East Asian
societies compared, 32
Patronage system
in Korea, 73, 75
zaibatsus and, xxii
Pax Pacificana, 107, 118
Personnel transfer policies,
152
Philippines, People's
Revolution in (1986), 65
Philosophy, social, neglect
of, 230
Pilot University Program,
205
Planning
central, failure of,
182–183
by development
administrators, 6
economic
mechanisms of state
intervention, 87–89
under Park, 86–87
vs. social, 13
educational, 204, 206
Pluralism, political
and advanced economy,
67–68
consequences, 68–69,
72, 75–76
defined, 20
desirability of, 56–57
influence in Korea,
20–21, 22
structures and
assumptions of, 68
Policy-making
bureaucratic role, 247, 251

by development
administrators, 5–6
elections and, 73–74
in local administrations,
152–153
public input into, 231
Policy research institutes,
in ROK, 90–91
Political development
dimensions of, 11
in Korea, 10
Political leadership
role in administrative
reform, 241, 244
see also Charismatic
leader
Political parties
coalition-building in
ROK, 78, 80–81
electoral systems and, 78
policy-making role, 153
in ROK, 70–72
Political regime
change in, 61, 64–65
indices of political and
economic power-
seeking, 62
types of, 61–64
Political science, public
administration and, 211
Political security state
(PSS), 63
Political welfare state
(PWS), 64
Politics
proposals for change in
ROK structures, 76–80
social forces and, 74
Population. *See*
Demographic change
Poverty, government
intervention to remedy,
184–185
Power, ethics and, in
Korean society, 126–127
Prefect, xxiii
powers of, 151
President
EPB and, 101–102
power of, 69, 158
over governing elites,
54–55
public administration
system and, 124–125
Rhee's view of role, 86
Presidential Commission for
Educational Reform (PCER;
1985), xxv, 206–207

Price Control Act (1961), 88
Price controls, abolition of, 89
Private sector
   dependency fostered by public administration, 130
   growth of, 89–90
   increased role in development needed, 134
Privatization, promotion of, 140–141, 143
Production, public administration role in increasing, 127
Productivity, improvements in, 110
Protectionism, growth of, 110
Public, limited role in policy-making, 92
Public administration
   academic programs in, 211
   after World War II, 210
   as agent of economic growth, 125–134
   American model, in Korea, xxvi
   analytical dimensions of, 3
   before Korean War, 123–124
   East Asian countries compared, xvii–xviii
   legalistic emphasis of, 211
   modernization and, 123
   reforms needed, 248–249
   research activities, 215–216
   research agendas, 216–219
   tasks of, 221–223
   see also Development administration
Public administration education
   American influence, 226–227
   curricula, 228, 231–232
   developmental stages, 224–225
   doctoral degrees in,
   ethnocentric orientation, 213
   goals and accomplishments of, 212
   integrating theory and practice, 218–219
   Japanese influence, 226
   postwar development of, xxv
   redefining purpose of, 216–217
   reform orientation, 214
   regional imbalance in, 223
   scholar/bureaucrat relations, 221, 222
   student profile, 228–229
   teaching methods, 232–233
   weaknesses, 234–235
   Western influences on, 212–213
Publications, in public administration, 229
Public enterprises
   efficiency of, 141
   managerial recruitment, 139–140
   types of, 166
   see also State-owned enterprises (SOEs)
Public sector, economic development of ROK and, 157
Public Utilities Rates Review Committee, 89
Pusan, industrialization of, 163

Rae, Douglas, 78
Recruitment, 7–8
   of governing elite, 43, 48–49
   of municipal workers, 173–174
   under Park, 87
Reform. See Administrative reform; Regulatory reform
Regionalism, in Korean power structure, 49–50
Regulatory reform
   need for, 250
   proposals for, xxviii
   switch to market orientation, 142, 143
Research, in public

Reunification Democratic Party, 71, 72, 73
   dissolution of, 80
   support for status quo, 79
Rhee, Ki-bung, 46
Rhee, Syngman
   cabinet appointments, 49
   as charismatic leader, 44–45
   dictatorial personality type, 47
   political emphasis of policies, 62
Riggs, Fred, on developing societies, 22–23
Roh, Tae-woo
   democratic reform promised by, 246
   electoral majority of, 80
ROK. See Korea, Republic of
Rural areas
   development of, 193–194
   growth of manufacturing in, 163
   transformation of, 116
   see also Migration, rural-to-urban

Saemaul (New Village) movement, xxiv, 125
   local government role in, 185, 187–188
   psychological effect of, 128
   reasons for, 124
Sartori, Giovanni, 78
Savas, E. S., on shrinking government role, 140
Scholastic Achievement Examination, 202
Schools
   administrative reforms, 208
   entrance examinations, 201, 207
   private, 202
   secondary, competition for entry, 200
Schumpeter, Joseph, on democracy, 23–24
Second National Comprehensive Physical Development Plan, 164
Security-oriented state
   ROK as, 63
   see also National security

Seoul
  administrative
    structures, 172–177
  growth of since Korean
    War, xxiii
  industrialization, 163
  influence of in cabinet, 49
  mayor of, 152
  need for metropolitan
    regional government, 179
  population statistics, 162
  public enterprises in,
    166–167
  revenue sources and
    management, 169–172
  tax structures, 170,
    171–172
  urban administration
    system of, xiv
Seoul National University
  Graduate School of
    Public Administration,
    xxv, 211, 215, 242
  graduates of, 229
  influence of
    diminished, 234
  origins of, 226–227
  influence of graduates,
    51
Shamanism, in Korean
  culture, 27
Shin, Hyon Hwak, 104
Smith, Brian, on
  centralization, 148
Social Democratic Party, 71
Social development
  agendas for, 4–5
  as alternative
    development strategy,
    12–13
  dimensions of, 11–12,
    13–14
  economic development
    and, xv–xvi, 193
  local government role
    in, 184–189
  needs, 248–249
  planning processes, 183
  strategies for
    implementing, 189–191
Social mobility, East Asian
  societies compared, 31,
  36–37
Social welfare services
  increasing demand for,
  113
  local government role in
    delivery of, 186

quality of life issues, 223
  in Western model of
    development, 115
Socioeconomic
  development, political
    consequences of, 239
Special accounts, in Seoul
  financial structure, 171
State
  role in postwar
    modernization, xix–xx
  see also Political regime
State-owned enterprises
  (SOEs)
  functions of, 174
  growth in, 88
  see also Public
    enterprises
"Strategic elite," 23
Student Defense Corps,
  199–200
Subsidies, state, to Seoul,
  171–172

Taoism, in China, 27
Taxation
  for education, 205
  indirect, as main source
    of ROK revenues, 89
  local, 152
  municipal, in Seoul,
    170–172
  state to local transfer
    needed, 171
Taxes, collection of, 88
Technical education,
  promotion of after
    Korean War, 200
Technology
  economic change in
    NICs and, 109–110
  increasing role, 221
  public administration
    role in advancing, 129
  see also Computerization
Textbooks, government
  control of content, 204
Tocqueville, Alexis de, on
  pluralism, 21
Tokyo University, influence
  of graduates, 32, 51
Training
  for local government
    officials, 186, 194
  materials for in public
    administration, 233
Training institutes, for
  public administration

professionals, 228
Tutoring, private, 202, 208

United States
  alliance with ROK, xxix,
    65
  influence on Korean
    public administration,
    226–227
  Korean policy of, 59–60,
    105
  public administration
    study in, 220
  universities attended by
    senior U.S.
    administrators, 51
  see also Public
    administration,
    American model
United States Regulatory
  Council, 142
Universities
  admission quotas, 203
  public administration
    programs in, 228
  student–professor ratio,
    203
  see also College entrance
    examinations;
    Education, higher;
    Public administration
    education
University students,
  dissatisfaction with
    status quo, 74
Urban development,
  control of, 176
Urban finance
  for development, 166–167
  types of, 167, 169
Urbanization
  problems of, 151
  rate of, 162
  reasons for, 163
  in Western model of
    development, 115
Urban policy
  interagency coordination
    in, 174–176
  main objectives, 163–164
User charges, institution
  of, 169

Violence, to maintain
  hegemony, 68
Voluntary organizations
  in social development
    programs, 195

see also
Nongovernmental
organizations (NGOs)

Waste management, in
Seoul, 167
Water supply systems,
interagency coordination
and, 175
Welfare. *See* Social welfare
Westernization,
modernization and, in
Korea, 125
Whang, In Joung, xx, xxi,
xxviii

on CMES, 250
Wilson, Woodrow, on
public administration,
220
Woo, Roh Tae
democratization policies,
xxvii
meeting with
Gorbachev, xxix
Wright, Arthur, on
Confucianism, 28–29

Yangban (aristocrats)
system, 31, 33
Yi dynasty, power

structure under, 44
Yi, Yun-yŏng, 45
Yonsei University, 220
Yoo, Jong Hae, xxvi
Yoon, Tae-rim, on
Confucianism, 28
Yoon, Woo-kon, on Korean
administrative culture,
30
Yushin system, 59, 101,
102, 103

Zaibatsu, xxii, 131
Zoning regulations,
176–177

Other important books from KUMARIAN PRESS:

DEMOCRATIZING DEVELOPMENT
THE ROLE OF VOLUNTARY ORGANIZATIONS
JOHN CLARK

THE FAMILY PLANNING MANAGER'S HANDBOOK
BASIC SKILLS AND TOOLS FOR FAMILY PLANNING MANAGERS
EDITORS: JAMES A. WOLFF, LINDA J. SUTTENFIELD, AND
SUSANNA C. BINZEN
MANAGEMENT SCIENCES FOR HEALTH

GETTING TO THE 21ST CENTURY
VOLUNTARY ACTION AND THE GLOBAL AGENDA
DAVID C. KORTEN

KEEPERS OF THE FOREST
LAND MANAGEMENT ALTERNATIVES IN SOUTHEAST ASIA
MARK POFFENBERGER

OPENING THE MARKETPLACE TO SMALL ENTERPRISE
WHERE MAGIC ENDS AND DEVELOPMENT BEGINS
TON DE WILDE, STIJNTJE SCHREURS, WITH ARLEEN RICHMAN

TRAINING FOR DEVELOPMENT
SECOND EDITION
ROLF P. LYNTON AND UDAI PAREEK

THE WATER SELLERS
A COOPERATIVE VENTURE BY THE RURAL POOR
GEOFFREY D. WOOD, RICHARD PALMER-JONES, WITH
M. A. S. MANDAL, Q. F. AHMED, S. C. DUTTA

WORKING TOGETHER
GENDER ANALYSIS IN AGRICULTURE
HILARY SIMS FELDSTEIN AND SUSAN V. POATS

❖   ❖   ❖

For a complete catalog of
KUMARIAN PRESS titles:

630 Oakwood Ave., Suite 119
West Hartford, CT 06110-1529

tel (203) 953-0214 • fax (203) 953-8579